GRAD
expectations

The essential guide for all
graduates entering the work force

ROB CROSS

Copyright © 2009 by Robert Cross

All rights reserved. No part of this book may be reproduced or transmitted in any form or by any means, electronic or mechanical, including photocopying, recording or by any information storage or retrieval system, without permission in writing from the author.

www.rob-cross.com

First published in Great Britain in 2009 by Ecademy Press Ltd,
6, Woodland Rise, Penryn, Cornwall. TR10 8QD
Tel: +44 (0) 1326 373057. www.ecademy-press.com
Company Registered in England – 5639586 VAT Registered – 971 4474 02

Typeset in Baker Signet 11/13pt by Zahra Ginieres Ridge
Cover Design by Zahra Ginieres Ridge, www.zgrdesigns.co.uk
Cover Photo by Harrison Keely

ISBN 978-1-905823-61-1

Printed and bound by
Lightning Source UK Ltd, Chapter House, Pitfield, Kiln Farm, Milton Keynes MK11 3LW
Email: enquiries@lightningsource.co.uk Voice: 0845 121 4567 Fax: 0845 121 4594
Lightning Source UK Ltd. Registered in England and Wales Company number 4042196
Registered office 5 New Street Square, London, EC4A 3TW

To all those leaving university with expectations and aspirations
— may you achieve whatever success you desire,
and may you make a positive difference in the world.

ACKNOWLEDGEMENTS

I would like to thank all the people who have inspired and educated me throughout my journey. Without your guidance, support and challenge I would not have found my place and purpose in the world.

I would like to thank all the people I have had the pleasure of working with over the last 10 years. I have never ceased to be amazed and inspired by what I have learnt from each of you.

I would like to thank Mindy Gibbins-Klein, The Book Midwife, who helped me turn all of my thoughts into the book you have in your hands today.

CONTENTS

Why Read This Book 9

INTRODUCTION 11

PART 1 - BECOMING A PROFESSIONAL 25

1. Is This What Professional Life Is Really Like? 27

2. Start By Managing Yourself 41

3. You Can Manage Your Boss 63

4. Manage Your Relationships…At Work 84

5. There Is A 'Right Way' To Make A Difference 97

PART 2 - WHO ARE YOU? WHY ARE YOU HERE? 119

6. Your Future…Really Now Starts Here! 121

7. Recognise The Crisis 131

8. Acknowledge Where You've Come From 143

9. Build Who You Are 157

10. Define What's Important…To You 177

11. Take Considered Action 193

12. Make It Stick…Maintain Focus 212

CONCLUSION - The Secret Is Showing Leadership 225

Afterword…Beginning Your Journey 231

Suggested Further Reading 232

Why Read this Book

Parties, friends, romance...I'm sure there are plenty of other things you'd prefer to do than read another book. That's right, university is over; there are no more exams to sit, and no more essays to write...*so that means you no longer have to read...or does it?*

But now that you've started your career, I've got some questions for you...

    Is work what you expected?

    Have all the things you were promised when recruited come true?

I'm guessing the answer to both questions is **NO**, especially if you're like the tens of thousands of university graduates around the globe who start fresh each year in their first professional job.

You see, what I've discovered as a university graduate myself, and then through working with graduates over the last 10 years, is that...

    Nothing prepares you for the professional world; not university, not your parents, and not even the work experience you've had before.

That's why I wrote this book. To help you not just survive in this new world, but to help you succeed by achieving what you want to achieve.

This book does what it says. It provides you with an essential guide to navigate through your first job after university. This book is written about you and for you. Whilst based on five fictional characters, the story captures what all people experience when they start their first job after university. However, rather than just tell the story, this book also provides you with the tools you need to succeed at the start of your career.

So if you want to do more than just survive at work, if you want to achieve what you desire, and define and fulfil your purpose, then go on the journey with Steve, Taylor, Jane, Simon and Angela as they join the professional work force. Accompany them from day one at World-Corp PLC, through their challenges and successes, and use the tasks that they use to guide your actions so you can achieve success by being yourself.

Now that you've picked this book up, grab a pen and, as you read on, use it to complete the tasks included. And whilst doing these tasks, keep an open mind and be prepared to take action because your success will only come from consciously applying the knowledge you gain throughout your journey beyond graduation.

Enjoy the journey...

INTRODUCTION

To Tie, or not to Tie – that is the question!

"Name?" the girl at the counter asked sharply but with a smile.

"Name?" the girl asked again, this time starting to lose her patience.

Simon snapped out of his daydream realising that he'd just reached the front of the line.

"Um, um, Simon," he blurted out, feeling like a complete fool.

"Surname?" the girl said sarcastically.

"Oh sorry," Simon responded, noticing the name tags on the table.

"Trimble," he said apologetically, "Simon Trimble."

"Great, here you are," the girl said, picking up a tag and handing it to him.

"Thanks," Simon replied shyly as he attached the tag to his suit jacket.

So I'm off to a great start for my new job, Simon thought to himself as he followed the signs to the World-Corp new joiners' induction.

At the top of a set of stairs which led down to a reception area, Simon stopped and looked in awe at the sea of faces below. From this mass of people all he could hear was a growing hum of voices. It seemed to him that almost all of the 350 new joiners had now arrived at the World-Corp head office ready for the official 10:00 a.m. start. Across the faces Simon could see that unmistakable sense of uncertainty and anticipation that always accompanies the first day at a new job.

"There's tea and coffee on the table over there," a polite voice said to Simon, snapping him out of his trance.

"Thanks," Simon said. He then descended the stairs slowly, wondering what he had got himself into.

Within the crowd most people had attached themselves to groups, choosing to make that uncomfortable introduction to people they'd never met before. Others, who were too shy to approach complete strangers, distracted themselves on the crowd's periphery with their mobile phones or sipping at the tea or coffee they had just picked up.

Feeling completely out of place and very self-conscious, Simon helped himself to a cup of tea. With his cup in one hand and a folder in the other, he then made his way to the edge of the swarm and surveyed the faces, hoping to see someone he might recognise. On the first scan there wasn't a single familiar person. However, just as he finished his initial sweep something dawned on him; all the guys in the room were wearing ties. Quickly doing a second sweep of the group, his eyes darted backwards and forwards confirming that not a single other guy had made the same choice as him that morning. With this realisation, a feeling of dread quickly formed in Simon's stomach.

What was I thinking? Simon muttered to himself. *How can I be the only one here not wearing a tie?*

His hands then became sweaty as the potential implications rushed through his mind.

So I'm sure they'll think I'm trying to be some 'media' type, or that I'm not taking it seriously enough.

These thoughts quickly escalated to images of him being escorted out of the office on his very first day.

That's it! My career is over before it's begun, Simon muttered, disgusted with himself for making such a poor decision.

As the feeling in his stomach intensified and he began to feel physically ill, out of the corner of his eye Simon saw something: a brethren, another guy who had chosen to go tie-less on his first day. On seeing this person, Simon quickly made a line straight for him. Nothing was going to get in the way of him joining forces with this other rebel. As Simon approached, the person glanced up from his mobile phone to see Simon stop a few short paces in front of him.

"So, here for the media roles are you?" Simon joked with a slight chuckle.

The guy looked at him quizzically.

"No, I'm here for the legal roles," this supposed ally responded, looking utterly confused.

"Oh," Simon replied.

Well I'm definitely off to a winner today, he thought to himself. *So how do I get myself out of this one?* Before he could come up with anything even remotely intelligent, an announcement came over the speakers.

"Could all new joiners please make their way into the auditorium and take their seats according to the seating plan," a well-spoken lady's voice requested.

Saved by the bell, Simon thought to himself.

He then set his attention back to his tie-less colleague.

"Well, that sounds like us then, great to meet you," Simon said, before spinning around and quickly joining the mass of people migrating towards the auditorium entrance.

And so it Begins

The auditorium was actually a large open room, full of what seemed like hundreds of round tables each with a number planted firmly in the middle. At each table, six chairs were spaced evenly around, with a drinking glass, notepad and pen in front of them. Also on each table were two bottles of water and a small bowl of sweets. At the front of the room was a stage with a speaker's lectern placed to the left of a giant white screen.

As people slowly made their way through the entrance into the room, each person scanned the tables looking for their number. A few individuals, on looking around the room, quickly realised they'd forgotten their table number and made their way back through the crowd to re-check the seating plan.

Amazingly, at precisely 10:00 a.m. everyone had found their place and was seated at their table.

Simon found his table, number 47. As he sat down he gave an acknowledging glance to the others who were already seated. There were two guys and three girls, each of whom had written their name on the piece of card provided. On the cards the names Taylor, Steve, Jane, Angela and Liz were written. Below her name, Liz had also written the word 'buddy'. Simon quickly wrote his name on a piece of card and displayed it for the others to see. As he went to open his mouth to say hello to Angela who was sitting to his right, the lights dimmed and the first speaker came on stage.

"Welcome to World-Corp PLC," the person announced, "and congratulations for joining such an amazing company! Each of you is one of the 350 people who we have deemed suitable to join our thriving family of 75,000 people across the world. From over 10,000 applicants you have proven yourself to be what we are looking for. So you have proven yourself above 9,650 others and that is something to be proud of."

Around the room people listened intently as presentation after presentation filled the next two and a half hours. Each presenter, including the CEO, reinforced the World-Corp story. The company was a large world-wide corporation with a diverse portfolio of operations from manufacturing and technology through to finance and insurance. It had a strong values-based culture, meaning that people were measured constantly against living the values. It was also described as a meritocracy, so if you worked hard and made a difference then you were rewarded. The final presentation informed them of World-Corps' excellent Corporate Social Responsibility record by telling the story of the work under way with various charities, the environmental initiatives and also volunteering opportunities. All in all, a good company to work for.

Breaking the Ice

After the final presenter finished, an announcement was made that lunch would now be served in the reception area. Just as they all stood up, Liz quickly introduced herself.

"Hey guys, just to let you know my name is Liz and I'll be your buddy for the next two years. We'll have a better opportunity to get to know each other after lunch, but if you have any immediate questions then just let me know."

Everyone gave Liz a quick smile as they followed her out to the reception area where they joined a queue for the food. Whilst standing waiting, Jane decided to ask the first question.

"How long have you worked for World-Corp, Liz?" she asked.

"Five years now," Liz replied.

"Wow, you must really like it here then?" Angela asked.

"I love it. World-Corp is a really great company to work for," Liz replied.

"The press hasn't been too kind to World-Corp over the last few months," Steve said in a slightly negative tone as the group fell silent.

"I mean, I'm glad to be here, but it isn't all that rosy is it?" Steve continued, as if hoping to get some reassurance from Liz.

"Every company has its own sets of issues, Steve," Liz responded quickly, "and we're no different. However, what we're very good at here in World-Corp is looking at those issues and seeing how to turn them into opportunities."

"I agree," Taylor blurted out, almost butting in over the top of Liz. "World-Corp is a strong company with a great track record, and we should be proud to be here."

Finishing as abruptly as he started, Taylor looked around for a vote of confidence from his new-found friends.

"Ah, the front of the queue," Liz announced as she ushered each person through by handing them a plate.

The rest of the lunch break was largely uneventful as Liz, Taylor, Steve, Simon, Jane and Angela made small-talk, getting to know each other in what felt like an even more crowded room than before.

At precisely 1:25 p.m., the same well-spoken lady's voice came over the speakers requesting that people make their way back into the auditorium.

Knowing Me, Knowing You

Just as everyone sat back into their seats, the first speaker reappeared on stage.

"Welcome back, everyone," she announced. "I hope you all had a great lunch and are ready to continue on for the afternoon. You hopefully will have noticed that we've deliberately sat you at certain tables. The people at your table will be your support group for the next two years while you remain on the new joiner development programme. At each table we have also allocated a buddy who has been in the business for a few years, and who will be there to help you every step of the way on your journey in World-Corp."

Each person at the table quickly gave the others a glance, recognising that they were now a team.

"So with all this in mind," the presenter continued, "what we would like you to do now is get to know each other. Your buddies will lead the activity, but what we want you to do is introduce yourself with your name, what you studied and at which university, where you live, and why you chose to work for World-Corp. Just remember that you've all got the job now, so please be honest on the last point."

As the speaker finished, each person drew their attention to the centre of the table, wondering who would introduce themselves first.

"Let me go first," Liz announced, noticing the tension.

As she positioned herself to speak, Liz, who was clearly professional by any standard, leant slightly forward and brushed her chestnut-brown hair back with both hands, tucking it behind her ears. With her elbows resting on the edge of the table and her hands clasped in front of her, she momentarily looked each of them in the eyes before starting. Simon couldn't help noticing how blue her eyes were when she looked at him.

"My name is Elizabeth Jamieson, or Liz for short," she started. "As I said at lunch, I have worked for World-Corp for five years now and, in fact, was sitting exactly where you are almost five years ago to the day. After doing a variety of roles I am now a senior consumer marketing manager and I manage a team of five people. I studied English Literature at Newcastle University, but travelled for a year before I joined World-Corp. The reason I joined World-Corp was that I didn't really know what I wanted to do with my career and I really liked the opportunities that were being offered here. And I have to say that I haven't been disappointed."

"Wow, you really do love it here," Jane remarked with a smile.

"I really do," Liz replied. "If I didn't, I wouldn't be here. Now who wants to go next?"

"I will," Taylor burst in.

Spinning their heads around, they all stared at Taylor.

Now that's a bit odd, Steve thought to himself, wondering why Taylor was so enthusiastic.

"OK Taylor, thanks for volunteering," Liz responded with a feeling of unease.

Before he opened his mouth again, Taylor seemed to go through a form of ritual in preparing to speak. First he tightened the double Windsor knot that held his red tie perfectly in place on his white shirt. He then fiddled with each of his immaculately shiny silver cuff-links that seemed to match his rather expensive-looking Omega watch. As he leant forward, partially mimicking Liz's movements, slight folds appeared in the sleeves of his navy pin-stripe suit when his elbows finally came to rest on the table.

"My name is Taylor Johnson," he said with an air of authority in his voice. "I'm 24 years old and have worked for a year and a half as a senior project manager for Project Success Ltd. My father is a top surgeon here in London and so is my brother."

At that moment, Simon shot Jane a knowing glance across the table. Without either saying anything they both knew exactly what the other was thinking: *Who is this guy?*

"I didn't want to be a surgeon," Taylor stated. "My future is in the corporate world, which is why I studied Natural History at Loughborough, rather than medicine. Although Natural History was good, I'll probably do an MBA in the next year or two. I joined World-Corp because I want to get to the top, and I don't care how hard I have to work to do it! I live in South Kensington with my parents."

Simon and Jane's eyes met again. This time, however, there was no knowing glance but rather an overt rolling of the eyes by Simon which brought a slight smile to Jane's face.

"Thank you Taylor, most interesting," Liz said. "So who's next?"

Reluctantly, and feeling slightly guilty at making fun at Taylor's expense, Simon volunteered.

"I'll go next," Simon indicated.

Feeling himself get immediately flustered, Simon quickly unbuttoned the cuffs of his blue shirt before rolling up the sleeves. Just as he was about to speak, he hunched forward, scratched his head, slightly messing up the look which he'd carefully modelled on Beckham's latest style that morning, and then nervously picked up his pen from the table. His eyes, although looking at the others, rarely made direct eye-contact.

"Simon Trimble is my name," Simon stammered. "I live here in London and play football for a local team. I studied Business Management at London University. The reason I joined World-Corp was, well if I'm going to be really honest, was that all my mates were joining big corporations so I thought I'd better as well. I applied to lots of different companies and World-Corp was the first to offer me a job, so I took it!"

"Thanks for your honesty, Simon," Liz responded with a smile. "What position do you play?"

"Striker," Simon responded immediately, feeling good that Liz had taken an interest.

"Great," said Liz. "So who's next?"

Feeling as though she didn't want to go last, Angela responded quickly.

"I'll go," she said.

"Thanks Angela," Liz replied.

Angela picked up the notes on her answers to the questions before leaning back in her chair. Although feeling a little nervous, she composed herself by adjusting her petite gold watch and by flicking back her curly brown hair from her face. Once she felt at ease, Angela confidently crossed one leg over the other and started.

"Hi everyone, I am Angela Jones and I also live here in London," Angela started. "Well, I've actually only just moved here from Manchester. I studied Business Management at Manchester University focusing on Economics and Business Law. The reason I chose to join World-Corp was that I think it is a really great company. I researched a lot of different companies and World-Corp kept coming out on top, especially for the project opportunities and its CSR track record, which is really important to me. So actually I only applied to World-Corp, and luckily they accepted me."

"Great, thanks Angela. I'm sure you won't be disappointed," Liz said. "So, who's going to be last?"

"I'll go next," Jane said, hesitating to see if Steve would get in before her.

"Excellent, thanks Jane," Liz responded.

Although not standing, it was easy to see that Jane wasn't as tall as Angela or Liz. Feeling incredibly nervous, she sought to compose herself by adjusting her watch in the same way as Angela had and then by checking that her blonde hair was still held back by the large clip that she had carefully placed that morning. Leaning forward, Jane also crossed her legs and then picked up a pen as a source of comfort. As she spoke, Jane lifted her head slightly to look at the others.

"My name is Jane Wolton," she said softly and slightly uncomfortably. "I've just moved back in with my parents outside of London. I went to Oxford but only studied English Literature. I joined World-Corp because I really didn't know what I wanted to do and my uncle who works here suggested I join."

"What does your uncle do?" Liz asked politely.

"He works in manufacturing," Jane responded, looking briefly at Liz.

"Your uncle's not Tom Wolton the Global Manufacturing President is he?" Taylor exploded with excitement.

"Yeh, but I didn't get the job because of him," Jane fired back, feeling accused.

"Don't worry Jane," Liz defended her. "I've met Tom on a couple of occasions and there is no way he would let such a thing happen. Plus, our recruitment processes are incredibly robust and objective."

Jane smiled shyly at Liz and then glared at Taylor who was oblivious to how he had made her feel.

"So last but not least," Liz continued, "Steve it looks like you're next."

Steve shuffled in his seat as if not really wanting to be there. His black suit jacket was already on the back of his chair, rather than trying to hide his poorly-ironed white shirt that looked as though it had been just been stuffed into the top of his trousers that morning. As he leant back even further in his chair, Steve scratched his head, leaving his already messy hair in an even more dishevelled state. He then scratched the stubble on his chin before playing with the buttons on his shirt.

"Yeh Steve, Steve Lily," he said casually.

"Live in London. Studied Engineering at St. Andrews. Joined World-Corp because it seemed like a good company," Steve concluded abruptly.

"Oh," Liz exclaimed, surprised at Steve's briefness, "Did you apply anywhere else?"

"Yeh, a couple," Steve responded. "But World-Corp was the first to offer me a job."

"Right," Liz responded, looking over Steve with a sense of reservation.

"OK, well, welcome to World-Corp and it is lovely to meet you all," Liz continued. "As was said earlier, over the next two years we will work together to support you and help you to find your feet and really make the best of the opportunities you have. We'll also work together to support your development through the various training activities that you'll go on. Now, does anyone have any questions?"

After a short pause, Angela broke the silence.

"When do we find out what projects we have?"

"Well, there is one more presentation to go and then you will be given all of your necessary equipment and allocated to your projects. Once you have this you will need to go and make the arrangements to meet your manager," Liz replied.

"Excellent, thanks," Angela replied.

"So do we start with our projects tomorrow?" Simon asked.

"Yes, your managers are expecting you. So once you're given their contact details it would be a good idea to give them a call," Liz stated.

"That's great," Taylor said. "I'd hate to waste any time getting started."

There was a short pause as they each wondered what their first real day at work would be like.

"By the way everyone, there's welcome drinks tonight at the bar over the road if you're interested," Steve said, taking everyone's attention off work.

One by one they nodded, agreeing to tag along so they could meet some other people. The main speaker then came on and announced that there was tea and coffee outside for those who wanted to stretch their legs. The group then proceeded out towards the reception area for refreshments.

What's Expected

After taking the opportunity to grab a drink and something to eat, they were again herded back into the auditorium. Although it was only 2:30 in the afternoon, with the initial nerves and anticipation of the day, they were all feeling tired.

Once they were all seated, the lights dimmed and the screen behind the stage lit up.

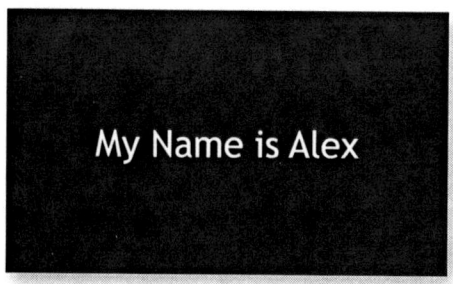

Immediately, the members of the group looked at each other. *Who the hell is Alex?* they all thought. A slight grin came to Liz's face.

Within a few seconds of the name Alex appearing on the screen, a tall, professional-looking guy strode confidently out on to the stage. He wore a slick-looking black suit and a white shirt with no tie, which Simon noticed immediately. Once in the middle of the stage, the figure stood there analysing each of the faces before him, rather like a predator sizing up its prey. Everyone instinctively stiffened slightly and rose to sit up in their seat.

"Hi everyone, my name is Alex," he said loudly and confidently, easing the anticipation of the crowd. "Welcome to the start of your journey. Yes, *your* journey. Not mine. Yours!"

Without taking her eyes off the front, Angela reached for her notepad and pen. Noticing this, Simon and Jane did the same, thinking it was the right thing to do.

"Let me tell you something about this journey that you are embarking on," Alex continued. "Whether you have defined it or not, your journey will have a destination, or a purpose, much like when a stream flows from the mountains to the ocean. But like a stream, your journey will not be a straight line from when you leave this room today. I can guarantee you that you will experience many twists and turns as the unexpected happens and new opportunities arise."

Alex paused and then walked slowly across the stage.

"So whilst I'm sure that many of you will be considering what your desired destination may be, I encourage you to always be ready to learn, and always be on the look-out for opportunities as you travel along your path. And as you do this, you will find that the journey and the experiences you have each day will be as important and as fulfilling as the destination itself."

Alex stopped walking and stared at the faces in the crowd.

"That's right; by recognising that the journey is as important as the destination, you will find that your journey and your life, will be a wonderful experience."

Not a single person shuffled or dared move to draw attention to themselves.

"So what is the secret to succeeding at World-Corp, and in this new professional world beyond graduation from university?" Alex asked rhetorically.

"Easy," he responded. "It's the same as the secret to making a difference and gaining fulfilment in your lives, and throughout your journey."

At that point a second slide flicked on to the screen.

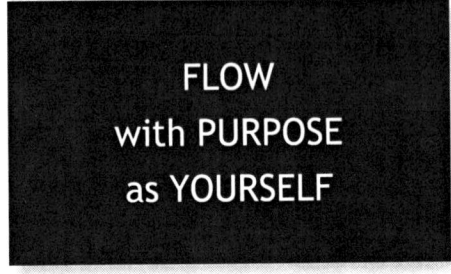

"The secret is to flow, with purpose, as yourselves," Alex said. "By 'flow', I mean that like the water flowing from the mountains to the ocean, you need to be fluid and flexible in how you travel through the journey of your life. If you remain too rigid you will almost definitely miss some of the great opportunities that may come your way. By 'with purpose', I mean that you need to have a plan. Know what your purpose is and have a plan to fulfil it. And finally, 'as yourself' means that we want you to be yourself no matter what. We recruited you because of who you are, and that's all we want from you. We want you to be yourselves."

He paused yet again, taking the time to look across the crowd.

"But in seeking to do this there are a few things you should know."

A third slide then flicked on to the screen.

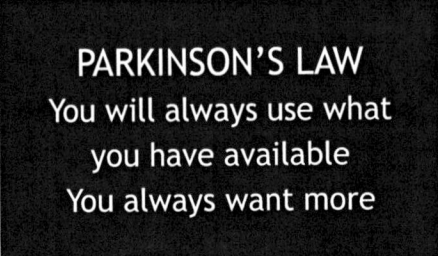

"In seeking to make a difference and gain fulfilment, the first thing you should know is that you will always have to deliver what you need to, with what you have available. And whether it is time, resources or money, you will always want more. This is known as Parkinson's Law and it applies to everything, including your salary. Yes, that's right everyone, regardless of how much you get paid you will always spend it all and you will always want more!"

A slight laugh rolled across the crowded room. A fourth slide flicked on to the screen.

> **PARETO PRINCIPLE**
> 20% of your Effort
> produces
> 80% of your Results

"As you will never have enough time or resources, the second thing you need to recognise is that 20% of your effort produces 80% of your results," Alex read from the slide. "This is known as the Pareto Principle. It means that you must focus your energy on doing that which will have the greatest impact in any particular situation. Failing to do this could result in you having a lesser impact or in wasting valuable time, effort and energy."

At the end of this sentence, the fifth slide appeared on the screen.

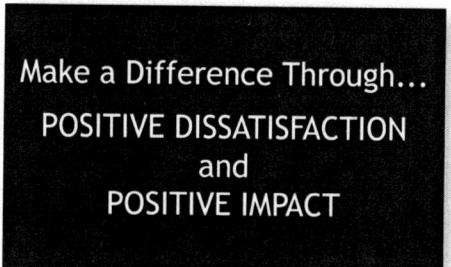

"So what we expect from you in our, and now *your* business, is that you will seek to make a difference. And how you do this is through positive dissatisfaction and through positive impact. At World-Corp and in life it's OK to be dissatisfied with things. We all know that the world is not perfect. But rather than just be annoyed that things don't work, we want you to be thinking about how to fix them. Then we want you to do just that: fix them. This is the way you can have a positive impact. This the way you can make a difference."

A sixth slide is appeared.

> **This Is About**
> **SHOWING LEADERSHIP**
> *You have Influence!*

"In seeking to make a difference, I want you all to recognise that you have influence, especially over yourself. And we expect you to exercise this influence in a considered way. What we call this in World-Corp is Showing Leadership."

Alex paused again and then slowly walked back across the stage.

"At World-Corp, yes we *want* you to be leaders but, more importantly, we *need* you to Show Leadership. We need you to know what you're trying to achieve in every instance, your definition of success, and then we need you to consciously focus your energy and effort on that which you can influence to achieve it. If you do this, you will make a difference not just for World-Corp and the people around you, but also for yourselves."

As he finished the statement, Alex paused. He looked across the room and, as he did so, every new joiner felt as if he was looking directly at them.

"So here is my final statement," he said flicking on to the next slide.

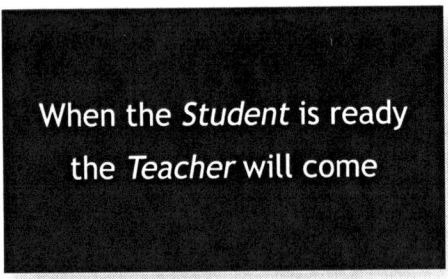

"With this ancient Chinese proverb I can tell you that the lessons and knowledge you need to make a difference and gain fulfilment in your lives are all around you. It is up to you, however, whether you are prepared to see them and, more importantly, it is up to you whether you are prepared to apply them."

Once again, Alex paused for a few moments as everyone in the room took in his message. At the table, Angela was frantically capturing every word, while the others sat fully engrossed with what was being said.

"So I encourage you to consider the destination of your journey, your purpose. Then

I encourage you to develop your conscious awareness so that you can spot and take advantage of the opportunities that come your way and which will help you fulfil your purpose."

People remained silent as Alex looked up at the screen. Looking back towards the crowd he then finished his speech.

"Now, before I go I want to say thank you for your time today, and thank you for allowing me to pass on some of the knowledge which I have learned throughout my journey. Congratulations on joining a great company. I wish you all the best for the start of your journey, and please seek me out if I can help you in any way."

He paused yet again.

"And finally, always remember: flow with purpose as yourselves. That is how you will make the greatest difference. That is how you will gain fulfilment."

With that, the room erupted with applause. Even Steve clapped along with the others.

Getting Started

As the applause died down and once Alex had left the stage, each person drew their attention to Liz.

"So now we give you your laptop and mobile phone etc., and then we put you in touch with your project manager," Liz explained.

They all stood, picking up the notes they'd written and then proceeded to follow Liz, ready to embark on the first part of their journey.

PRINCIPLES TO REMEMBER

Flow, with Purpose, as Yourself
Be fluid and flexible about how you travel your journey.
Know what your purpose is, have a plan, but remain nimble as you seek to fulfil it.
Be yourself no matter what.

Parkinson's Law
You will always use what you have available. You will always want more.
Ensure you use your time and resources wisely.

Pareto Principle
20% of your effort produces 80% of your results.
Always focus first on the vital few things that will deliver the greatest results.

When the Student is ready, the Teacher will come
The lessons and knowledge you need to make a difference and
gain fulfilment in your lives are all around you.
It is up to you whether you are prepared to see them and
whether you are prepared to apply them.

Show Leadership
Always define what success means to you – your desired outcome.
Consciously focus your energy and effort on that which you can influence to
help you achieve your definition of success.

Part I
Becoming a Professional

I.
Is This What Professional Life Is Really Like?

Rumours and Reputations

"Have you heard the latest rumour about Taylor?" Jane asked Simon as they caught up for a coffee.

"No, what is it now?" Simon replied.

"They're all calling him the wannabe ladies man," Jane said with a smile.

"That figures," Simon replied, "especially after he tried cracking onto every girl in the place during the drinks after induction. I actually thought that Angela was going to hit him at one stage, that's why I had a chat with him."

"He's definitely not making any friends, that's for sure. Perhaps that's why he's not in the office so much at the moment. He's probably trying to keep a low profile," said Jane.

"So a whole month has gone, how's your project going?" Simon asked, seeking to change the subject.

"Well, like Steve I had a lot of problems getting hold of my project manager at the start. Can you believe that he went off on holiday without telling anyone I was coming? If it weren't for Liz putting me in touch with someone else I don't know what I would have done. So I've really only just got started," Jane replied.

"Unbelievable," Simon responded, getting frustrated for what Jane had to put up with. "I heard that Steve's project manager was just too busy to take any time to see him as well. I mean, why did he ask for a new joiner if he wasn't going to make the time to even see him?"

"I agree," Jane said, shaking her head.

"By the way, did you hear what Steve did?" Simon asked again, changing the topic.

"No, what?" Jane asked curiously.

"Well, apparently the fool lost all his stuff after one of the nights out. That's right: his laptop, his bag, his identity pass and his mobile phone. All of it."

"What?" Jane remarked.

"Yep, everything. He had to go in front of HR to explain why they shouldn't sack him. He's pretty lucky to still be here if you ask me. He said that it was stolen, but I think we know the truth," Simon said, shaking his head.

"That probably explains why he's so negative at the moment," Jane replied.

"Yeh, he's had a pretty tough run. I mean no manager for the first couple of weeks and then no laptop. I think I'd be negative too if that were me."

Jane nodded in agreement, feeling thankful that at least she was working and had met her manager a couple of times.

Checking In

The day after Simon and Jane had caught up, each of the group received the same email invitation from Liz for what she called a 'check-in' meeting.

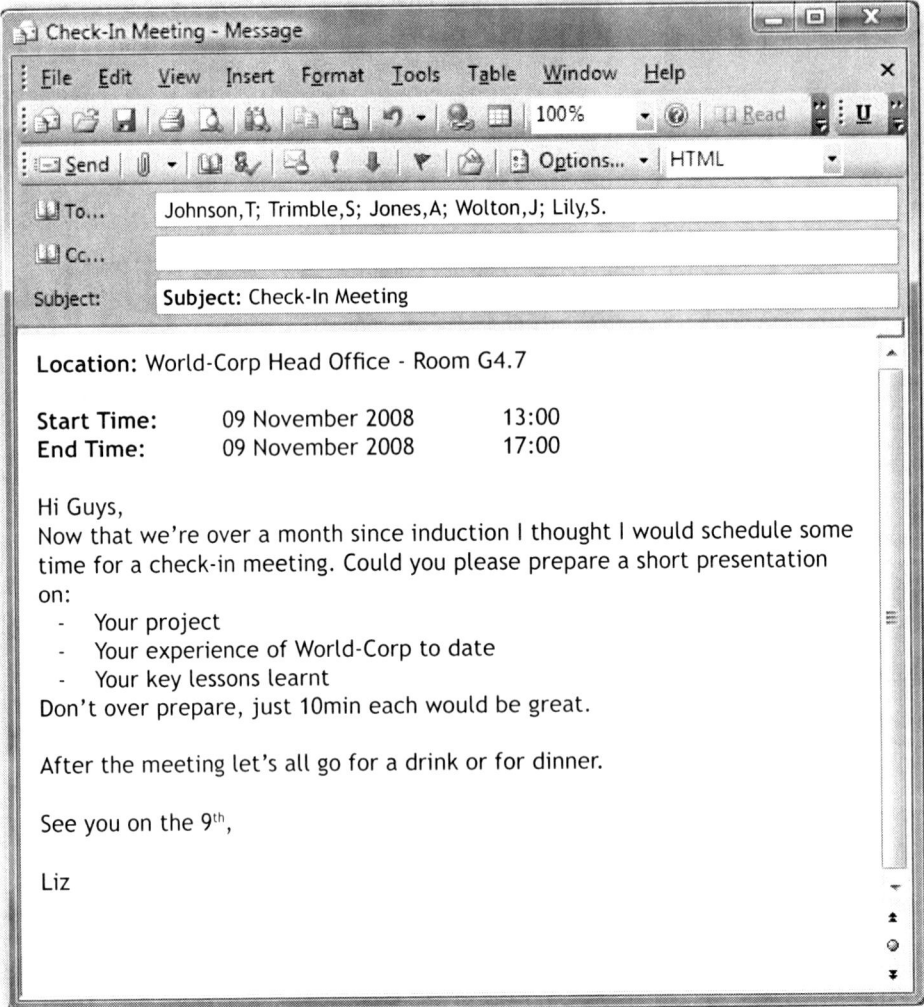

On the 9th Simon and Jane decided to catch up for lunch before wandering into the meeting room where they found Liz with her laptop open and just finishing a call.

"Hey guys. How you going?" Liz asked with a smile.

"Good thanks. And you?" Simon replied

"Great," Liz replied enthusiastically.

"Unfortunately Taylor is running slightly late. He said he was coming back from Leeds. It sounds like he's doing a lot of travelling for his project at the moment," Liz continued.

"Mmm," Simon mumbled, looking at Jane.

"I guess that's because he's an important man," Simon went on to say out loud.

Liz looked at both of them and smiled.

A couple of minutes later, Angela burst into the room looking slightly rushed. Steve sauntered in shortly afterwards.

Just as they were all settled, Liz went to start but was interrupted by Taylor throwing the door open. In his hands he had a long coat, a fancy-looking laptop briefcase and behind him was a small overnight case on wheels.

"Sorry I'm late everybody. I got caught in the foyer with my boss and the MD," Taylor blurted out without caring if they were listening.

As Liz looked up, Taylor continued.

"I'm more than happy to go first with the presentations if you want, Liz. I prepared mine on the train this morning while sitting across from this hot blonde."

"OK Taylor, you can go first," Liz replied, feeling herself getting frustrated. "But do you mind if I say a few things first?"

"No, not at all," Taylor responded, removing his laptop from the briefcase.

"Well, as I was about to say," Liz continued, glancing at Taylor, "today is an opportunity for us to check in to see how each other is doing and to see what's working for you and what's not. With the presentations, hopefully you've had the chance to reflect about how things have gone and what you've learned over the last month. I'm sure the time has just flown by for all of you."

They all nodded their heads, feeling amazed that they'd been in the business over a month.

"So Taylor, do you want to kick us off?" Liz asked politely.

"Sure thing; I assume there's no LCD projector to display my slides?" Taylor responded as he looked around the room.

"Oh well, you'll all just have to follow on my laptop then," he said as he spun the computer around for the others to see.

Taylor's presentation was slick. He'd produced 20 Powerpoint slides detailing every aspect of his job and his reporting chain. Throughout his presentation, he dropped in name after name while the others gradually lost interest. When Liz butted in after ten minutes, Taylor had only covered the first eight of his slides.

"It sounds like you've been doing some really interesting things, Taylor. You seem to be doing really well and making a name for yourself," Liz stated.

"Well, that's what I'm here for," Taylor replied.

"So what hasn't gone well?" Liz asked.

"Nothing," Taylor responded, wondering why she would ask such a question. "Everything is working exactly as it should."

"Mmm..." Liz responded.

Taylor then continued for another ten minutes before Liz drew him to a close. The others were now looking and feeling drained after Taylor's version of the 'look how great I am' show.

"Shall we have a quick break?" Liz suggested once she'd managed to silence Taylor.

"Great idea," Steve replied, feeling like he'd lost the will to live.

Upon returning to the room, each person then took it in turns to present their story. From their stories, Simon, Jane, Steve and Angela were all struggling with poorly-defined objectives and having difficulty getting time with their manager. As a result, none of them were sure of what they should be doing from day to day.

"I think I've managed to carve out a few things to focus on," Angela said. "I think people are seeing me as someone who's helpful. But although I'm busy, I'm definitely not challenged. In fact sometimes I think that I'm too busy, as it seems like the more I do, the more people want me to do. If you know what I mean."

"Sounds like you need to learn how to say no," Liz remarked.

"I think you might be right," Angela replied. "But it's not always that easy, Liz."

Jane was struggling with complete boredom.

"I just seem to be doing a lot of very basic data analysis and looking through spreadsheets," she said, feeling completely disheartened. "Initially it was interesting because it was new, but now I'm just bored. And my team are so busy that I can't seem to get any time with them to get other things to do."

"Well, my life just seems to go the same as Jane's," Steve said. "You know, complete boredom, and then into complete chaos when my boss decides to throw another pointless crisis my way to deal with."

"I'm just ticking along," Simon explained.

Your Future Starts Here

As each person told their story, the others listened feeling a real sense of sympathy, aside from Taylor who was still basking in his own glory. At the end of the presentations, they sat there in silence feeling quite depressed about their experiences.

"Well, what I've learnt from all this is that I couldn't stand to do this for the next two years, let alone for the rest of my career," Steve said breaking the silence. "I mean, the recruiting advertisement said 'Your Future Starts Here' but if this is my future I don't want it. This isn't what I signed up to: bad managers, boredom and feeling like I'm getting nowhere fast."

"I agree," Jane burst out. "I feel like I'm losing my mind. There has to be something better than this. Did I really go to university to get here?"

"Why don't you just get your uncle to fix it?" Taylor butted in without thinking.

"Because I don't need my uncle to fix it, thank you Taylor," Jane snapped back.

"Well all I can say is: *So is this what professional life is really like? Is this what I have to look forward to for the next 40-plus years?*" Simon asked.

All the others, even Taylor, nodded as they contemplated what Simon had just asked.

Work is a Scary Place

Throughout the discussion, Liz stayed quiet. However, a minute or so after Simon had finished his last statement, she decided to speak.

"Let me tell you about what I discovered when I was at the same stage as you five years ago. Because, believe it or not, I also went through exactly what you are going through today."

They all looked up at Liz, surprised that she understood where they were coming from.

"My first project in World-Corp was much the same as what each of you are experiencing," she said. "I fluctuated between extreme boredom and uncontrollable chaos, without much in between."

Liz paused and smiled, as Steve raised his eyebrows.

"After I'd been here about two months, it all came to a breaking point one Friday when I went down to see my parents for the weekend. I was feeling extremely frustrated and as low as I ever had. As I walked into the kitchen where my parents were, Mum asked me how things were going with the new job. At that point I just burst into tears right there in front of them. They both stood there completely startled when I blurted out that it was awful and I couldn't stand another day of it, let alone doing it for the rest of my career."

Liz stopped and took a sip from her bottle of water, as the others sat shocked by what she was telling them.

"That night, after I got a grip of myself, we sat in the lounge and I told my parents all that was happening. At the end my father said, *'well when you're new to the professional world, work can be a scary place.'* *You can say that again*, I replied to him.

As I thought more about my predicament over the weekend, I came to realise that prior to joining World-Corp I didn't realise that life would be like this. I thought that once you started work and 'became an adult', life would get simpler. You would have money in your pocket. You would get responsibility and be recognised for what you did. I believed what they said in the brochures, that I would have to work hard but I would be learning and developing as I went.

The more I thought, the more I questioned whether I had studied the right course at university. Perhaps I should have chosen a different degree or different subjects. Perhaps I should have picked a different university. I then felt like I had forgotten most of what I had learnt, which made me question whether I had actually learnt anything at all. I even remember questioning whether I'd missed the subject explaining what working life was really like."

"So what did you do?" Jane asked anxiously.

"Well," Liz said, continuing the story, "all of this led me to really doubt myself and feel insecure about who I was and what I was capable of. As I was getting no clear instructions and no real feedback, I doubted whether I was doing the right things, which made me withdraw further away from responsibility. And in doing this, I focused on the things that were simple and easy to complete, meaning that I stopped learning.

I think that this was made worse by being surrounded constantly by people who I perceived to be really talented. Because I was feeling so bad about myself, I started believing that I could never be as good as them no matter how much I tried. Unfortunately, some people who I worked with also had chips on their shoulders. It seemed that they had worked many years to get to where they had, and they didn't appreciate us new joiners coming in and trying to take over the place, or so they said."

"And finally, for some reason I felt like I had to compete with my peers, not that anyone was telling me to, but it just seemed like I should, which meant that I started losing friends."

Liz stopped and took another sip of water as the others sat silently.

"So feeling quite insecure and not knowing what to do, I started working harder and harder. I often felt like I was coming to work and putting on a mask as I entered the building. And my mask was me trying to be the person who I thought I should be in this new environment. After only a few weeks, it seemed that I was stuck on a hamster-wheel just running constantly trying to be someone who I wasn't."

"So what did you do?" Angela asked, desperate for the answer to Jane's question.

"Well," said Liz, looking first at Angela and then at Jane, "it was probably not so much what I did initially, but what I realised."

"And what was that?" Angela asked eagerly.

"I realised that I had stopped being myself," Liz explained.

"That's absurd!" Steve scoffed. "How could you stop being yourself?"

"No, that makes perfect sense," Jane remarked. "Just the other day one of my friends said the same thing to me. She said *'Jane, where have you gone? Why have you stopped being you?'*"

They all focused their attention on Jane.

"See, I didn't know what my friend meant, but hearing you talk about feeling like you were putting on a mask, Liz, that's exactly how I feel. It's like when I walk through the door each morning I take a deep breath and put on my confident face for the day ahead. Then I just sit there waiting for something to do, but too worried what people will think if I go out and ask them," Jane finished.

"Well, I don't feel like I'm wearing a mask," Steve sighed, "but I'm not happy, that's for sure."

"Me neither," Simon and Angela both replied.

Your Past Success was Due to You Being You

"When you realised that you were no longer being yourself, what did you do?" Jane asked, focusing the group's attention back towards Liz.

"Well," she said, "I decided that I wasn't happy and that I needed to do something about it."

By this time, Taylor had taken more of an interest in the conversation and had closed his laptop.

"So, what did you do?" he asked bluntly.

"Well, I'm not sure that I personally did anything right at that point," Liz replied directly to Taylor. "But before I left my parents' house that weekend, my mother did say something that brought me right back to reality."

They all focused their attention on Liz, hoping to hear the 'golden secret'.

"My mother said to me, 'Liz you've achieved some really great things in your life, and all of those things you've achieved through being yourself. So, why don't you just get back to being yourself?'" Liz replied to them.

Liz paused again, looking to see the reaction on each of their faces. It seemed as though, whilst all of them were looking directly at her, each of them was lost in their own world trying to make sense of what they'd heard. Angela broke the silence first, still not quite happy that she had been given the answer she needed.

"Liz, I understand what you're saying, but I'm still not sure how that helps," Angela said, feeling frustrated.

The others nodded in agreement with Angela, hoping that Liz would continue.

"Well," Liz replied, "my mother was right. I had achieved a lot of things through my schooling. I had also played some sports and travelled to different parts of the world. I'd finished university with reasonable grades. I had a great group of friends. And that was all due to me being me. At no stage had I pretended to be someone I wasn't."

"But I'm sure in each of those things you could have done better," Taylor butted in, almost insulting Liz without meaning to.

"Perhaps," Liz replied with a measured response. "It's true that I could have done better, but I guess that you can always compare yourself to others who have done more or achieved greater things than yourself; and there are always people who have. For example, I could look at my degree and say, *well I didn't get my PhD in the subject, so I haven't achieved as much. Or, yes I went to the Himalayas but I didn't climb Everest.*"

"That's right," Taylor continued confidently. "Surely if you had really wanted to achieve great things, then that's what you would have done."

"Perhaps," Liz replied again. "But, I didn't want to do those things so I chose not to. At the time my choice was probably less conscious than it is today, but I still chose not to."

Jane and Steve both scowled at Taylor who finally took the point that he wasn't helping the situation.

"But on the note of making comparisons, Taylor," Liz turned to look at him, "you can also compare yourself to those who have achieved less, as well. There are many people who wanted to go to university, but never did. Or who want to travel the world, but never have. So when looking at your achievements, it is always better to make the right comparison, if you feel you need to make a comparison at all."

Liz focused her attention back to the rest of the group.

"The key here is to recognise what you've achieved and acknowledge, even if only to yourself, that your achievements throughout life are due to you being you."

They all paused again, taking in what they had heard.

The time was now 3:30 p.m. Looking around the room, Liz could see that each person was still trying to find the nugget of knowledge they sought to find.

"Do you mind if we have a break, Liz?" Steve asked, breaking everyone's concentration. "I think that tea has gone straight through me and it's not going to be good if I sit here for any longer."

At that point, everyone let out a brief laugh.

"Sounds like a good idea, Steve," Liz replied, still smiling. "I'd hate for there to be an accident. Let's meet back here in ten minutes."

They all left the room, with Steve making the break straight to the gents. Simon wandered back to his desk and checked his email, while Angela and Jane took the lift down to the first floor café with Taylor hot on their heels trying to make interesting chit-chat. As they stood in the queue to purchase some more drinks for the group, Taylor started moving uncomfortably close to Jane. Just as the hairs on the back of her neck started to stand up and she was feeling like he was sitting on top of her, Taylor spoke.

"So Jane, what's the chance of you introducing me to your uncle?" he asked.

Jane and Angela both spun around in absolute amazement. Jane, tempted to tell him exactly what she thought, decided to hold back.

"Why sure, Taylor," she said calmly. "But I must warn you that Uncle Tom doesn't like brown-noses, he tends to want to fire them on the spot. So are you sure you want to meet him?"

"No, that's not what I mean," Taylor stammered. "It's just that I have some really great ideas on new management techniques in World-Corp that I'm sure he would want to hear."

Angela and Jane turned back to place their drinks order.

"You're unbelievable, Taylor, don't you ever give up?" Angela stated angrily without looking at him.

As soon as they received their order, the girls headed back to the elevator without waiting for Taylor.

We Hired You Because of Who You Are

Once back in the room, the atmosphere had turned a little frosty due to Taylor's advances in the coffee queue. Liz noticed that things had changed, but chose not to ask what was going on.

Angela, rather than dwell on the inappropriateness of Taylor's request, decided to break the tension.

"Liz, I really get what you're saying, but I'm not sure how this all helps me at work," she stated carefully, hoping to tease further information out of Liz.

"I struggled with the same thing," Liz replied. "That is until I stopped and thought about it some more. See, on the train back to London on the Sunday night I realised that one of my achievements was getting a job here. When I was hired into World-Corp we were in a recession which meant that competition for jobs was really fierce. I think that we had about 15,000 people applying for 300 positions, and I got one. That's pretty good, don't you think?"

The realisation started to seep into the group as they considered what that meant for themselves.

"That's right," Simon interrupted. "Even for us competing against 10,000 to get this job is a pretty great achievement. And I know for sure that I didn't pretend to be someone I wasn't through the interview. In fact, quite the opposite; I made sure they saw the real me."

Angela agreed with a nod, whereas Steve and Jane remained silent, thinking back to the recruitment process, wondering whether they had decided to put on a mask that day. Without saying anything, both of them concluded that they hadn't. Taylor was still seemingly tuned-out.

"It's easy to forget how big an achievement that is," Liz continued, "and I know that in the past some people have felt like they were the ones who slipped through the net and made it in when they shouldn't have. Now that may be true in some cases, but I doubt it. I can tell you that we know exactly what we're looking for. Our recruiters have been doing this for a very long time and our processes are pretty robust, meaning that we spot the fakes who come through the crowd. And we used the same model to recruit all of the great people who are working in the company today. If you think about some of the most talented people you've met, they were recruited in the same way as you were. So there's no randomness in the process!"

Liz stopped, looking at each person, ensuring that they understood the extent of their achievement.

"What I started to appreciate, and what I hope each of you appreciates as well, is that we hired you because of who you are. It's just as Alex said at induction. So, whatever each of you did during the recruitment process, it was noticed by us and we wanted you. Just remember, 10,000 people is a pretty big crowd. But each of you stood out in that crowd, both on paper and in person. So you've each proved that you deserve to be here."

A sense of relief filled the room as each person relaxed slightly into their chair. One by one, they no longer felt as though they were on guard or having to prove themselves.

"Remember what one of the speakers said at induction?" Liz asked as people returned their attention to her. "They said that you've already got the job here, so you don't have to compete against anyone. In my view, that means that all you need to do now is take off your mask and be that person we hired – be yourself. By doing that you'll start to really make a difference here."

Silence filled the room again as the words 'be yourself' rung in their ears.

"Just be yourself," Jane said softly. "I think that makes sense."

Another minute or so of silence passed before Steve decided to speak up.

"Well, that's a lot for an afternoon," he exclaimed. "It must be time to knock off, surely? Who's up for a drink after work?"

"Great idea," Liz replied, seeking to ease the mood. "I'll pay for the first round. Is everyone interested?"

Taylor, having sat quite uncomfortably throughout most of the session, quickly flicked up his wrist showing everyone his expensive watch as he checked the time.

"Sorry guys," he stated quickly. "I might be a little late as I need to catch the MD before he heads off. But I'll see you over there afterwards."

Jane found herself looking directly at Steve; they were both thinking the same thing about poor Taylor.

Once packed up, Liz, Steve, Jane, Simon and Angela wandered over to the pub opposite the office. As Liz purchased the first round of drinks, they all stood around a tall table in the middle of the room. After Steve's earlier indiscretion he was on his best behaviour and maintained a constant vigil over their laptop bags and coats.

After such an intense day, they all avoided talking any more about work. Instead, they focused on travelling, the clubs they were in at university and other amusing stories about their lives before World-Corp. By 7:00 p.m. Taylor still hadn't shown up so Steve gave him a call. Once the call went straight to voicemail, Steve announced that they should all go for dinner.

Good News – Just be Yourself

Over the weeks following their check-in meeting, Simon, Angela and Jane each found their rhythm a little better and were worrying less about some of the challenges they had described to Liz. Taylor was still excessively busy. Steve, on the other hand, was still suffering.

"I just don't get it," Steve said to Simon as they caught up before the Christmas break. "I just can't get my boss to listen to me."

"What are you going to do?" Simon asked.

"You know what, mate, I don't care. I'm off skiing tomorrow, so I'll forget about it for a couple of weeks and then see if he's any different after Santa visits him."

On the final day of work before the Christmas holiday, Angela, who had been thinking more and more about what Liz had told them that day, sent the others an email.

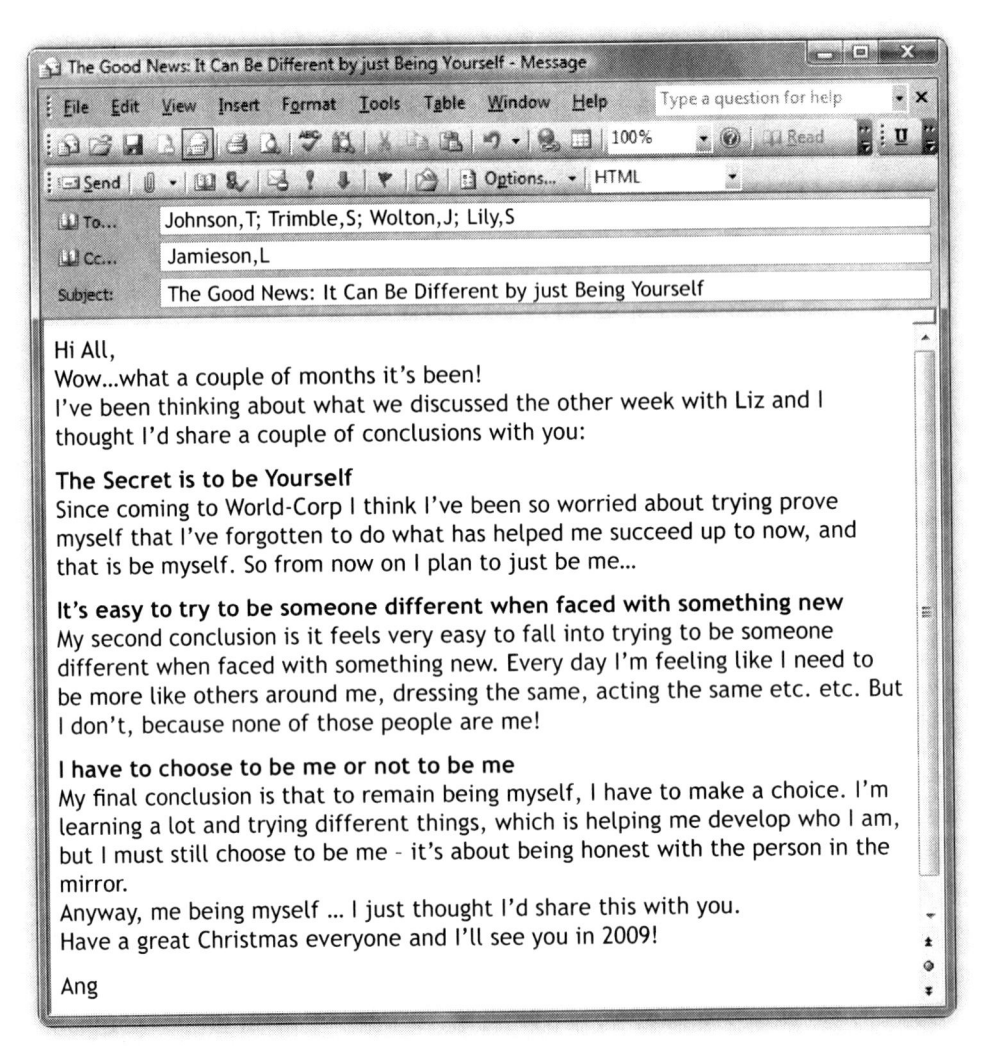

The Good News: It Can Be Different by just Being Yourself - Message

To...: Johnson,T; Trimble,S; Wolton,J; Lily,S
Cc...: Jamieson,L
Subject: The Good News: It Can Be Different by just Being Yourself

Hi All,
Wow...what a couple of months it's been!
I've been thinking about what we discussed the other week with Liz and I thought I'd share a couple of conclusions with you:

The Secret is to be Yourself
Since coming to World-Corp I think I've been so worried about trying prove myself that I've forgotten to do what has helped me succeed up to now, and that is be myself. So from now on I plan to just be me...

It's easy to try to be someone different when faced with something new
My second conclusion is it feels very easy to fall into trying to be someone different when faced with something new. Every day I'm feeling like I need to be more like others around me, dressing the same, acting the same etc. etc. But I don't, because none of those people are me!

I have to choose to be me or not to be me
My final conclusion is that to remain being myself, I have to make a choice. I'm learning a lot and trying different things, which is helping me develop who I am, but I must still choose to be me - it's about being honest with the person in the mirror.
Anyway, me being myself ... I just thought I'd share this with you.
Have a great Christmas everyone and I'll see you in 2009!

Ang

After sending her email, a flurry of replies shot through cyberspace between Jane, Simon and Angela. Taylor ignored the note and Steve had already left to go skiing in France.

PRINCIPLES TO REMEMBER

You are the common factor throughout your life.

Your past success was due to your being you.

It is easy to try to be someone different
when faced with something new.

The secret is to make the choice to be yourself.

TASKS FOR THE READER

Recognising your Achievements

As '*you*' are the common factor throughout your life, it is important to understand and be proud of what you've achieved up to today. Use the table below to capture your most memorable achievements – *what have you achieved that you are most proud of?* As you consider what you've done over time, make sure you make the 'right' comparison when thinking about your key achievements.

DATE	ACHEIVEMENTS

Just Remember:

Never forget your past achievements, as these successes were due to you being you.

2.

Start By Managing Yourself

The First Training Session

"So, three days out of the office at our first training session," Simon said to Jane, Angela and Steve as they settled into their train seats ready for the long journey down to Wales.

"Yeh, I can't believe that they're sending all 350 of us down to Wales for three days," Jane replied.

"Only 30 people at a time though, isn't it?" Steve asked, wondering how all the new joiners would fit into the one venue.

"There were only 30 names on our invite," Simon responded.

The train groaned as they slowly started moving out of Paddington station towards their destination.

"So what did you get up to for Christmas?" Angela asked Jane.

"Just went home to see the family," Jane replied. "To tell you the truth, after a pretty hectic couple of months I really just felt like a break."

"Me too," Simon said with a sigh. "Unfortunately I made the mistake of agreeing with my girlfriend that we should have both our families over to our little one-bedroom flat for Christmas. We were basically sitting on each other and the place was like a sauna with so many people in it."

"Ha, that'll teach you," Steve laughed. "You should have come skiing with me."

"What, and end up with a twisted knee like you, you must be joking!"

"Well, no pain no gain, mate," Steve replied to Simon with a smile. "At least it got me out of the office for a couple of weeks, even if I did have to come back early."

Simon, Angela and Jane all shook their heads at Steve.

For the rest of the trip they swapped stories about their Christmas break and the horror gifts they'd received over the years. Simon, Angela and Jane were all careful not to talk about work for fear that Steve would hijack the conversation and reinforce his own sense of misery.

"Where's Taylor?" Steve asked during one of the few pauses in the conversation.

"Don't know," Simon replied. "He never got back to me."

"Oh," Steve responded before changing the subject.

The venue for the training was a converted 18th century mansion house that was surrounded by lush gardens which had piles of snow spread across them. The driveway into the mansion curved from the main road past a visitors' car park until it looped around a large fountain that was positioned in front of the building's main entrance.

As their taxi drove off, Steve, Simon, Angela and Jane walked into the reception. Just as Angela was about to tell the lady behind the counter her name, they were all distracted by the sound of loud thudding music coming from behind them. Outside, a slick-looking, black two-door Mercedes had just rolled up and was parked almost blocking the front doors. As the door to the car opened, out jumped Taylor wearing his aviator sunglasses as if he were Tom Cruise in Top Gun. Heading straight for them, there was a quick bleep as the side-lights of the Mercedes flashed, indicating that the car had locked.

"Nice car," Simon stated as Taylor approached. "Yours?"

"No, it's my father's. He's away at a medical conference in Las Vegas this week, so he let me use it," Taylor replied boastfully.

"Where do I park?" Taylor snapped at the receptionist.

"Sorry sir, I was just checking in your colleagues here, so I'm afraid you'll have to wait," the receptionist replied, not intimidated by Taylor's steely glare.

Taylor spun round impatiently, tearing off his aviators and sliding them coolly into where his shirt was buttoned up. Ignoring his reaction, the receptionist continued checking Angela, Jane, Steve and then Simon into their rooms.

The Dreaded Introductions

As per the instructions provided, at 1:30 p.m. after lunch all the new joiners assembled in the main training room, which was laid out with round tables in a similar style to the initial induction. Naturally, each of the colleagues gravitated to a table with their support group. Taylor had decided to change out of his expensive jeans and shirt and was now dressed much the same as the others in more casual clothing. He even chose to join the conversation by asking the others how their Christmas break was and what Santa Claus had brought them.

"Welcome to Learning how to Manage Yourself training," the trainer announced loudly from the front of the room, encouraging the crowd to quieten down.

"Now, I've worked with new joiners from World-Corp for the last five years, and each time I've been constantly impressed by the quality of people I've seen," he continued. "So here's my challenge to you: it's my expectation that you will be equally as impressive, if not more impressive, than all those before you."

The room went completely silent.

"Now let me tell you what we've got in store for you over the next few days," the trainer said as he displayed the agenda on the large screen at the front of the room.

The agenda didn't give too much away other than that the rumours about 7:00 a.m. starts for physical exercise were true, and that whole blocks of the days were set aside for something called 'experiential exercises'. Despite the opportunity, no one asked any questions.

Looking around the room Jane recognised a few faces that she had met before at various social events or around the office. *It would be good to get to know a few more people,* she thought to herself.

"Right, now I want each of you to stand up and introduce yourself, starting with you," the trainer said loudly as he pointed at Jane, instantly grabbing her attention.

Jane's face went bright red. She hated this part of any new session. The dreaded introductions were the worst bit, and going first was never good.

Standing up slowly, Jane was too embarrassed to think of something clever to say.

"Hi," she started softly, "my, my name is Jane and I'm working in finance."

Within a few seconds she was back in the comfort of her chair, hoping that her cheeks were now returning to their natural colour.

Around the room, others felt the same sickening anxiety as they waited for their turn.

It's More Common Than You Think

"So now we all know each other," the trainer said once the introductions were over, "I want you to consider where you are right now."

Just as the trainer finished his sentence a new picture lit up the large screen.

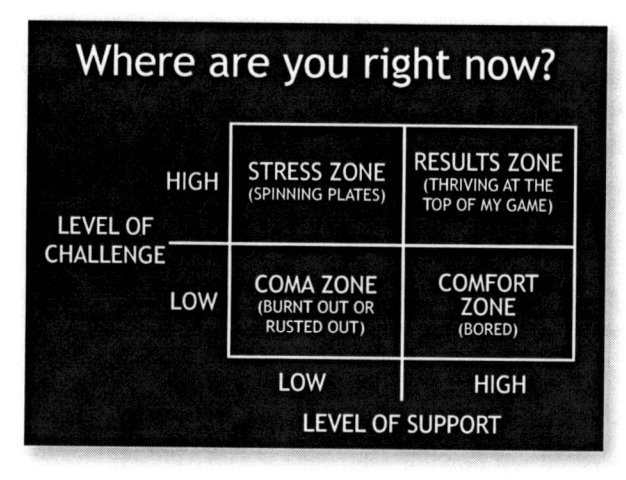

Where are you right now?

LEVEL OF CHALLENGE	STRESS ZONE (SPINNING PLATES)	RESULTS ZONE (THRIVING AT THE TOP OF MY GAME)
HIGH		
LOW	COMA ZONE (BURNT OUT OR RUSTED OUT)	COMFORT ZONE (BORED)
	LOW	HIGH

LEVEL OF SUPPORT

Everyone's eyes quickly focused on each of the descriptions in the boxes as they sought to answer the question being asked.

"I'm definitely in the comfort zone, rapidly moving towards the coma zone," a blonde girl called out from the back of the room, clearly frustrated with her experience so far.

"I'm bored out of my mind at work," she continued.

"I know how you feel," another person said, "I think I started from day one in the coma zone."

"You're lucky," yet another person yelled out, "I haven't stopped doing 50-plus hour weeks, so I'm definitely in the stress zone headed towards burn-out."

As more people spoke up, Jane, Angela, Simon, Taylor and Steve couldn't help but feel relieved that others were also feeling the same highs and lows as them. Just as the trainer regained control over the eruption of voices, the blonde girl spoke up again.

"This is all great," she said sarcastically, "but I've been here for three whole months and there is no way I see myself ever getting to the results zone."

People sat amazed at her being so forthright but, before she could continue, a redheaded guy from the front butted in.

"I agree," he said angrily, "this isn't what it said in the brochures for World-Corp. It said that we'd be challenged and that we would grow and develop. But all I'm feeling is frustrated and that I'm going backwards fast."

He paused for a moment as the rest of the room fell silent.

"I have to ask, but is this what professional life is really like? Because if it is, I think I've made the wrong choice. I can't ever imagine myself getting to the results zone, and I can't imagine doing this for the rest of my career," the redheaded guy continued, still with an angry tone in his voice.

Many others around the room nodded, knowing exactly how he was feeling.

"Well," the trainer said, remaining calm but positive. "Let me tell you the good news for all of you who are not in the results zone. It is possible to get to, and stay in there, just by doing one simple thing."

"And what's that?" the blonde girl asked, still sarcastically.

"Well, it's to be yourself," the trainer replied without hesitating.

At that point, Jane, Angela, Simon, Taylor and Steve all shot glances at each other, and a small smile came to each of their faces. They'd heard this before.

The rest of the new joiners sat silently contemplating what the trainer had said. A few thought about challenging what he was suggesting, but chose not to.

"So, the purpose of the next three days is to help you do one thing and one thing alone, and that is manage you, yes the person in the mirror," the trainer said slowly but confidently. "And what this means is that we will be seeking to equip each of you with some techniques to take control of the most valuable asset you have – you!"

The trainer then paused for a moment to wait for a challenge, but none came.

"Let's have a break, and as you leave the room I want you to consider this: you are your greatest asset and over this asset you have complete control, especially over what you think. That's right, you control you. Those who accept this in their lives will make a difference and will gain fulfilment and those who don't accept this won't. It is that simple."

"Wow, I knew Liz was right," Angela said to Steve as they headed out for a break.

"I'm still not sure I get it," Steve replied as he winced while bending his knee a little too much.

How Do You Work?

On the screen as they arrived back in the room was a single question: **How do you work?**

Each of their faces showed their confusion as they puzzled over what it meant.

"What we are now going to do for the rest of the afternoon," the trainer said once the last person was seated, "is help you answer that very question."

"The first thing to consider in seeking to understand how you work is to consciously understand what impact you have. That is, when you say or do something, what is the result? By asking this question you can see whether the result you had is the result you wanted. The second thing to consider is to understand how what you're thinking and what you're feeling at any moment influences what you say or do, and hence the impact you have."

Everyone sat there, still looking puzzled. The trainer then flicked up a new picture on to the screen.

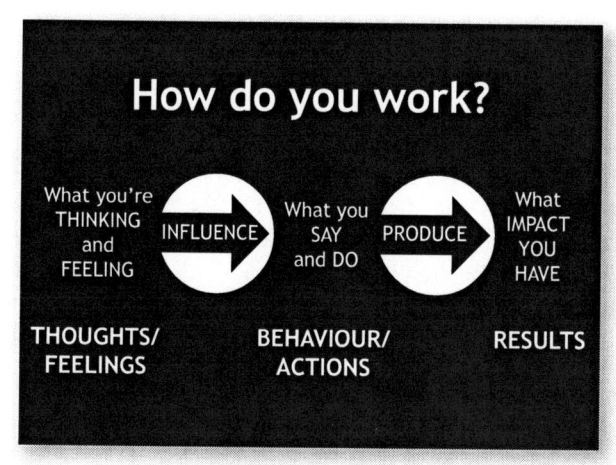

How do you work?

What you're THINKING and FEELING → INFLUENCE → What you SAY and DO → PRODUCE → What IMPACT YOU HAVE

THOUGHTS/FEELINGS   BEHAVIOUR/ACTIONS   RESULTS

"Now the key to building this understanding is being more conscious about what you do and why you do it. This requires you to ask three questions: One, what do I want to achieve? Two, what do I need to say or do to achieve that? And Three, how is what I am currently thinking or feeling influencing my behaviour? By asking these questions you can really focus on choosing the right thoughts, feelings and behaviour to help you achieve the results you desire."

As those in the room listened, Simon started to feel a little stupid.

"Do you know what he's on about?" Simon whispered to Angela during one of the trainer's pauses.

"I'm not sure," Angela whispered back, "but I'm guessing that we'll know soon enough."

Simon eased back into his chair, feeling a little better that he wasn't the only one not getting it.

"In seeking to build this understanding of how you work, the first thing we're going to do is an activity to get you to reflect on how your results in a particular situation were impacted by your behaviours and actions, which were driven by your thoughts and feelings," the trainer said.

"What I want you to do is consider a situation from your time in World-Corp when you haven't achieved the results you wanted. For this situation I want to you to capture what you wanted to achieve and then the results that you actually produced. Then capture what you were thinking and feeling at the time and what you said and did to try to get the results you wanted. Finally, I want you to consider how what you were thinking and feeling, and what you said and did, stopped you from getting the results you wanted."

They all remained silent, thinking about the task.

"Once you've written this on a sheet of paper, I want you to discuss it with a partner. The key here is to really think about what you were thinking and feeling in the situation and how that influenced your behaviour, which stopped you from getting your required results," the trainer then instructed.

Each of them did what they were asked, although they found it difficult to remember what they were thinking or feeling at the time.

"In my situation," Jane said to Simon when they paired up, "I remember feeling really nervous and almost scared of my boss. So when I spoke to him I ended up being unclear about what I wanted, which resulted in me not getting the information I needed to complete the task. I felt like such a fool afterwards as all I had to do was ask the right question, but instead I was just a bag of nerves."

"I think I was a too 'in your face' with my boss," Steve said to Angela recounting his situation. "At the time I was thinking that this guy is hopeless and I know better than him. So the way I ended up behaving was quite arrogant in telling him what we should be doing. You can just imagine how that went down."

Taylor, who didn't really seek to partner with anyone, struggled to come up with a situation where he didn't get the results he wanted.

"Things always just seem to work for me," he replied when Simon asked.

"So it's amazing how much what you think and your feelings influence your impact in the world," the trainer announced, bringing everyone's attention to the front. "The good news with this exercise is that because you can actually control what you think and feel, you can influence your behaviour at any time. By controlling these things you can ultimately have a far better impact in any situation."

The trainer paused, looking at the faces in the room. He could see that they were all looking a bit weary and were ready to freshen up before dinner.

Recognise Your Impact

"Now tonight over dinner," the trainer said before letting them leave the room, "I want you to get to know someone you haven't met before. As you do this, I want you to focus on how what you think and feel impacts on others, and on how you get to know new people. I want you to try and be really conscious at any moment about what you're thinking and feeling, and how this is influencing what you're saying and doing."

Everyone agreed without thinking too much about what was being asked. At dinner, most followed the trainer's instructions by sitting with people they didn't know. Taylor deliberately positioned himself next to a French girl and, without waiting to be asked, proceeded to tell her how fantastic his impact was on others. The girl listened patiently while Taylor retold the 'fig jam' (Fuck I'm Good Just Ask Me) story.

As Taylor finally paused to take his first mouthful, the French girl reached for her glass of wine.

"Would you like me to tell you what your true impact is on me?" she then said with a strong French accent.

"I would love you to," Taylor replied as he turned to look into her eyes, expecting the reinforcement of his perceived greatness.

"Well," she said quietly, "you have to be the most arrogant, over-confident person I have ever met. Not all English men are like this, because my boyfriend is English and he is lovely, but you are not. Throughout the whole of dinner you have only spoken about yourself with not a single question directed at me. So your impact on me is quite negative."

The food Taylor had just put into his mouth almost fell out as he stared at her in astonishment. Snapping out of it, he quickly looked around to see if anyone else had heard what she said, but it looked as though they were all deep in conversation. Angela, however, who was sitting on a table nearby, heard every word.

The French girl then continued eating as if nothing had happened. Taylor, on the other hand, scoffed down his meal in silence and then pretended his mobile phone rang, so he could excuse himself from the table. No-one really noticed him leave.

A couple of tables away, Jane was sitting next to a tall American guy. As she spoke, he listened as if fully captivated by her words. Feeling completely at ease, Jane told him her World-Corp story. When she reached a natural conclusion, he spoke up.

"I hope you don't mind me saying this Jane, but I think that how you think and feel about yourself means that you really hold yourself back," the American guy said in his strong New York accent.

"What do you mean?" Jane responded, feeling concerned by such a remark.

"Well, you seem like a really great and confident person. But I think that because you don't believe in yourself, you're just holding back when there's no need to," he continued. "My advice is start letting the world see how great you are. Pick up the phone more, meet people more and use that great personality to get out of that introverted shell of yours!"

"That's easy for you to say, you Americans are great at that type of thing," Jane responded cheekily.

"That's what most people think, but it's not true. I tell you it takes a lot of concentration and energy for me to meet new people but I know I have to, so I do," the American fired back with a grin.

"You're right. I think it is something I really need to work on. At university I got over my shyness, but here I haven't managed to. I guess I don't want to have to put on a mask to push myself out there though," Jane thought out loud.

"Who said you have to put on a mask? What I do when I know I need to make more of an effort is just borrow behaviours instead. That way I'm not compromising who I am, but I am picking the right behaviours to have the impact I need. Which, I might add, then influences what I think and feel about myself when it goes well," the American said, noticing that people were heading to the bar.

"Shall we follow?" he then said motioning to leave the table.

"Mmm…borrowing behaviours, I think you might be right," Jane said slowly, not wanting to break from his gaze. "Yeh, let's follow."

Most people had now moved into the bar, with a couple heading off for an early night. Taylor was nowhere to be seen. Steve, in fine form, was at the bar surrounded by people and telling a story about his skiing adventures. Laughter erupted as Steve comically re-enacted how he twisted his knee.

Simon and Jane, along with a few others, found themselves in the lounge room. They had formed a circle with their chairs around a small table that held their drinks. Rather than talk about the day's events, they chose to re-tell stories about the horrors of their first couple of months.

As the night went on, the people in the bar slowly disappeared leaving only Angela and

Steve. Now alone, Angela told Steve about Taylor's incident with the French girl.

"You know, I feel sorry for Taylor," Steve announced looking out of the window.

"Really, why?" Angela responded, astonished. "The guy is a creep! He's hit on just about every girl at World-Corp."

As he lowered his glass after taking another sip of beer, Steve looked at Angela and then out of the window opposite the bar.

"I know he's a creep, and I don't blame him hitting on you by the way, but I think the guy just doesn't know who he is. See how he rolled up in his old man's Mercedes thinking he was king of the world. None of us really care about that, but with him it's like he's trying to prove something that he doesn't need to prove."

Angela stood silent, still fixated on Steve's first comment about not blaming Taylor for hitting on her.

"So I think that we should give the guy a bit of a break and help him out a little," Steve continued, giving Angela a wink as he took her arm and led her into the lounge room.

As they walked in, Steve announced to all that the king and queen of World-Corp had arrived and they would now right all the wrongs in the company. Everyone laughed and made space for them to join. The party continued until 1:00 in the morning when people decided to finally call it a night. Steve, well drunk and still pretending to be the king, walked Angela to her room. Much to Angela's surprise, just before turning away towards his room, he kissed her on the cheek.

"Goodnight my fair queen, I will see thee on the morrow," he said before spinning around and stumbling to his room.

Always Make Conscious Choices – *Create a Gap*

After being rudely awoken by their alarms, everybody was up and ready for their 7:00 a.m. exercise session. It had snowed overnight so people came down wearing as many layers as they could, ready for the cold. Before they headed outside, Angela sauntered over to Steve who was looking a little the worse for wear.

"Good morning Your Highness, how's the head?"

"Excellent thank you, my lovely queen. Nothing a few headache tablets couldn't fix. All ready for a run out in the snow?" he responded with a smile.

Before she could answer, they were all ushered outside.

Following their exercise, showers and breakfast, everyone reassembled in the main training room. Once in the room they were directed to move seats so they could get to know some other people. Much to Taylor's horror, the only seat left was next to the French girl from dinner. As soon as he sat down she glanced at him to acknowledge his presence. Taylor instantly felt sick. *Be a man about this*, he thought to himself. He then turned to face the

French girl.

"I just want to apologise for being such an arse last night. What you said was right, and I'm really sorry," Taylor said as respectfully as he could.

The French girl turned to face him.

"Merci," she said with a smile.

"So our first session today is on the need to make conscious choices," the trainer announced, drawing everyone's attention to the front.

He then flicked up the first slide on to the screen.

> You may not always be able to choose your circumstance
>
> *but you can always choose how you respond!*

"No matter what circumstance you face, you can always choose how you respond," he said. "In life, whether in or outside of work, you will not always be able to control the situations in which you find yourselves. Sometimes you will just seem to end up in places that you didn't expect or plan for. Despite this however, you can always choose how you respond in those situations."

He paused for a moment to allow people to take in what he'd said.

"An extreme example of this is the many stories you hear about prisoners of war who have survived the most awful atrocities because they believed in this theory; they chose how to respond despite the terrible predicament they faced."

He paused again.

"Now, in choosing how you respond to any given situation, one of the most powerful choices you can make is in regard to the attitude you adopt," the trainer continued as the next slide appeared on the screen.

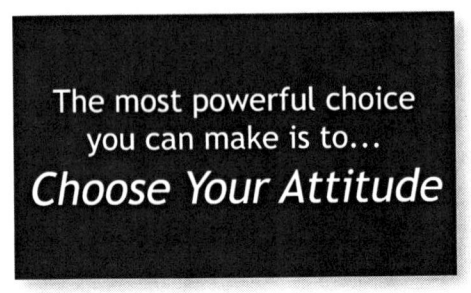

> The most powerful choice you can make is to...
>
> *Choose Your Attitude*

At this point, Steve, whose hangover had decided to return now he was seated, could not contain himself.

"That's rubbish! I don't choose to be pissed off at work, but because I have a bad manager, and because I'm either bored or manically busy, I get frustrated."

Steve's explosion resulted in a flurry of responses as people argued for and against the concept of choice.

"You still choose your attitude whether you like it or not," one person said. "It just means that the choice is unconscious because you're unconsciously choosing to be a victim."

Although deep down Steve started to agree with the trainer, he decided to keep it to himself to save face.

"One of the things I want each of you to consider is what attitude you choose at work. Are you a negative, glass half-empty type of person, or are you a positive, glass half-full type of person?" the trainer asked. "Because if you are negative then you're likely to be draining the energy of those around you, but if you are positive you are likely to be energising others."

He then flicked the next slide on to the screen.

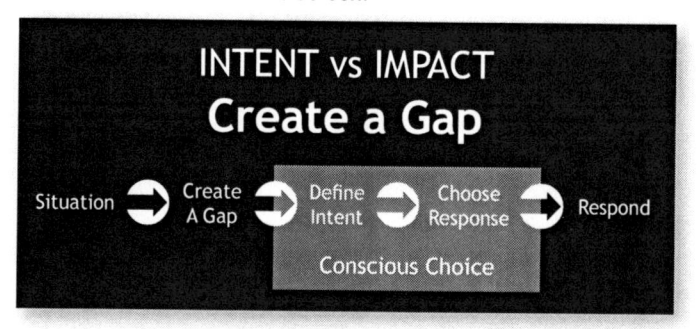

INTENT vs IMPACT
Create a Gap

Situation → Create A Gap → Define Intent → Choose Response → Respond

Conscious Choice

"In order to make conscious choices," the trainer announced, directing their eyes to the screen, "you have to consider your intent versus your impact."

Confusion swept across the faces in the room.

"What I mean is what you hope to achieve in any situation you might face; what your definition of success is," the trainer continued. "By defining this up front, you can be more conscious about the thoughts and feelings you develop, and ultimately what you say and do to achieve it. You can therefore respond consciously, rather than just react instinctively."

At that point the redheaded guy piped up.

"So are you saying that in every situation we face we must define what we want to achieve, or our intent as you call it, before we do anything?"

"Absolutely," the trainer responded enthusiastically. "Or at least define it to the level you can within the time available. This is so you avoid just reacting instinctively."

"So if my boss phones up and demands that I have something completed by the end of the day, you're saying that I should define my intent in the situation, rather than just say yes and do it?" the redheaded guy challenged back.

"That's right," the trainer continued. "We'll talk about how you do that, but your intent in that situation might be to deliver the best for World-Corp, your boss and you. So rather than just instinctively say yes, you might ask a few questions first. This way you can seek to define what success would look like before taking action."

"But that's easier said then done, especially if they're demanding," the redhead challenged.

"That's why you need to diffuse the situation a little, by creating a gap," the trainer replied.

"A gap? What's a gap?" the redhead fired back.

"A gap is a mental pause where you decide what your intent is in the situation and then you consciously choose how you are going to respond – what you're going to say and do – to achieve it. A gap need only be a second or two as you take a deep breath, provided you use that pause properly," the trainer explained.

The redhead sat there contemplating whether to ask another question, but decided not to.

"Right, let's do an activity," the trainer announced, seeing that people needed a little more convincing.

"Think back to the task from yesterday where something didn't work out the way you had hoped. In other words, your intent didn't equal your impact. For that situation, consider what your true intent was in the situation; what was the success you wanted? Then consider what you could have done differently to ensure that your intent equalled your impact. That is, what else could you have said or done?"

The trainer paused.

"Once you've thought about this, discuss it with a partner and get them to give you their thoughts on your perceived intent and then what you might have said or done differently to achieve it. You might also want to ask them what they think your attitude is at work."

As a few people got up to go to the bathroom, much to Taylor's surprise the French girl spoke.

"So what do you think your attitude is?" she asked softly.

"Well," Taylor started without thinking what he was saying, "I think I'm pretty positive at work most of the time, but I'm pretty negative about myself."

As he finished his statement, Taylor realised he'd said too much and quickly changed the topic.

"What part of France are you from?" he asked hurriedly, hoping that there wouldn't be any follow-up questions.

"Paris. And, I think you might be right," she responded with a smile before standing up and heading towards the ladies' bathroom.

Standing outside the room, Steve was grappling with what he'd heard that morning.

"Do you believe that stuff about choosing your attitude?" he asked Simon who was standing with him.

"Yeh, I think I do," Simon responded. "Most of the time I would consider myself to be a glass half-full kind of guy, but I know I let some of the crap at work get to me when I shouldn't, which means I am choosing to be negative. What do you think?"

"I don't know," Steve replied, looking away.

"Would you say I am positive or negative?" he then asked Simon hesitantly.

"If you want the truth, mate," Simon looked him in the eye. "Outside of work definitely positive, your majesty, but when it comes to work I'd say definitely negative. I think you just need to take some of who you are outside of work and inject it into here. And to do that I think that all you need to do is create a gap and choose a different attitude...if you don't mind me saying so."

"Mmm, a gap," Steve mumbled.

Keep Focused – *Stay in the Present*

"The key thing to remember with creating a gap," the trainer stated once everyone was ready for the next session, "is that it takes practice. At first it is tough to do because you have to consciously pause rather than unconsciously react. But as you get better at it, you'll find that it is as simple as taking a breath."

The trainer paused as he prepared to change topic.

"In organisations today, and the world for that matter, there is a constant stream of information bombarding us. Whether it be from email, mobile phone, Blackberry, instant messenger or just people looking for time with you, it is very easy to get distracted."

Isn't that the truth, Simon thought to himself.

"So this afternoon we're going to take you through some techniques to help you keep focused by prioritising, controlling your distractions and through staying in the present," the trainer continued.

The new joiners were then separated into five equal teams of six and then allocated to another facilitator.

"The task you are going to undertake is an office simulator," the trainer announced, seeking to get their attention. "This task is designed to test your ability to keep focused and manage your priorities."

Each of the groups was then ushered into its own room that was equipped with two laptops, a mobile phone and a fixed telephone. For the next 90 minutes they were then subjected to a constant flow of information and requests via email, telephone and from people rushing into the office.

"So how did it go?" the facilitator for Simon's group asked once the 90 minutes was over.

"It was impossible," one of his new colleagues stated. "There was no way we had enough time to do everything."

"Who said you had to do everything?" the facilitator asked.

"Well, no-one," Simon responded, looking puzzled. "But people were asking for it, so that means we should deliver."

"Perhaps," the facilitator responded with a smile. "But surely some tasks were more important than others and surely some of them were not your problems to fix?"

As she finished her statement, the facilitator handed each team member a sheet of paper with four boxes on it.

Priority Matrix

	NOT IMPORTANT	IMPORTANT
URGENT	PRIORITY 3	PRIORITY 1
NOT URGENT	PRIORITY 4	PRIORITY 2

"So after lunch let's try this activity again," Simon's facilitator said as they each looked at the sheet. "This time, however, I want you to really prioritise the tasks you're given against their importance and urgency. You should really only be focusing on your Priority One and Two tasks. And I want you to check to see if those in Priority Three and Four are really someone else's problem that has just been passed to you."

They each nodded.

"What I also want you to do is manage your distractions. This means working off-line on email and diverting your phone to voicemail, and only checking them periodically. You could even try signing off from instant messenger."

"But we live in a world of instant communication," said another of Simon's colleagues.

"That's the idea of all this technology."

"That's true," said the facilitator, "but we don't need instant communication to be effective. We've just come to rely on it because it's there. Just try what I've suggested and see what happens."

After lunch they re-did the simulator task. For 90 minutes they tried the prioritisation techniques and removing distractions. To their surprise, they managed to deliver all of the most important requirements well within the allocated time and they were able to push back to the originator that which wasn't important; and all of this without responding instantly to a single request.

Once all the groups were back in the main room, the trainer asked people what they thought.

"It's great," Angela announced, "I can already see my to-do list shrinking due to this. And being given permission to not respond instantly to emails or calls is fantastic. I never thought that I didn't have to be available all the time."

Another person piped up.

"I'm still not sure," he said, "I mean I just don't know how my boss will react if he can't get hold of me."

"Well," Angela said, giving her own advice, "you could always tell your boss the best way to get hold of you and then manage every other distraction. For example, you could turn your email off and keep your phone on silent so you aren't distracted by the calls, and then ask him to text you if he needs you."

"I'll try," the person responded to Angela, still a little wary.

"Ultimately," the trainer continued, "these are techniques for you to try and tailor to your particular circumstance and style. The key here is to make sure that you keep focused on that which is most important and urgent each day, your Priority Ones. Then remove distractions that may prevent you from achieving this. As an example, one of my techniques is each morning before logging on I capture the top three priorities I must do that day. This helps me keep focused."

People around the room nodded as they considered what they might try.

"The final thing I want to talk about today is staying in the present," the trainer continued.

The present? Jane thought.

"The most powerful thing to help you keep focused is to stay in the 'present'," the trainer explained. "This means keeping all of your conscious attention on what you're trying to achieve in the present moment. Now to do this you must learn how to catch yourself when your mind starts to drift off, or when a distraction comes your way. To stay in the present you must also learn to avoid dwelling on the past or worrying about the future," the trainer continued.

"But how do you stop dwelling on the past?" Jane heard herself ask.

"Well, the past is just that – the past. There is nothing you can do about it if you don't have a time machine," the trainer responded with a smile. "But you can learn from it, and by learning from it you can help to shape your future."

"That's easy to say, but how do you shape your future?" another person asked.

"You plan, and then take action against that plan," the trainer replied quickly.

"It all sounds so simple," the person responded, "but nothing is ever that easy."

"That's true," the trainer replied yet again, "but if you never try you'll never know."

"So tonight over dinner, I want you to think about how you can keep focused, by remaining in the present. To do this, can I suggest that you first consider where you spend a lot of your time? Do you dwell on the past, worry about the future or are you always in the present moment?" the trainer asked.

Over dinner that night people were buzzing over the various revelations they'd had that day. Taylor, after making another gaffe by trying to take over in the simulator, decided to keep a low profile. Noticing this, Steve sought to help him out by inviting him to join them at the bar once everyone had finished eating.

"So where is my beautiful Queen?" Steve asked in a regal manner as he approached the bar after dinner.

"Here I am, Your Highness," Angela responded, playing along.

As they leant shoulder to shoulder on the bar out of earshot of the others, Steve whispered to Angela, "Well my fair Queen, whilst I seek to be in the present, I cannot help but wonder what our future has in store."

Angela tilted her head slightly in Steve's direction.

"We'll just have to see, won't we?" Angela whispered back as her brown eyes lit up.

"Fancy finding somewhere quiet?" Steve replied with a mischievous smile.

"Mmm, I think that would be nice," Angela said softly.

As the crowd in the bar grew and the noise became louder, Steve and Angela attempted to slip away without being noticed. Once they were well out of sight, Steve reached down and gently took hold of Angela's hand. A shock flew up her arm as she felt his tender touch on her skin. Leading her by the hand, they walked towards a smaller training room. Once the door was closed behind them, Steve turned until they stood face to face. Without being able to take the anticipation any longer, Steve leaned forward and kissed her. Angela's arms reached around Steve as the intensity of their passion revealed itself.

Whilst standing as a part of one of the groups in the bar, Simon spotted Steve and Angela leaving. He nudged Jane who was standing next to him and nodded in their direction.

"Mmm," Jane responded to Simon with a smile.

After a very full day, by 11:30 p.m. most people had left the bar for bed.

Learn Constantly

The next morning as Jane was walking down the hall ready to assemble for their physical training, she spied Steve slowly coming out of Angela's room, hoping not to be noticed. Looking up he saw Jane standing there smiling.

"Morning," Jane said with a smile.

"Morning," Steve replied quickly, trying to hide his embarrassment. "All ready for the morning training?"

"Yes, are you?" Jane responded.

"Will be in a few minutes," Steve said as he turned and headed for his room.

Throughout the physical training and breakfast, Steve and Angela sought to avoid each other as much as possible so people wouldn't notice that something had happened between them.

Jane was quick to tell Simon what she'd seen, which gave him valuable ammunition with which to make fun of Steve. Every time Steve looked his way, Simon would give him a smile and a disapproving shake of the head.

It was the final day of their training and they were due to finish just after lunch.

"What we are going to spend today on is the need to 'Learn Constantly'," the trainer said. "To do this we're going to focus on reflective learning and feedback. Reflective learning is where you take the time out after an event and objectively ask yourself three questions: What went well? What didn't go well? What could I have done differently? Feedback is where you get others to tell you their perception of you to test your self-concept and really uncover your blind spots."

"Now, rather than considering a specific event from your time in World-Corp, what I want you to do is use these three magic questions to pair up and get some honest feedback."

A feeling of dread instantly developed in many of the new joiners' stomachs.

Honest feedback, Jane thought to herself, *I'm not sure I like the sound of that.*

"For feedback to be effective," the trainer continued, "it has to be relevant and timely. It has to focus on the behaviour and not the person. It also has to be developmental and consistent. Feedback, as they say, is the breakfast of champions, so I really encourage you to seek it out whenever possible."

Once the trainer had finished speaking, they all paired up and found a comfortable place to talk. To avoid working with Angela, Steve volunteered to join Taylor. Simon and Angela also paired up, leaving Jane to work with her American friend.

"So, shall I start with giving the feedback?" Steve asked Taylor once he'd prepared a few things to say.

"Sure," Taylor responded, not knowing what to expect.

"What I really like about what you do is how you search for the positive in everything you're doing, and how you're so professional," Steve said as Taylor listened carefully. "But I have to say, what I find really frustrating is how you constantly 'big up' what you've achieved which seems like you're trying to prove how much better you are than everyone else."

As he finished, Steve instantly felt that he might have gone a little over the top, but he also believed that Taylor needed to hear it. Taylor sat there, completely unsure of what to say.

"Well, I can't help it if I'm getting involved in some really important stuff," he retorted, going on the defensive.

"I'm not saying it's not important, mate, but I am saying that you're starting to get a bit of a reputation as someone who brags too much, a real overstater if you know what I mean. And I think that because of this, people don't want to have anything to do with you," Steve said, deciding not to soften his approach.

"Angela told me what happened with the French girl the other night, and I think that's a clear example of it," Steve continued.

Taylor sat in silence, realising that Steve did in fact have a point.

"Listen Taylor, I'm only telling you this because I think you're a good bloke and I'd hate to see you not liked by the rest of them. Just think about it," Steve finished, sitting back in his chair.

"Thanks," Taylor said, easing back also. "Do you want some feedback now?"

Steve agreed, expecting Taylor to deliver it with both barrels.

"Well, what I really think is that you're good at entertaining people. I mean, I'm jealous of how easily you become the life of the party. What you need to improve though, especially at work, is your outlook on things."

Steve leant forward looking puzzled, waiting for the explanation.

"Every time I hear you talk about work, you seem to be really negative and focus on blaming everyone else for your problems. You always come across like you're a victim. So what I think you could do differently is take responsibility for yourself and start to manage your greatest asset – you, as the trainer says."

Wow, Steve thought to himself, *I didn't expect that.*

Steve and Taylor then sat there in silence, both contemplating what they'd been told.

"All right guys?" Simon asked as he approached, interrupting their thoughts.

"Time to head back in," he continued.

As they walked towards the room, Steve thanked Taylor for his feedback, although he was still not sure of what to think.

In the room the trainer reinforced the need for people to take time out after each critical event, or even at the end of each day, to reflect on what they'd learned and what they could do differently next time. He also encouraged them seek feedback whenever they could from those they worked with.

"Without feedback how do you know how you're doing?" the trainer asked. "And without reflection how do you learn? As a first boss of mine once said, *'making a mistake once is a learning opportunity, making a mistake twice is a character flaw'.*"

The Need for Practice

As the clock ticked over to 12:00 noon the trainer commenced his summary.

"So, over the last couple of days our focus has been on helping you to understand that you are your greatest asset, and that you must learn how to control this asset if you are to have a positive impact. Beyond this, we have sought to equip you with some techniques to help you to manage yourself more effectively.

The trainer then reiterated the key points from the three days. As he did so, people realised how much they had covered and why they were so tired. The trainer then made a final statement before allowing them to head out of the door.

"Just remember that your career is a journey, and the only common factor in that journey is you. So I encourage you to start to manage yourself on that journey. For you to get better at managing yourself, the secret is to remain conscious about what you are doing and why, and what you're thinking and feeling in any given moment. To do this, you need to practise with the tools we have given you – and remember that perfect practice makes perfect."

On that note, people went up and thanked the trainer for his time before they headed out to the reception to pick up their bags ready for the trip home. As they waited in the reception for taxis, Angela and Steve deliberately held back, hoping to miss the rest of the group. With only their support group left, Simon asked Taylor for a lift to the station. As Taylor brought the Mercedes round to the door, Simon looked over to where Angela and Steve were standing.

"Sorry guys, looks like only me and Jane will fit, so you'll have to wait for a cab."

"No worries," Steve replied as he gave Simon a wink to say thanks.

PRINCIPLES TO REMEMBER

Start by Managing Yourself

Challenge versus Support
Know where you are in any given moment, and then recognise what
you need to do to get to the results zone – *more challenge or more support?*

Understand How You Work
Know what impact you want to have.
Be conscious about what you're thinking and feeling.
Choose your behaviour and actions.
Recognise your impact on others.

Always Make Conscious Choices
You may not always be able to choose your circumstance,
but you can always choose how you respond.
One of the most powerful choices you can make is
in regard to the **attitude** you adopt.
Understand your intent, and create a gap to ensure your **Intent = Impact**.

Keep Focused
Always prioritise Urgent versus Important.
Remove distractions – *don't be afraid to turn things off!*
Stay in the present – *learn from the past, plan for the future – don't dwell or worry.*

Learn Constantly
Reflect and Learn – *what went well, what didn't go well,
what could I do differently next time?*
Seek Feedback – *understand others' perception of you.*

TASKS FOR THE READER
Start by Managing Yourself

As *you* are *your greatest asset*, it is essential that you take control over yourself. This includes over what you think and feel, and over what you say and do. This will help you have the impact you desire.

Task 1: Where are you right now?

It's important to know whether you are at the top of your game at any moment. If you're not, what are you going to do about it?

Circle which zone you think you're in right now:

Where are you right now?

LEVEL OF CHALLENGE	LOW LEVEL OF SUPPORT	HIGH LEVEL OF SUPPORT
HIGH	STRESS ZONE (SPINNING PLATES)	RESULTS ZONE (THRIVING AT THE TOP OF MY GAME)
LOW	COMA ZONE (BURNT OUT OR RUSTED OUT)	COMFORT ZONE (BORED)

Why do you think you are in this zone?

If you're not currently in it, what action do you need to take to get yourself into the results zone?

Task 2: Always Make Conscious Choices

Recognising My Attitude
L – to Life: W – to Work

Glass Half Empty ←—————————|—————————→ Glass Half Full
(Negative)   (Positive)

Choosing your attitude in any situation is one of the most powerful choices you can make. On the continuum from glass half-full to glass half-empty, mark where you think others would describe your attitude to life (mark with an L) and to work (mark with a W).

What actions will you take to move your 'L' and 'W' marks further to the right?

Task 3: What will you do next?

What are the two key things you will do differently to manage better your greatest asset - you?

ACTIONS	BY WHEN

3.
You *Can* Manage Your Boss

Perfect Practice Makes Perfect

Following the training course, the next few months flew by for the group. To see what they'd learnt from the course, Liz caught up with each of them in February.

"Things are going all right," Simon told Liz when they met. "I'm prioritising and planning a lot more which is helping me keep focused. I'm also trying to be more positive which actually feels good."

"I've really been trying to push myself forward," Jane said to Liz. "But although I'm feeling more confident, I'm still finding it hard to get noticed. My boss just seems so busy all the time."

Taylor missed his meeting with Liz, but managed to get hold of her on the phone later that day. As usual, his story was the same: always busy, always important. However, Liz could tell he was sounding tired having spent almost the entire time at World-Corp in the stress zone, mostly for the wrong reasons.

"Just remember, Taylor," Liz said at the end of the call, "your journey is a marathon, not a sprint. There is no need to be in such a hurry all the time."

Taylor, oblivious to the comment, thanked her and said goodbye.

In catching up with Angela, Liz found that the whole Wales experience resulted in an epiphany.

"Liz, it's been great," Angela said, beaming. "I've shrunk my to-do list, pushed things back to their rightful owners and concentrated on delivering my top priorities. I've even learned to turn off my phone, instant messenger and email at periods during the day so I can get things done."

The only downside for Angela was that her relationship was starting to drag her down. She never mentioned Steve's name but as Taylor was a terrible gossip, Liz knew who Angela was talking about.

The final person Liz caught up with was Steve, who had rescheduled several times. When he finally did make it he was late. As he swaggered up to the table with a cup of coffee in hand, Liz noticed that he looked like a broken man. It appeared that the first few months at World-Corp had not treated Steve well.

"How's things Steve?" Liz asked.

"Not too bad," Steve responded.

"A boss of mine once said that the statement *not too bad* is actually a double negative. So how are things really going - good or bad?" Liz asked again, not letting Steve off the hook.

"Well, if you really want to know, things are awful," Steve answered as he slumped down in the chair.

"They just don't treat me as a human," he then blurted out. "It's like I'm their little new joiner and they just keep piling on the crap day after day. I wouldn't complain, but it's not even interesting crap."

As he spoke, Liz noticed that his body matched his attitude; he was half sitting, half lying in the chair. Seeing this, Liz fired a sharp comment at Steve to see how he'd react.

"Steve, why don't you sit up straight and tell me what's really going on?"

Steve, looking Liz in the eye, shuffled in his seat and sat upright.

"Well…I'm just not enjoying this at all. I did all right at university, but here it feels like I've taken a step back. I mean, I don't mind World-Corp, but I hate my job."

"What would it look like for you to love your job?" Liz asked.

"I'd be challenged. I'd be working hard, but I'd be enjoying what I was doing. And I'd have a manager who cared," Steve responded after thinking for a moment.

"Do you see any opportunities where you could get that within your team?" Liz asked.

"Sure, but that would require my idiot of a manager to give those tasks to me, rather than waiting for someone else to have the time to do them."

"Well, why don't you just pick them up yourself?" Liz continued. "There's nothing wrong with using your initiative to make things happen. And there's nothing wrong with asking for forgiveness and not permission. That's what I would do."

Steve looked directly at Liz as if testing her resolve. At that point, Simon and Taylor's feedback about needing to be more positive drifted into his mind.

"Mmm, I'll see how I go," Steve replied without wanting to commit.

"Well, I'd like to see you do that Steve. After all, it would be nice to see some of that positive social Steve be brought into World-Corp," Liz said as if reading his mind.

"We have another catch-up in a couple of weeks, so let's talk again then," Liz said, ending the conversation.

Half Year Reviews

With the onset of March, the time had come for their first six month performance review.

In preparation for this, Liz forwarded them the relevant guidance from HR. However, knowing how confusing this can be sometimes, she also arranged for them to meet in the London head office.

Angela was the first to arrive in the room, followed by Taylor who was keen to impress Liz after missing their last meeting. Jane and Simon entered a couple of minutes later, and Steve strolled in five minutes late without even an apology. As he walked in, Angela looked up at him and gently shook her head in despair.

Liz explained the full review process for new joiners. It focused on them needing to be rated against what impact they had made and also how their impact rated in terms of behaviours against World-Corps' values. They all saw this as simple enough to do, given that the process was accompanied by a special electronic template.

"But how do we prove that our ratings are correct?" Simon asked at the end of Liz's description.

"Through providing feedback from those who have benefited from what you've delivered and from those you've worked with," Liz responded. "It's also important that your boss signs off your ratings. They must agree with what you've captured."

At that point Jane erupted.

"But my boss would have no idea what I've done."

"I'm not sure my boss would know either," Simon followed with.

"Well, there goes my rating," Steve sighed. "I doubt whether my boss would even care how I've been doing."

As Liz looked at each of them, it seemed as if only Angela and Taylor were happy with the process.

Building a Relationship with Your Boss

"You know, your relationship with your boss is one of the most important relationships you have at work," Liz stated, realising she needed them to focus.

"What do you mean?" Jane asked.

"Well, if you each think about your situations, your relationship with your boss and how your boss perceives you has a huge impact on your success and also your happiness at work," Liz said.

"You can say that again," Steve said as the others nodded in agreement.

"So wouldn't it be wise to build and manage this relationship in a proactive way?" Liz asked.

"That's exactly what I do," Taylor butted in as if he were an expert on the matter.

"She doesn't mean 'brown-nose'," Jane replied sarcastically.

Liz went on to explain the importance of the relationship each of them had with their boss. She reinforced that this relationship impacted not only on their happiness and sense of self-worth as people, but also their manager's sense of self-worth as a boss.

"I've yet to meet a manager at World-Corp who doesn't want to be a good boss," Liz said, looking directly at Steve. "It's just that sometimes they either don't know how to, or they get too distracted from trying to."

Steve looked up, considering making a snide remark but thought better of it. Liz then stood up and drew a picture on the board.

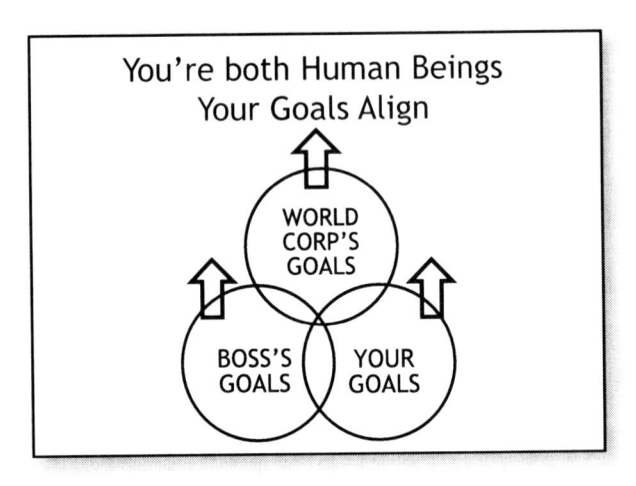

```
You're both Human Beings
Your Goals Align
       ⇧
   WORLD
   CORP'S
   GOALS
  ⇧         ⇧
BOSS'S    YOUR
GOALS    GOALS
```

"This is the foundation of your relationship with your boss," Liz stated. "Firstly you're both humans, which means that you're both a product of your past and your environment, and neither of you is likely to be perfect. I know I'm definitely not perfect as a person or as a boss."

"And secondly," Liz continued, "your goals, your boss's goals and the goals of World-Corp are actually all aligned. We are all professionals and we all want to do well so we can feel valued and fulfilled from the contribution we make and, by doing this, each of us and World-Corp will prosper."

Everyone around the table nodded in agreement, except for Steve who was contemplating the imperfections of his boss.

What Do You Know About Your Boss?

"So how do you build a relationship with your boss?" Jane asked.

"Building a relationship with your boss is much like how you would build any other relationship; first you have to get to know them," Liz responded.

As she finished her statement, Liz asked each person to take a blank piece of paper and a pen. She then asked them to write what they knew about who their boss is - as a person, as a professional and, last of all, as their boss. As they all considered how well they knew their boss, Liz provided a few prompts.

"Now, it is important to respect the personal and professional boundary but, as a person, does your boss have a family, are they married and / or have children? Does your boss have any hobbies or things they are passionate about in their spare time? Does your boss have any dreams about the future? What makes them feel valued as a person?"

Each of them captured what they knew against the questions. Most knew a few things, apart from Steve and Jane who really struggled. Taylor, on the other hand, seemed to know every detail.

"As a professional," Liz continued, "what experience does your boss have? Where have they worked in the past and what sort of work have they done? What are their professional aspirations? What image do they portray at work?"

"And finally," Liz said, "what do you know about them as a boss? What are their objectives and what things do they need to deliver? What issues or problems are they currently facing? What's keeping them awake at night?"

Each of them in the room, including Steve, was now scribbling frantically as their thoughts poured out.

"One more thing," Liz said as they each reached a natural end. "On the bottom of the paper I want you to write two areas where you think you can help your boss by releasing some of the stress on them. Then I want you to write two areas where you think you might add to the stress of your boss, and consider how you might stop doing this."

Each of them stopped for a moment and considered the questions being asked before writing their ideas.

"So as you take this away," Liz concluded, "my challenge for you is to invest some time in getting to know your boss and building that relationship with them."

They all nodded.

"Shall we have a quick break to stretch our legs and go to the bathroom?" Liz suggested.

Know What Your Boss Expects From You

While the others were coming back into the room, Liz asked Taylor how he knew so much about his boss.

"I always try to make an effort," Taylor responded. "After all, the more I know about my boss, the better the relationship I can build, and the more he'll want to help me succeed."

Once they were all seated and before Liz could continue with her review guidance, Jane asked a question.

"I can understand building a relationship, and I'll definitely try to do that, but I'm just not sure what my boss expects of me."

Steve and Simon both agreed.

"What do you think they expect?" Liz asked.

"I don't know. I guess they want me to work hard and deliver what he needs," Jane responded, struggling to think of anything.

"That's part of it," Liz explained. "As a boss myself the first thing I expect is that my people not only work for me, but also *with* me."

Liz could see that Jane, Simon and Steve were puzzled.

"You see, the majority of managers don't want to have to micro-manage you or treat you as a subordinate. We have to manage our time too," Liz continued.

"Yes, some may do," Liz added quickly, seeing that Steve was about to give his thoughts, "but the majority don't. What we want is for you to work with us as adults and peers."

"Managing people takes a lot of energy," Liz continued, "and whilst it's very rewarding and often a lot of fun, it is energy that we prefer to focus on helping you develop rather than telling you how to do each and every detail of your work. So the first thing your boss expects is that you seek to work with them and not just for them."

"What else?" Simon asked, wanting the next insight.

"Well, what do you think?" Liz responded.

Angela jumped in quickly before Simon could answer.

"When I was on my placement year in between my third and fourth years at university, one of my bosses said that what she expected was for me to prove my competence and confidence," Angela stated confidently.

"Go on," Liz requested as Angela paused, wondering if she'd said the right thing.

"Well, my boss expected me to always deliver what I said I would in the time that it was required, and this is what she referred to as proving my competence. She said that if I needed help then I should just ask for it, and if I was going to fail then I should fail fast and recover fast."

"What about proving your confidence?" Steve asked, feeling proud of his girlfriend.

"Proving my confidence was also about being prepared to have a go and stretch myself. In other words being prepared to step outside of my comfort zone," Angela continued as she looked at Steve and smiled.

With that statement, Angela stood up and drew a picture on some flipchart paper.

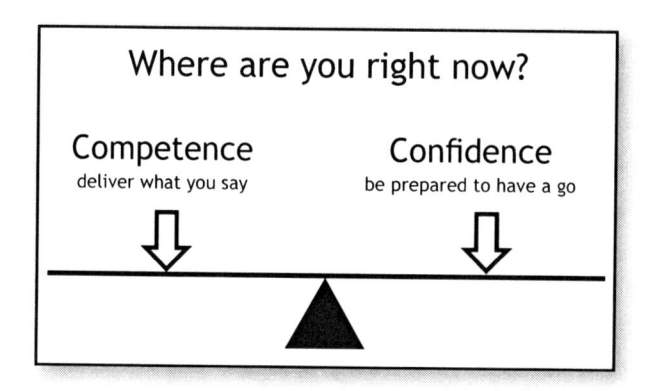

Where are you right now?

Competence	Confidence
deliver what you say	be prepared to have a go

"My boss said that she expected all of her people to prove themselves through balancing their competence and confidence. She said that she had seen many people who were very capable but who struggled to get noticed because they never stretched themselves by having a go at something new. She also said that she had seen many people whose confidence outweighed their competence, and hence they failed repeatedly because they leapt into things without knowing what they were doing."

"But how do you make sure you get it right when you do stretch yourself?" Jane asked, slightly worried.

"Well, my boss taught me this process," Angela replied as she drew another picture.

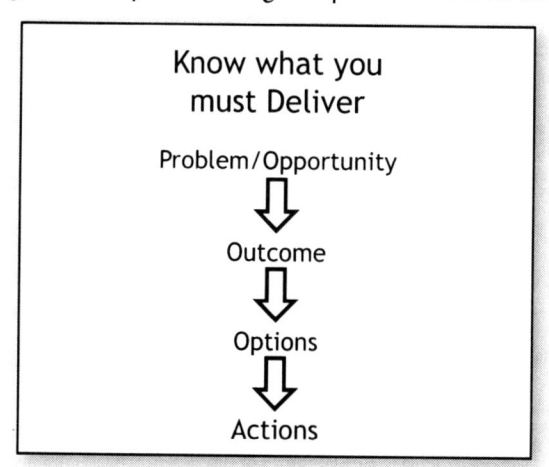

Know what you must Deliver

Problem/Opportunity
⇩
Outcome
⇩
Options
⇩
Actions

"My boss said that whenever I was given a new task I should always plan first what I needed to deliver and this involved considering the Problem/Opportunity, Outcome, Options and Action."

Jane and the others listened as they took notes.

"Problem/Opportunity is all about fully defining the problem or opportunity being faced.

This meant getting to the true root cause of what was causing the problem or opportunity to arise. Outcome referred to the need to fully define what success looked like against the problem or opportunity. This needs to be as full a definition as possible including when it needed to be delivered by," Angela said before pausing to let the others catch up.

"Options referred to understanding all the possible solutions available to achieve the desired outcome. Once identified, they could then be assessed against the cost versus the benefits for achieving the outcome, to identify which is preferred. And finally, Action involves identifying what needs to be done, by whom, and by when to implement the preferred Option to achieve the desired Outcome."

"So you always follow this process?" Jane asked.

"Absolutely," Angela replied. "It's always the first thing I do with any task. I always ask; *'What is the real problem or opportunity, and what does success look like against this?'* And then *'What are my potential solutions?'* and ultimately *'What action will I take?'*"

"That's great, thanks Angela," Liz said as Angela took her seat. "And I have to say I use that very same process every day."

"So the second thing your boss expects is that you prove yourself through proving your competence and confidence. And to do that you must focus on Problem/Opportunity, Outcome, Options and Action," Angela concluded excitedly.

By this point it seemed that Angela's enthusiasm had rubbed off on the others, especially Steve who felt compelled to contribute.

"I think the third thing is to ensure there are no surprises," Steve announced.

Everyone, especially Angela, turned to focus on Steve, slightly surprised that he had got actively involved.

"In the last six months," Steve continued, not wanting to lose momentum, "things have gone really badly when my boss phoned asking why I hadn't told him about a specific issue. On one occasion, it was a disaster because the President of Manufacturing - your uncle, Jane - called my boss asking questions when I should have let him know about some delays."

Each person cringed.

"On that occasion my boss phoned me and said *'Steve, I just need timely truth from you. I don't mind if things aren't going as they should, but I need to know about it sooner rather than later so we can do something about it',*" Steve recited as if he were his boss.

"So the third thing that our bosses expect is definitely no surprises by giving them timely truth," he then summarised proudly.

Angela led a round of applause as Steve, in true social-Steve fashion, stood up and took a bow. After seeing the adulation Steve received, it was now Taylor's turn to contribute.

"The one thing that I always do is make sure I align our expectations," Taylor announced, pausing for his own round of applause.

"What do you mean?" Simon enquired.

"Well, whenever I go to work for a new boss I always make sure I fully understand what they expect of me, and also that they understand what I expect of them. 'Getting on the same page' I call it," Taylor continued, feeling a little disappointed at the lack of praise from his colleagues.

As the others started to tune out, Jane decided that she wanted to know more.

"So you sit with your boss and discuss expectations at the start of your project?" she asked.

"That's right. I make sure I schedule some time so I can really understand what they expect of me against my objectives and deliverables, working hours and approach, and also what they need from me in the form of support or information," Taylor said, firing a quick glance at Steve.

"Then," Taylor continued, "I express to them, politely of course, what support I will need from them to be able to meet their expectations."

Jane stared at Taylor, feeling as though she'd just been given a magic solution.

"Thanks Taylor. So I guess the fourth thing your boss expects is that you align expectations by getting on the same page," Liz concluded. "Is there anything else anyone can think of?"

"No, that's great," Jane said in an excited tone.

"Well, the last thing I would like to include is to show loyalty," Liz added in a serious tone. "It is really important for any boss to be able to trust the people who they work with. This means you should never seek to undermine them to others, no matter what you think of them, and you must seek to show that they can trust you. It's OK to disagree with them, but do so respectfully and not in public."

At that point, Steve squirmed slightly in his seat knowing that he had broken many of these final points by bad-mouthing his boss to others. *What if that got back to him?* he thought to himself.

Now 'Wow' Them

Realising that their meeting had run over time, Liz asked if people could hang around a little longer.

"Sorry, I couldn't possibly spare any more time," Taylor stated. "I've got a meeting with the MD which I just can't miss."

Just as Taylor left the room heading for his meeting, Angela asked a question.

"Liz, I think that I've been OK in terms of living up to my boss's expectations. I seem to get good feedback and I have regular meetings to see how things are going etc., so I guess I know my boss likes what I'm doing. But that's not enough; I want my boss to be delighted with the impact I'm having."

"Well, you need to learn how to wow them," Liz remarked with a smile.

"That's it," Angela responded excitedly, "but how do I wow them?"

Reaching into her folder, Liz pulled out a piece of paper that looked like it had been carried with her for a few years and positioned it in the middle of the table. They all leaned forward to see what was written on it.

WOW YOUR BOSS

Focus your Contribution
Fix what's keeping them awake at night

Provide Solutions not Problems
Don't pass on issues to your boss

Get Noticed
Subtly blow your trumpet

Ask for Forgiveness, not Permission

"I was told this by my first mentor about three years ago. At the time I was complaining that whilst I was considered good by my boss, I wanted to be seen as great. It felt like I had the knowledge and skills to do well in World-Corp, but I just wasn't getting noticed in the way I wanted," Liz explained.

"So my mentor told me to try these things. First I had to focus my contribution by really understanding what was keeping my boss awake at night and then seeking to fix that. Obviously I kept doing my day job, but I also used my initiative to fix what wasn't working or to make the best of the opportunities I saw for the team. Remember Alex's presentation at induction? Well this is all about that: Positive Dissatisfaction and Positive Impact," Liz stated.

"But didn't you need your boss to tell you what to do?" Simon asked.

"No, not always," Liz replied. "That's where the bottom statement comes into it: ask for forgiveness, not permission. See, most of the time I would just fix the things that I felt I could fix easily. If at any time I felt I was really stretching myself, I would test my ideas with my boss, but most of the time I would just get on with it. That is, I'd ask for forgiveness when things went wrong, which they occasionally did, rather than asking for their permission to do it in the first place."

"But surely there were times when you really risked making a monumental mistake?" Simon asked again.

"Absolutely," Liz replied. "But on those occasions, if I felt that something was particularly risky I would ask myself whether I would be happy explaining it to the CEO if he saw my picture and story on the front page of the newspaper the next morning. If I ever said that I wouldn't be comfortable, then I'd find another approach."

"What I found surprising was that almost immediately I started doing things, my boss started recognising my contribution," Liz concluded.

"That's fantastic," Angela exploded. "What's next?"

"Next is making sure that you don't pass on your problems to your boss." Liz replied. "They should never feel like you are just pushing things on to them rather than sorting it out yourself."

"But sometimes I just don't know what the solution is," Jane said.

"That's true," Liz replied, "but you can go some way to figure out what the solutions might be. This is where I really use the Problem/Opportunity, Outcome, Options and Action process to help me structure my thinking. You see, by using that process you can easily come up with what you think the true problem is, as well as what you think is the desired outcome and what the preferred options might be. Even if you get this wrong, at least you are not going to your boss with a completely blank sheet and expecting them to solve it for you."

Simon and Steve both slid back into their chairs contemplating Liz's advice.

"The next thing to wow your boss is to make sure you get noticed by subtly blowing your own trumpet," Liz continued, looking at the sheet of paper. "It's no good achieving great things if you don't get recognised for it. After all you're not a charity, as a boss of mine once said."

"But how do you do that without behaving like Taylor," Steve asked as the others sniggered.

"Mmm," Liz replied, choosing to ignore the remark about Taylor. "When I first came into World-Corp I found it really hard to know how to get noticed without feeling like I was bragging about myself."

She then stood up and drew another picture on the board.

```
        B       C                              A
        <------------------|------------------>
        Under-Stator                    Over-Stator
```

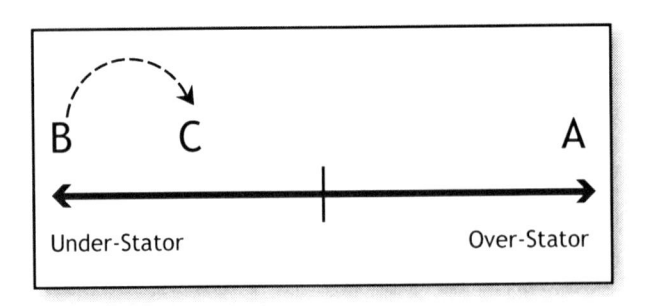

"What I was told by a manager at the time is that the there is a continuum between those who are under-stators and those who are over-stators. Under-stators are people who always seek to down-play or even ignore their achievements, whereas over-stators are people who will always seek to exaggerate what they've achieved."

I'm definitely an under-stator, Jane thought to herself.

"Now, for those people at A, they need to learn how to tone it down a bit otherwise they will quickly get ostracised by their peers and by those above them," Liz continued. "For those people at B, they need to recognise what impact they've had and start making it known. The challenge for under-stators, however, is that even a little jump from say B to C can feel like you're becoming an over-stator. That's why when subtly blowing your own trumpet, you need to focus on the outcomes you've delivered and the impact you've had, rather than who you are."

"But how do you do that?" Jane asked.

"I guess for under-stators," Liz replied, focusing her attention on Jane, "the challenge with subtly blowing your own trumpet is that you've first got to be honest with yourself about the impact you've had. And a good way to do this is to test with others when you think you've done something well."

Jane and the others nodded, still taking in every detail.

"So to subtly blow your own trumpet," Liz continued, "what you need to do is to figure out who needs to know about what. It won't be the whole world, but there will be certain people that need to know about the impact you've had. Once you've identified this target audience, you can then work out how to do just that; let them know about the impact you've had. And by focusing on the impact, you no longer need to talk about you as a person. But by virtue of you being the one who delivered that impact, you are naturally creating an association that people can recognise."

Each of them sat back in their seat contemplating what they would do next.

"Since we're still on managing your relationship with your boss, can I also encourage you to do two things?" Liz added after a short pause.

"The first is to focus on your image, both in and outside of work."

"What's image got to do with anything?" Steve said, feeling as though the comment was directed at him.

"Well, as we all know, people make judgements about you within three seconds of setting eyes on you. And whilst we all know that you shouldn't judge a book by its cover, we all still do. So can I encourage you to consider the image you portray at work through how you dress, what you say and what you do. Also consider the image you portray outside of work and what you show the world through things like Facebook etc. Because all of these things influence people's perceptions about you, and ultimately you want to ensure these perceptions are positive."

Liz paused before finishing her statement.

"So, whilst image is not everything, it is important for you as professionals to recognise that it is something," she concluded.

They all sat in silence thinking about what Liz had said. Steve in particular felt a little self-conscious about his image.

"The second is to learn what you can from every boss you have. Throughout your journeys you'll have both good and bad bosses. Despite whether they're good or bad you should learn what you can from each one in terms of what they do well and what they don't do well. And with what you learn, you can then seek to be the best boss you can when you become one."

Each of them nodded as they contemplated becoming a boss.

"So, that's how to wow your boss," Liz concluded before she went on to explain the remainder of the review process.

A Difficult Boss

At the end of the meeting Steve waited for Angela.

"Fancy dinner tonight at my place?" Steve asked quietly.

With Steve's project not going well he'd become quite a difficult person to be with and Angela was getting cold feet in the relationship.

"Yeh, why not." Angela decided to agree after seeing a glimpse of the old Steve during the meeting. "Let's meet in the foyer at 5:30 and we can head off from there."

"You got it babe," he said playfully, with a cheeky smile.

Steve's idea of dinner was a pizza and a bottle of red wine, which they ate in picnic style on a rug on the lounge floor. From the moment they left the office there was a sense of tension in the air between them, as neither felt entirely comfortable. Just as they sat there looking at the pizza crusts left in the box, Steve broke the silence.

"That stuff that Liz was talking about today was interesting, don't you think?"

Angela looked at him, noticing that he obviously had something on his mind.

"I mean, I know Liz is right, and it all makes sense, but I just don't think I can do it," Steve said quietly without looking up from his glass.

At that point Angela noticed a tear rolling down his cheek. Steve dared not look up for fear of showing Angela that he was crying.

"I...I...I just can't do this any more," Steve stammered as his tears began to run more freely.

Angela instinctively put her glass down and then took Steve's out of his hand. She then held him as tightly as she could, hoping to comfort her lost boyfriend. Steve turned and buried himself in her embrace.

"You won't tell anyone I cried," he mumbled, still locked into Angela's grasp.

"Of course not," Angela replied stroking his hair and wondering what to do to help him.

During the night Angela convinced Steve to give Liz a call about what was happening. Whilst Angela desperately wanted to help Steve, she didn't quite know how to.

As promised, Steve called Liz the next day and they met in a café that afternoon. Whilst trying to hold himself together Steve explained everything that was happening. How he felt like his boss didn't trust him at all and how he was micro-managing every little thing he did. How he felt that he was losing his mind with frustration at not doing anything interesting. How he hated coming to work each day. And mostly how he knew all of this was having an impact on him and Angela.

As Steve spoke Liz listened, never shifting her gaze. Once Steve had come to a natural end he felt as though a huge weight had been lifted from his shoulders. Just by sharing he now felt a lot better.

"So what do I do?" Steve asked, almost pleading with Liz.

"It sounds to me that you have a difficult boss," Liz responded without answering the question.

"Difficult is one way to describe it," Steve replied with a sigh.

"The key with difficult bosses," Liz started, "is that while their behaviour may not be excusable, it is explainable."

Steve tilted his head trying to understand what Liz was saying.

"When you're in the heat of the moment it's hard to see, but if you're able to create a gap you will notice that all people's behaviour is driven by a need to fulfil some form of motive," Liz continued as the look of confusion on Steve's face grew.

Seeing this, Liz grabbed a piece of paper and drew a rather elaborate picture.

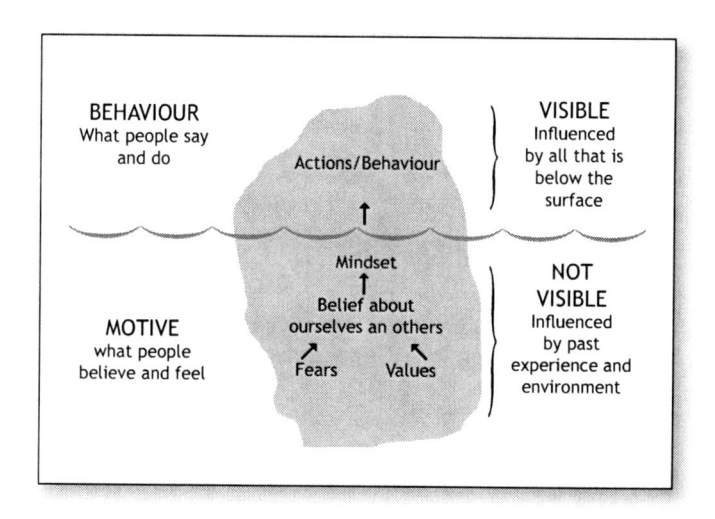

```
        BEHAVIOUR                                VISIBLE
        What people say                          Influenced
           and do          Actions/Behaviour     by all that is
                                   ↑             below the
                                                 surface
        ~~~~~~~~~~~~~~~~~~~~~~~~~~~~~~~~~~~~~~~~~~~~~~~
                                Mindset
                                   ↑             NOT
                             Belief about        VISIBLE
          MOTIVE          ourselves an others    Influenced
         what people          ↗       ↖          by past
        believe and feel   Fears    Values       experience and
                                                 environment
```

"Much like an iceberg," Liz explained, "whilst we see what a person says and does - their behaviour - there is a lot that we don't see in terms of the motive driving that behaviour: what they believe, think and feel. So when dealing with difficult people it is essential that you focus on responding to their motive, or what you don't see, rather than their behaviour, or what you do see."

Liz paused briefly as Steve took in the detail of the picture.

"Right, what do you think is driving your boss's behaviour?" Liz asked, breaking Steve's concentration.

"Well, I think the guy is really insecure, which is why he tries to bully me and the other team members." Steve responded promptly.

"And what do you think he's insecure about?" Liz asked.

"I think he's under a lot of pressure and really trying to prove himself in the company. I also think he sees some of the others as a bit of a threat to him," Steve answered thoughtfully. "Which I guess is why he didn't really appreciate me dropping him in it with the President, or why he didn't respond well to me suggesting heaps of new improvement ideas."

"That's right," Liz replied. "Now with people like that it is critical to respond to their motive, not their behaviour and that means firstly making them feel safe."

Once again Steve tilted his head.

"So if you've identified that your boss is potentially feeling insecure because he feels threatened, which is what's driving his behaviour," Liz continued, "how might you make him feel safe?"

"Well, I guess that I need to prove that I'm on his side," Steve said confidently.

"And how would you do that?" Liz asked.

"For starters, I could seek to ease some of the pressure on him. Then I could start to build a relationship. We're both mad Chelsea supporters so that should be easy. And I guess I could make sure I'm proactive in delivering what he needs, especially information."

"That's great," Liz responded to Steve's suggestions. "Being proactive is definitely the key, and I think if you do that you'll find that your boss will respond really well. He may never be perfect, but at least you will prove to him that you are on his side and things will improve."

As they stood up and walked back to the office, Steve's mind was a race with the things he could do. Just before the reached the front doors, Steve swung around and gave Liz a big hug.

"Thank you," Steve said, before he strode confidently off into the office.

PRINCIPLES TO REMEMBER

You Can Manage Your Boss

Build a Relationship with your Boss
Recognise and get to know them as a person.
The foundation of your relationship is that you're both humans and your goals align.

What Your Boss Expects
Work with them, not just for them.
Prove your Competence and Confidence.
(*Problem/Opportunity > Outcome > Options > Action*)
Ensure no Surprises – *Deliver Timely Truth.*
Get on the same Page – *Align Expectations.*
Show Loyalty.

Wow Your Boss
Focus your Contribution - *Fix what's keeping them awake at night.*
Provide Solutions not Problems - *Don't pass on issues to your boss.*
Get Noticed - *Subtly blow your trumpet.*
Ask for Forgiveness, Not for Permission.

Respond to a Difficult Boss
Understand and respond to the motive driving their behaviour, not just the behaviour.
Make them feel safe.
Build a relationship.

TASKS FOR THE READER
You Can Manage Your Boss

Your relationship with your boss is one of the most important relationships you have at work. Your relationship with your boss has a significant impact on your success and also on your happiness at work. It is therefore critical that you manage this relationship with them proactively.

Task I: Building a Relationship with your Boss

Before you can build a relationship with anyone, you must know some things about them. Keeping aware of the personal and professional boundary, what do you know about your boss?

As a Person... (family, married, children, hobbies etc...
As a Professional... (experience, aspirations, image at work etc...)
As a Boss... (objectives, targets, current issues etc...)

Identify two areas where you think you complement your boss:

1.

2.

Identify two areas where you think you add to the stress of your boss:

1.

2.

Identify two areas where you think you can improve your relationship with your boss:

What will you do to improve your relationship with your boss?	By When
1.	
2.	

Task 2: Knowing what Your Boss Expects

Building an effective relationship with your boss relies on you both being on the same page with respect to your expectations of each other.

What do you think your boss expects of you, and how and when will you check this with them?

How can you better meet these expectations better?

What will you do?	By When

What do you expect of your boss, and how will you let them know?

Task 3: Seeking to wow your Boss

Wowing your boss involves really showing them how you can make a difference. A key area to focus on with this is to resolve what is keeping them awake at night.

What do you think is keeping your boss awake at night?

What can you do to wow your boss – what can you do to ease what's keeping them awake at night?

What will you do?	By When

Task 4: A Difficult Boss (if required)

If you believe that you have a difficult boss, it is essential to understand what you think is driving their behaviour. Through understanding this you can then seek to make them feel safe by responding to the motive driving their behaviour and not the behaviour itself.

What motive do you think is driving their behaviour?

How can you make your boss feel safe?

How can you build a relationship with your boss?

4.
Manage your Relationships…at Work

A Fresh Start – New Projects

"What project did you get?" Simon asked Angela as they all caught up for lunch at the beginning of May.

"Can you believe they're putting me in charge of a team of four?" Angela replied. "I've never managed people before. What about you?"

"My project's similar to his," Simon replied pointing at Steve. "Yet another virtual team spread across the country. At least this time I get to work with a real customer, even if it is with making sure our service is up to scratch."

"Nothing like virtual teams!" Steve said, shaking his head. "Who'd have thought we would never even get to meet the people we work with face to face."

"I bet you're glad to get away from your last boss, though," Jane said.

"Sort of," Steve replied. "To be honest, Liz's advice really helped and we actually started to develop a good relationship. Once he realised I was on his side and he started to feel safe with me, we hit it off all right. We even go to the football together sometimes. And would you believe that I'm even helping him with some of the things I've learned…yeh, I'm helping him!"

"Help from Steve, that's exactly what he needs," Simon said, teasing Steve.

"Wow, that's great," Jane added, also smiling, "my next project is similar to you guys, although I get to deal with our suppliers."

"I'm in sales," Taylor butted-in over the top of Jane. "I've even been given sales targets I've got to meet."

Each of them looked at Taylor hoping that they weren't going to be subjected to another 'look how great I am' story.

A New Challenge – Delivering Through Others

As each of the group progressed in their new projects, a range of different challenges arose. Taylor was faced with trying to reach sales targets with some tough customers. Initially he relished the challenge, but quickly found that these people were immune to his so-called charms. He was even thrown out of one customer's office after upsetting her with his attempts to impress. In their roles, Simon and Steve also found themselves facing some unforgiving customers. Their challenges were making sure that what World-Corp delivered was the same as what was promised. Jane, although not customer facing, struggled to get World-Corp's external suppliers to do what they said they would. Even Angela, who thought it would be easier to deliver what was needed because she was now a boss, was struggling as her team failed to deliver consistently what was needed. As Angela sat there one day frustrated that things were not going how she wanted, she struck up a conversation over instant messenger with Jane.

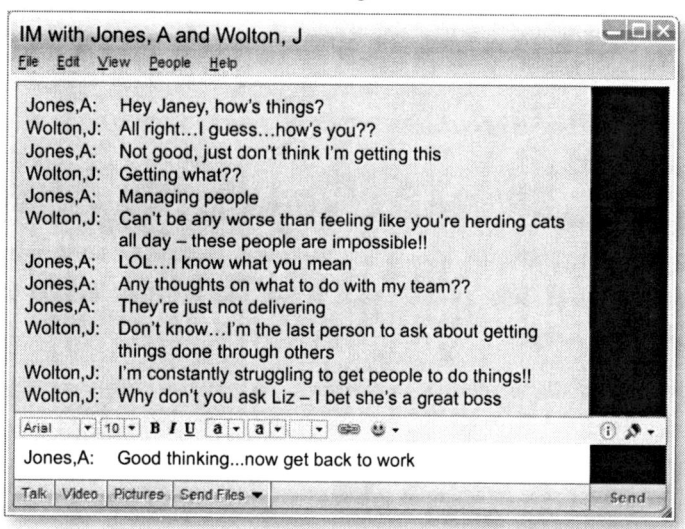

```
IM with Jones, A and Wolton, J
File  Edit  View  People  Help

Jones,A:    Hey Janey, how's things?
Wolton,J:   All right…I guess…how's you??
Jones,A:    Not good, just don't think I'm getting this
Wolton,J:   Getting what??
Jones,A:    Managing people
Wolton,J:   Can't be any worse than feeling like you're herding cats
            all day – these people are impossible!!
Jones,A;    LOL…I know what you mean
Jones,A:    Any thoughts on what to do with my team??
Jones,A:    They're just not delivering
Wolton,J:   Don't know…I'm the last person to ask about getting
            things done through others
Wolton,J:   I'm constantly struggling to get people to do things!!
Wolton,J:   Why don't you ask Liz – I bet she's a great boss

Jones,A:    Good thinking…now get back to work
```

Later that day Angela dropped Liz an email hoping to catch up with her for a coffee, only to receive an out-of-office message saying that Liz had headed off for a two-week vacation.

I'm not sure I can wait that long, Angela thought to herself.

Just at that moment, Angela's phone started flashing. It was her new boss. Although they got on well, Angela could tell from his voice that he wasn't happy. Her team had missed another delivery deadline and he wanted to know why. It seemed that despite her best attempts they were just not providing her with timely truth. Angela told her boss quickly that she would sort it out by the end of the day. Feeling the pressure and in sheer desperation, Angela sent out an invitation to her support colleagues asking for an emergency meeting in Jim's Wine Bar opposite the office for the next day. The title of the invitation was simple; **I NEED HELP!**

The next day, Simon, Jane and Steve walked down the stairs into Jim's Wine Bar together, to find Angela already sitting at a table in the back corner vigorously making notes. Taylor had replied that he too would join them, but it was likely he would be late due to customer meetings.

The wine bar, which was in the basement below one of the large city buildings, was quite dark inside, lit only with a variety of odd candle-shaped lights around the room. Scattered between the various brick columns supporting the building above was mismatched antique-looking wooden furniture. On the walls were black and white pictures of London in the early 1900s. They'd all been to the bar before, so they knew it was a nice place but it was slightly expensive for their modest new joiner salaries.

As each of them sat down piling their bags into a corner, Angela looked up.

"Thanks for coming guys, I really appreciate it," Angela said with a tone of real appreciation in her voice.

"How can we help, Miss?" Simon asked in a deep voice, poking out his chest and taking his best Superman stance.

As she sat down, Jane was quick to shatter Simon's fantasy by gently slapping his chest causing him to exhale suddenly. The waiter, who was pleased to see some guests, then wandered over and took their order. Once he was out of sight, Angela described the challenges she was facing.

"My team are just constantly missing deadlines," she said with a tone of despair. "It's like they don't care and they never put in extra hours to fix the problems we face. So now I'm taking on the work of five people as I'm doing their jobs as well."

Just as Angela finished her explanation, the waiter returned with a couple of bottles of wine, some glasses of water and some crisps.

"On the house for some beautiful ladies," the waiter said in a strong Italian accent, referring to the crisps that he placed on the table.

"Thanks," Steve said, pulling up his collar and then flicking his hair back, "I did make an extra effort this morning."

The waiter smiled and winked at Angela as she elbowed Steve in the ribs.

"So you see my problem guys," Angela stated drawing everyone's focus back to the issue at hand. "I really need your help."

Simon spoke first as they all noticed Taylor walking through the room to join them.

"Angela, you're not the Lone Ranger on this one. With you it's your people, with me it's the team I work with. So I'm definitely feeling the same."

"Me too," Jane said. "It just seems hard to get people to do their jobs."

"So I guess what I think we need to do here is work out how we manage our relationships...at work," Steve said unconsciously.

"I agree," Taylor announced as he fell into his seat and helped himself to a glass of wine. "I have to figure out how to build a better relationship with my customers, as I just feel they all hate me at the moment."

"Right," Angela said going into action mode, "let's get to it."

Know Who You Rely On

Rather than just giving Angela advice, they decided to all go through a process of capturing the same things.

"None of us can go it alone," Angela stated, "so let's first list who each of us rely on. You know, it could be our team, our customers, our suppliers, or anyone we need input from to deliver what we need to deliver, our key stakeholders my boss would say. I think it's worth listing people by their names, too."

They each quickly identified all the people they relied on. As they finished their lists, there was a common realisation about how dependent each of them was on others. They also realised that very few of the people they were dependent on were actually located in the same office or even the same country as them. This meant that building personal face-to-face relationships was almost impossible. Even Angela had only met two of her four team members in person.

"I think it would be a good idea to mark on a scale of 1 to 5, with 1 being terrible and 5 being fantastic, how good each of our relationships are with those we rely on," Simon suggested as the next step.

"Great thinking," Angela replied. As they did this, there were a lot of 1s, 2s and a couple of 3s on their sheets of paper. Taylor had even put for one customer a -1.

Build your Relationships - People are People

"So what's next?" Jane asked, feeling slightly dismayed by her answers.

"Looks like we've each got a lot to do to build our relationships," Steve said looking at his list. "What I learned most from my dealings with my last boss is that the statement of 'people are people' is absolutely true. When I finally took the time to get to know my boss as a person, a professional and then a boss, things became a lot clearer, and I could really focus my energy on doing the vital things to build a relationship with him. Remember the old Pareto principle from Alex!"

"So, why don't we figure out what we know about each of the people on our list as people and as professionals," Simon suggested, building on Steve's ideas.

"Great thinking," Angela exclaimed admiringly.

Each of them then followed Simon's instructions and first captured what they knew about each person as a person: do they have a family, are they married / or have children? Do they have any hobbies? Do they have any dreams about the future? What makes them feel valued as a person?

Then they captured what they knew about each person as a professional; what was their experience? What are their aspirations? What image do they portray? What are their objectives? What things are creating pressure on them?

Once they had gone through all the questions they could think of, they compared their notes. Angela was particularly disappointed in herself.

"If this were my boss, and this was all he knew about me, I would be horrified," she announced to the others. "I really need to invest some time getting to know my people."

Each of them nodded, realising that they should do the same. Jane then took a deep breath.

"I guess the key thing here is to make sure we get to know those people because we want to, not because we have to. We all know what it feels like to have people be insincere, and interest without sincerity makes you a fraud," she said looking at her notes.

"We should also respect people's boundaries," Simon added. "I can't stand people being too pushy with me, so I'd hate to do that with others."

They all nodded.

Get on the Same Side

Feeling like they were all getting somewhere, Simon realised that only Taylor had touched his drink.

"Wow," he remarked, "who'd have thought that we'd actually get some work done. I guess it just shows what you can do when you're on the same side."

"That's it!" Jane said excitedly almost knocking the drinks over. "We now have to work out how we get all these people on the same side."

"Fantastic," Angela squealed. "But how do we do this?"

Taylor, after taking a long sip from his drink, answered first.

"Well, an old boss of mine at Project Success used to repeat a quote from President Lyndon Johnson about J. Edgar Hoover from the FBI in the 60s. It went something like *'It's probably better to have him inside the tent pissing out, than outside the tent pissing in'.*"

Everyone laughed, realising what Taylor had just said.

"I think you're right Taylor," Simon said. "We need to work out how we get these people inside our tent."

"But why would people want to get inside our tent?" Steve asked.

"I guess because they want the same thing we do, and there's something in it for them," Jane said releasing a stream of consciousness.

"That's right! People want to get in our tent because we have the same mutual objective that they believe in. And, by achieving that objective, there is something in it for them," Angela said excitedly

"You got it," Taylor agreed, "You can't forget the old WIIFM factor – yep, What's In It For Me!"

With that comment, Angela instructed them all to take another sheet of paper. On it they wrote what they believed the mutual objective was for the people they relied on. They also captured what they believed the benefits were for each person from achieving that objective.

Build the Team

"Fantastic," Angela stated, feeling more excited. "I guess what I need to do now is get out there and build my team."

"Not just you," Jane replied, "I think we all do."

"In building a team it's important to recognise that they go through various stages like forming, storming and norming, before you get to performing," Simon stated, thinking back to what he'd learnt at university. "You remember from studying business, Angela, it's what Tuckman wrote: forming is where they come together, storming is where they seek to find what is acceptable, and norming is where you define the rules of the team."

"That's right," Angela said. "And it's important that you take people through this cycle quite consciously. I can't believe I haven't thought of that before. But I'm still not sure how you really build a team."

"Well, if a team is a group of people who work together to achieve a mutual objective, then you need to get people involved in defining that objective and determining the best way of delivering it," Simon said, still thinking back to his university lessons.

"I guess that's where the Problem/Opportunity, Outcome, Options and Action process would be a good way of getting people together to create suitable action plans," Steve suggested.

"I agree," Jane stated. "I think that we also need to really ensure that people are on the same page in terms of expectations. This was a big lesson for me from dealing with my boss, so it would have to work when trying to build a team."

"I think that the final thing to consider is the need to make sure there is a process for making decisions and learning within the teams," Taylor said. "My first ever boss always told me that a team must contribute to decisions if it is to be successful."

As they were talking, Simon was scribbling away on his napkin.

```
                    Building Your Team
                            △
                         Define
                         mutual
                         objective
                          Agree
                          WIIFM
                   Agree         Agree
                   how           process
                   decisions     for learning
                   will be made
         Problem/Opportunity-Outcome-Options-Action
```

"I think it looks like this," he announced, spinning the napkin around to show the others. "Excellent teams have a defined mutual objective; they know what is in it for each other; they've agreed how decisions will be made; and last of all they've agreed how they will learn and improve. And, they've also gone through the Problem/Opportunity, Outcome, Options and Action process to develop a plan to achieve their mutual objective."

"That's great Simon," Angela exclaimed. "So now all we have to do is get our teams together out of the office to discuss openly all of these things, and then create a plan that we all fully buy into for achieving our mutual objective."

"You're right Ang," Simon said as the others nodded.

Make Things Happen – Be a Role Model

As it had passed 6:30 p.m. the wine bar had started filling with people. Being fully engrossed in their discussion, still only Taylor touched the wine. With more people in the room, there was a growing hum of voices that filled the air. Following Steve's lead, each of them paused and sat back in their chair with a glass in their hand.

"Well," Steve announced, "it just shows what we are capable of when we start performing."

"You got it," Simon replied raising his glass in Steve's direction.

"I guess I'm still slightly concerned where we, as individuals, fit here," Jane said softly not wanting to ruin the mood.

"What do you mean?" Simon asked.

"Our role is to make things happen," Angela butted in before Jane could reply. "We have to be role models here."

"Role models?" Jane remarked.

"With all of this the key is action. So we have to role-model what's expected, especially in terms of making things happen using the attitude and behaviour expected within the team," Angela said confidently.

"I think you're right. Building the team won't work unless we drive it in the right way," Simon said.

"And the right way is to build trust," Steve announced. "You can't build trust without showing vulnerability at the right time."

"I agree," Simon replied. "One of the biggest lessons for me over the last few months is that I just don't know it all, and I've had to admit this as I've tried to get others' help. Whilst each time I felt like I was showing a weakness, I actually built trust by relying on them for their input."

"I'm not going to admit to the customer that I don't know what I'm saying," Taylor said, bursting into the conversation.

"Why not?" Steve asked abruptly.

"Because they will think I'm stupid, and it will look bad on World-Corp," Taylor snapped.

"No it won't," Steve snapped back, "they'll just understand that you're human. And, there's a difference between not knowing and not finding out, and not knowing and finding out later."

"You know that makes real sense," Angela said, breaking the argument. "I think that with my team I've only ever just told them what to do and never once asked for their input, or shown my vulnerability as you say. And all this does is at best get compliance, and at worst they just switch off even more."

Angela paused as the others stared at her.

"I think I need to ask them for their input more often," she concluded.

Stay on the Front Foot

"I'm hungry," Jane said as she waved to the waiter, breaking the silence after Angela's statement.

For the next few minutes they all scoured the menu. Once they'd ordered, the conversation became light-hearted as Steve announced how he would seek to show vulnerability by relying on everyone to do everything for him all the time.

"You just try that," Angela said with a smile, reminding him of who was the boss.

"Sorry, darling," Steve said, pretending to cower. "Would you like some more wine, my queen?"

"So how's your love life going Miss Wolton?" Angela asked Jane, changing the conversation. "Because I hear you're off to New York next week."

Jane went bright red and sought to deny everything.

"Just heading over to see a friend," she said.

"What about you, Taylor? How's your love life going?" Simon asked, seeking to save Jane from further questions.

"Just playing the field," Taylor replied, trying not to give too much away.

"What does that mean?" Jane asked, thinking that Taylor was being sexist.

"Well, I've just started seeing a girl from my gym," he replied quickly, seeing that the food was on its way.

"I guess that the thing I've learned about relationships," Steve said once the meals were placed in front of them, "is that to sustain a relationship you really have to stay on the front foot."

"The front foot?" Jane asked

"Yeh…you should always try to know what's going on with the other person; how they're feeling, what's happened in their day etc. And then, you need to really make sure you initiate the conversation when things aren't right. I think I've learnt that you can't just ignore the big white elephant in the corner, if you know what I mean," Steve then said as he looked towards Angela who'd stopped eating. "If there's something wrong, you have to get it out in the open with an honest conversation."

"I agree," Taylor said without thinking. "And you have to make sure that you reinforce when people do things well. You know…make sure you recognise and reward them in a way that makes them feel valued."

"And you have to remove barriers getting in the way," Jane said as they finished their meals.

Once the waiter had cleared away their empty plates, Taylor stood up, took some money from his wallet and threw it on the table before saying goodbye quickly.

"Wow," Simon said, once Taylor was out of sight, "now that was odd!"

Steve, Angela, Jane and Simon remained at the table for another couple of hours after Taylor left. They become more boisterous and playful as Steve sought to return to his fantasy of being King of World-Corp.

The next day back in the office, Angela in true Angela style, sent an email summerising what they'd discussed.

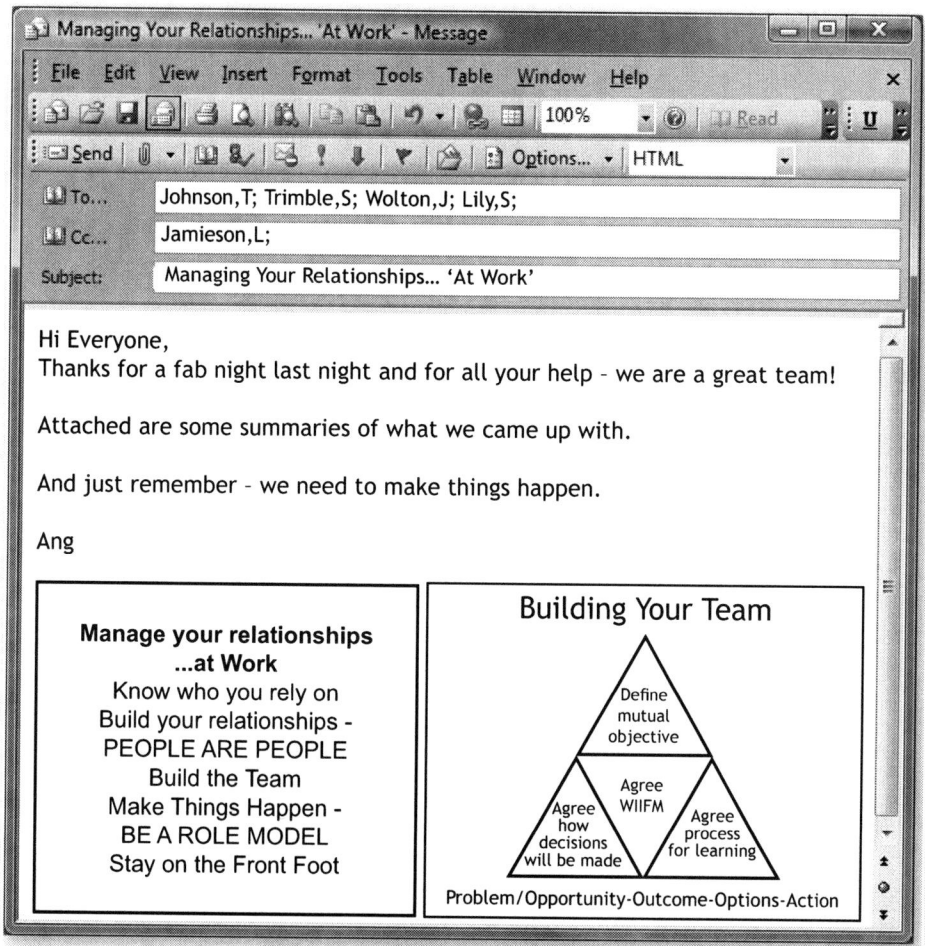

Managing Your Relationships... 'At Work' - Message

To... Johnson,T; Trimble,S; Wolton,J; Lily,S;
Cc... Jamieson,L;
Subject: Managing Your Relationships... 'At Work'

Hi Everyone,
Thanks for a fab night last night and for all your help – we are a great team!

Attached are some summaries of what we came up with.

And just remember – we need to make things happen.

Ang

Manage your relationships ...at Work
Know who you rely on
Build your relationships -
PEOPLE ARE PEOPLE
Build the Team
Make Things Happen -
BE A ROLE MODEL
Stay on the Front Foot

Building Your Team

- Define mutual objective
- Agree WIIFM
- Agree how decisions will be made
- Agree process for learning

Problem/Opportunity-Outcome-Options-Action

Once she got back from holiday, Liz sent the group a follow on email to congratulate the team on what they'd come up with. She also asked if she could send their material to her friend in the Learning and Development team who was really keen to use it to redesign some of the World-Corp training.

Upon reading the email from Liz, each of the group felt good about what they'd achieved.

Just imagine what we could have come up with if we were really trying, Steve wrote to them all.

PRINCIPLES TO REMEMBER

Manage Your Relationships…At Work

Know who you rely on.

Recognise that people are people when seeking to build your relationships.

Get on the same side – ensure that people are in the tent and not outside of it.

Build the team around a mutual objective.

Make things happen through role-modelling the desired attitude and behaviours.

Stay on the front foot to sustain your relationships.

TASKS FOR THE READER
Manage your Relationships...at Work.

Your relationships at work, whether formal or informal, are they key to your success. You rely on a range of people to help you achieve what you need to achieve. It is therefore critical that you recognise who these people are and that you seek to proactively manage your relationship with them, so that you are all contributing to achieving the same mutual objective.

Task 1: Know who you Rely On

Knowing who you rely on is the first step to proactively managing your relationships at work.

Who do you rely on, and why? What do you know about them? How strong is your relationship with them?

Who do you rely on?	What do you rely on them for?	What do you know about them?	How strong is your relationship? (1 - Poor : 5 - Strong)

What can you do to strengthen your relationships?

Task 2: Building the Team

Building a team requires that you know who needs to be on the team and that you consciously seek to take them collectively through the forming, storming, norming and performing cycle. The best way to do this is to get people together and discuss it openly.

What do you believe is the mutual objective for your team?

Who needs to be part of the team you are building? And what do they seek to gain from being in the team (WIIFM)?

Who	What is their role in the team?	What's in it for them to be part of the team - WIIFM?

What will you do to build the team?

What will you do to build the team?	By when?

5.
There is a *'Right Way'* to make a Difference

Change at the Top

Just before the summer, news leaked out that the CEO of World-Corp was retiring early. No-one understood the reason for his decision, but it was announced that he would be replaced by Tom Wolton, Jane's uncle. Although Jane had attempted to keep her relationship to the new CEO secret, news spread quickly amongst the new joiners thanks to Taylor opening his big mouth. For the rest of World-Corp, the first many knew about the change at the top was seeing it on the morning TV news.

Since their meeting in May at Jim's Wine Bar, Angela, Steve, Simon, Jane and Taylor focused on trying what they'd developed on managing their relationships at work. Taylor's attempt was short-lived as he reverted back to his original self. It seemed that although he produced some good ideas during their meeting, rather than practising what he preached, he kept trying too hard and ultimately applied far too much pressure in seeking to get to know and impress people.

"It doesn't sound like Taylor's doing well," Jane told Steve and Angela as they caught up for lunch on the day that her uncle was announced as the new CEO.

"What do you mean?" Steve asked.

"Well, I saw him this morning and he looked really upset. All he said was, *'Well, my customers still hate me and my now ex-girlfriend decided to leave last night'*," Jane replied, feeling sorry for him.

"I think that Taylor is just too impatient to wait for relationships to build and trust to form," Angela said. "I mean, now that I've stopped trying to drive things so hard and just started being myself and relating to people as people, things are going really well. I even have regular full team meetings and one-to-ones so that I can keep up with how the team are getting on."

"Ang that's great," Jane said, forgetting about Taylor's predicament.

"I think I need to learn some diplomacy," Steve thought out loud, reflecting on some of the things that hadn't gone well.

"No," Jane replied with a smile, "you need to learn how to create a gap."

Steve smiled, thinking back to the training course in Wales, and knowing that Jane was right.

"How have things gone for you, Jane?" Angela asked.

"Quite well I think," Jane said. "I arranged a workshop with the people I rely on, which I got one of the managers from my last project to facilitate. She was great and we ended up with a clearly-defined mutual objective and a plan to achieve it. So now we're all working more closely together."

Jane paused for a moment.

"You know, after seeing that manager facilitate the workshop, I think I'd like to do that one day," she concluded.

"You should Jane, you'd be great at it," Angela said encouragingly.

"I think Simon's doing well too," Steve said, seeking to change the subject. "So our session in Jim's was a real success."

"You can say that again," Angela said softly.

"So how was America?" she asked, directing all her attention at Jane who instantly went red.

The Need to Make a Difference

With the new CEO at the helm, people across World-Corp began wondering how things would change. Their first sight of this was a message from Tom distributed to everyone throughout the organisation. The message stated that although the performance of World-Corp was good, it needed to be better. He then set all 75,000 employees the challenge of making a greater difference in every aspect of what they did. For the new joiners based in Europe, they were all called to the London head office for a presentation from the new CEO and some senior managers, similar to their induction. This road-show, as it was referred to, was also held in other head offices around the world.

As the day of the road-show arrived, Jane was dreading it. She'd already received plenty of stick from many of the less mature new joiners, so the thought of sitting there while her uncle presented was unbearable. After the first few jokers approached, making jibes about being the boss's niece, Jane thought *Right, it's time to go on the attack.*

"I was talking to Uncle Tom about you last night over dinner," Jane said to the next person who made a remark, "and he said that he'd like me to put forward some people for him to have a chat with. So your name is now on the list if that's OK."

Very quickly word got around and, although she would never actually pass the names on, it provided her and Simon with that day's worth of entertainment.

"Our key focus now in World-Corp is on improving profitability, customer satisfaction and employee engagement," Tom announced in his presentation. "Whilst we've been performing well based on our past success, we've become complacent. And with the speed of change in the current market place, we have to start evolving with purpose to continue succeeding."

Once Tom had finished and left the stage, a familiar slide appeared.

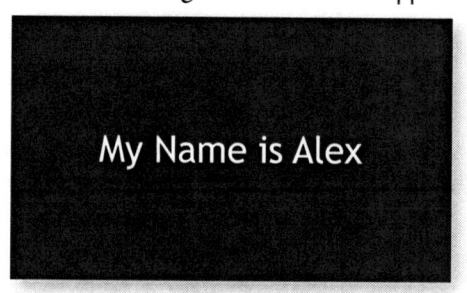

> # My Name is Alex

Once the murmurs from the crowd died down, as if re-enacting his entrance from the induction Alex strode confidently on to the middle of the stage. Standing again directly in front of the screen he surveyed those in front of him. The new joiners immediately shuffled in their seats hoping to show this figure on the stage how far they'd come in just under a year.

"Welcome back everybody," Alex broke the silence in a way that was larger than life. "So things have changed at the top, and what Tom has said is absolutely true. We need everyone at World-Corp to see how they can make a difference. That means Tom, that means me, and that means you."

The next slide appeared.

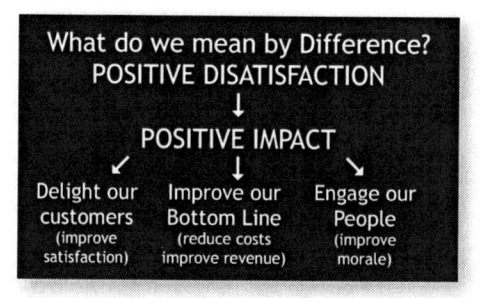

> **What do we mean by Difference?**
> **POSITIVE DISATISFACTION**
> ↓
> **POSITIVE IMPACT**
> ↙ ↓ ↘
> Delight our customers (improve satisfaction) | Improve our Bottom Line (reduce costs improve revenue) | Engage our People (improve morale)

"So what do we mean by difference?" Alex continued. "In simple terms, what this means is that in everything you do you need you to look how you can improve what you deliver and also how you deliver it."

The room was silent as everyone tuned in to what Alex was saying.

"It means that we all need to have a positive impact - a positive impact on our customers. They have to be delighted with what we deliver and that is both our internal and external customers. That's right, you each have internal customers who use what you deliver as well.

A positive impact for our bottom line means streamlining processes and reducing unnecessary costs where possible. We also need to look for new opportunities to improve revenue through increasing sales.

And finally, a positive impact for our people means we need to make sure that whatever action we take to improve things, it has to focus on better engaging the people of World-Corp. I want people to love working for World-Corp as much as I do," Alex announced in a sincere tone.

"And how you know where to make a difference is through positive dissatisfaction," Alex stated confidently. "As I said at the induction, it's OK to be dissatisfied with things. Tom has rightly pointed out that World-Corp isn't perfect, and if the CEO can say it, so can I. So as you see things that don't work or which could be improved, we need you to be thinking about how to fix them. And then, as I've said before, that is exactly what we need you to do – fix them. By doing that you will have a positive impact and you will make a difference - not just to World-Corp, but also to yourselves and those around you."

"So please," Alex started his conclusion, "as you leave this room, think about how you can make a difference. Look to where things aren't working or where they could be improved, and then think about what you're going to do about improving them. And as I always say, ask for forgiveness not for permission. Never wait to be given permission to fix something that's clearly broken."

On that note, Alex left the stage to another roaring round of applause.

An Idea to Make a Difference

In the days following the road-show session a new level of focus seemed to sweep across the new joiner community. Even some of the most cynical amongst them became more conscious about how they could improve what they delivered and how they delivered it. Exactly one week after they had all got together, Simon sent the group an email invitation.

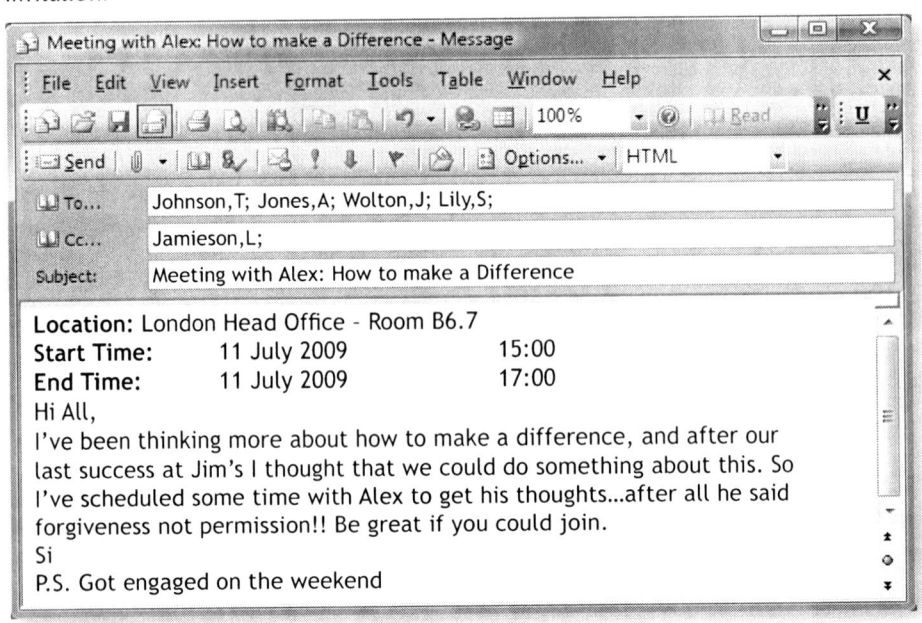

Meeting with Alex: How to make a Difference - Message

To... Johnson,T; Jones,A; Wolton,J; Lily,S;
Cc... Jamieson,L;
Subject: Meeting with Alex: How to make a Difference

Location: London Head Office - Room B6.7
Start Time: 11 July 2009   15:00
End Time: 11 July 2009   17:00

Hi All,
I've been thinking more about how to make a difference, and after our last success at Jim's I thought that we could do something about this. So I've scheduled some time with Alex to get his thoughts...after all he said forgiveness not permission!! Be great if you could join.
Si
P.S. Got engaged on the weekend

Steve and Taylor declined without really reading the note as they were both already scheduled to be in different parts of the country on the 11th. Angela accepted with a gushing email.

"You have to tell me every detail," Angela demanded as she called Simon straight after sending her reply. "I can't believe you didn't tell us you were thinking about getting engaged!"

Jane and Liz also accepted and sent notes congratulating Simon on getting engaged.

I bet your girlfriend is happy that you finally plucked up enough courage to ask, Jane wrote cheekily in her email.

No courage needed, Simon wrote back, *I am Casanova!*

When the day of their meeting with Alex arrived, Simon, Liz, Jane and Angela made it to the room a couple of minutes early. The meeting room that Simon had booked was quite long and narrow with the door at one end and windows that looked out on to the street at the other. Within the room was a large rectangular table positioned almost perfectly in the middle with six chairs around it. There was also a large whiteboard mounted on one of the long walls.

"Where should we get Alex to sit?" Simon asked Liz nervously

"Right at the end by the door would be fine," Liz replied with a reassuring smile.

At precisely 3:00 p.m. Alex entered the room. Simon jumped up immediately to shake his hand and the others followed quickly.

"Hey Liz, great to see you again," Alex responded sincerely when shaking Liz's hand.

Wow, Angela thought, *Liz is well-connected.*

Taking his suit jacket off and hanging it on the back of his chair, Alex took his seat seemingly at the head of the table.

"So how can I help?" Alex asked in a deep voice as he looked directly at Simon.

Simon stammered, feeling his nerves going into overdrive. *Pull it together Si,* he thought to himself trying to regain composure, *Alex is still a human.* Simon then took a deep breath and used the gap to think back to his well-rehearsed speech.

"Well, with Liz's guidance our support group has been coming up with some really great things over the last few months," Simon started, feeling his confidence grow.

"In fact, the basis of the 'Managing your Relationships at Work' training course for new joiners was something we came up with after a session in Jim's Wine Bar across the road," Simon continued with a wry smile, realising that he'd just revealed a little too much.

"Hey, that was you guys?" Alex replied enthusiastically. "I wish I had done that early in my career, then I might have avoided a few unnecessary challenges along the way."

Simon was now feeling more at ease and more confident that they were on the right track, so he continued.

"Well, because of that, myself, Jane, Angela, and also Steve and Taylor who can't be here today, thought that we could do something similar for making a difference."

"And what difference would that make to World-Corp?" Alex asked looking Simon straight in the eyes. "I mean what impact would that have for our company in terms of bottom line, customers or our people?"

Simon's confidence evaporated instantly as he felt like a rabbit in the headlights under Alex's gaze.

"I think it would have an impact in all areas," Angela said confidently, realising that Simon was in trouble.

Alex shifted his attention towards Angela, but not before giving Simon a wink and a smile of encouragement.

That's why this guy gets paid the big bucks, Simon thought to himself.

"Say more on that," Alex said, now giving his full attention to Angela.

"Well," she said, "if we can help people to improve the value of the impact they have through showing them how and where to focus their energy, and also how to take action with others, then they can seek to make a difference in all three areas."

"It's like you said at our induction," Angela continued, "we have influence and what we," she waved her hands motioning at the others around the table, "are trying to do is to extend our influence."

Alex paused, processing everything he had heard, while Simon, Angela and Jane shot each other nervous glances.

"I love it," Alex erupted, almost jumping out of his chair. "What I would really like to see is for you to capture what you believe are the principles for people to make a difference, but in a way that shows a journey, or story, where they can see it in practice."

Each of them looked slightly puzzled at Alex's challenge.

"See, if people can follow the principles through a simple story, we can not only give them the tools and permission to try things for themselves, but they will also develop courage to do it because they can see how it has been done before," Alex explained.

Alex then proceeded to get up out of his chair and move past Liz to the board on the wall.

"As I see it, there are three areas of focus," he said as he wrote down his thoughts.

Angela was surprised that two of the statements were taken directly from her.

> # Make a Difference
> Know where to Focus
> Take Action with Others
> Continue Evolving with Purpose

Rather than giving any further explanation, once he had finished writing Alex spun around to face the others.

"So the challenge is set," he announced, looked at each of them.

"When are you going to have it done by?" he asked openly.

They all looked at each other not knowing what to say.

"By the end of August," Jane announced whilst looking at the others.

"Perfect," Alex replied. "Set up a meeting for the end of August and then we can work out the next steps."

"Liz, are you OK to help these guys with this?" Alex said, focusing his attention towards her.

"Absolutely," she replied confidently, "but I'm not sure they need much help from me."

On that note, Alex thanked each person for their help. He then grabbed his jacket and left the room.

Knowing Where to Focus

The day after their meeting with Alex, they all decided to get together to develop a plan. Steve, who was in London, also joined them but no-one had heard from Taylor.

"Right, the first thing we need to do is work out where to focus," Jane said, recounting Alex's ideas.

"How do we do that?" Simon asked.

"Through positive dissatisfaction," Steve announced confidently. "I think first we have to identify something that we each think needs to be fixed."

In considering this, they talked about a variety of ideas including why some customers weren't happy with World-Corp, and how some of the processes and systems they relied on were not efficient. Jane also told a story about how her suppliers consistently failed to deliver what was needed. As the discussion continued, it dawned on them that much of their customers' dissatisfaction could always be traced back to a few simple causes within the business.

"I think that focusing on our suppliers, and in particular our procurement processes, has got to be a good option," Simon stated, drawing a conclusion from their discussion.

"I agree," Jane said. "I've been let down by the late delivery of essential equipment quite a few times over the last couple of months. And I know that this impacted on our customers, our team and also the bottom line."

"So how do we figure out what's not working in procurement?" Steve asked, agreeing with Jane's points.

"Good question," Angela responded, "I think we need to get in there and talk to them. But first I think that we need to really define what business they are in."

"What business they are in?" Jane asked, feeling confused. "What do you mean?"

"Well, I read an article the other day by a guy called Paul Sloan, and he said that *Black and Decker's business is not to make drills, but to enable people to make holes*. So I think that we should really focus on understanding what outcome procurement are seeking to fulfil to us as their customers. So they're not in the procurement business, they are in the..." Angela said as she struggled to finish her sentence.

"They're in the business of getting us what we need, when we need it, and at the right cost," Steve completed Angela's statement.

"That's it!" Angela said excitedly, reaching for Steve's hand across the table.

"So the first principle of knowing where to focus," Jane started to summarise, "is to find what's not working or where the opportunities exist through positive dissatisfaction. And then we must define what business they are in, for the area we are focusing on."

"That's right," Simon replied, smiling at Jane. "But then I think that we need to get in and talk to the people in procurement to find out what's working, what's not working and what they could be doing differently."

"Ah, the three magic questions," Steve replied, reminiscing about their Wales training course.

Using some contacts provided by Liz, the team arranged to talk to those in the procurement team. When they first started setting up meetings, people were cautious about saying too much. The team therefore had to use all they'd learned about building relationships to get people to open up. As they continued their meetings however, Angela, Steve, Simon and Jane found that those on the team had a lot of ideas on how to improve things when asked the three magic questions. Steve also focused on speaking to people about who their customers were and what they thought their customers expected of them.

"So do you see yourselves as having internal customers?" Steve asked a couple of the team's members.

"When you put it that way, I guess we do," one person responded. "I suppose it's our internal customers who respond to World-Corp's external customers."

Following their meetings, Jane and Angela also decided to talk to people who they saw as internal customers of procurement. From these discussions they discovered what people's expectations were of the procurement team in terms of both their needs (what was essential to them) and also their wants (what was desirable). They also uncovered some specific issues that could be dealt with.

After a solid week of data collection the team got back together in the same room where they had met with Alex. They pored meticulously over all the information and opinions they'd collected. Taylor, who'd managed to join them, brought a new objective viewpoint into the process.

"So what's really causing that?" he would ask, seeking to identify the root cause of the issues.

From their analysis they came up with numerous issues to focus on.

"We should really only focus on two or three issues at a time," Jane said. "Remember Alex's comment from induction: 20% of your effort will achieve 80% of your results. And that you will always use the resources you have, and you will always need more. So let's just focus solely on the vital things that will make the greatest difference with the resources we have."

"Great thinking, Jane," Steve responded. "We definitely have to make best use of our limited time."

"So the key points we have," Simon summarised, "are firstly to reduce the number of incorrect orders being placed by changing the ordering process. This is currently slow, manual and confusing for the procurement team's internal customers. Secondly, to reduce the amount of inventory we hold by improving the spares purchasing process. We currently hold far too many parts on the shelves that we just don't need. And thirdly, to increase the speed of delivery by improving the distribution process, which currently results in slow and expensive delivery of equipment to its requester."

"Excellent!" Angela said excitedly. "Shall we go for dinner?"

"Sorry, can't make it tonight. Wedding planning," Simon explained as he rolled his eyes.

"Sorry, me neither," said Jane, "I have to meet someone at the airport."

"The airport? You didn't tell us that Captain America is coming over," Angela said, using the nick-name they'd affectionately given Jane's new boyfriend.

"Yeh," Jane said, not wanting to reveal too much. "He's arriving tonight and we're going to take a few days off to go to the countryside."

"Wow!" Angela's face lit up like a Christmas tree. "Things are moving along, aren't they?"

Take Action with Others

Without wanting to break momentum, once Jane was back from her long romantic weekend they scheduled another meeting. After they had all arrived in the room, Angela probed Jane for the juicy gossip on her love life. Jane, however, refused to reveal a single detail other than to say that she had a great time.

"Right, let's get to it," Simon announced, seeking to save Jane from any further questions.

They decided to start with a quick recap of all that they had done so far and make sure they still felt that they were on the right track. Liz kindly offered to play devil's advocate by challenging their approach and assumptions.

"So what's next?" she asked at the end of their explanation to her questions.

"Now we need to determine how to take action with others," Steve announced as he found the note from the original meeting with Alex.

They all sat there in silence as they considered what exactly this meant.

"I guess that the key part of this is 'with others,'" Jane spoke up first. "I think that we need to test our ideas with all those we've already spoken to, especially with those in the procurement team who will have to help make this happen."

"I agree," Simon said, smiling at Jane. "So I think we need a plan for which of us will talk to who."

"Can I also suggest that when you talk to these people, you present your ideas and analysis as a straw-man," Liz added.

"What do you mean by straw-man?" Steve asked.

"A straw-man is a term for work in progress, and by presenting it as such you are seeking to get the people who would be involved in making things happen to help shape the concepts and plan with you. This will help them take ownership of the ideas and help you avoid presenting them with a final solution, or *fait accompli*," Liz explained.

"Great thinking," Simon replied enthusiastically.

Over the following few days, they presented their straw-man, as Liz had called it, and got ideas on the concepts they were developing. From their discussions, further ideas and enthusiasm were generated about what could be done. However, some of those within the procurement team, especially some of the senior managers, required some more convincing.

"I think that I can do something a little creative here," Steve announced to Jane who had just told him about a particularly tricky meeting she had attended.

To help explain what they were seeking to achieve and to build strong sponsorship from the top, Steve created a scale model in the form of a pile of fake money that represented how much unnecessary stock World-Corp was holding and how much cash was being wasted through poor processes. Along with Jane, he then took this model directly to the office of the Vice President for Procurement.

"So this is what we think we can save by just doing these three things," Steve said confidently, pointing to a large pile of fake World-Corp dollar bills that had the VP's picture on them.

"That's in the millions," the VP said, looking directly at Steve.

"That's right," Steve said. "We actually think that it's about £5 million a year."

On hearing the amount, the VP instantly requested that Steve tell the same story to his direct reports.

"Can you also break down the amounts that each department can save?" the VP requested. "And make sure you put their picture on the dollar bills for their department."

When Steve did this, a new level of enthusiasm was generated towards **the change**. It seemed that the fake bills stirred some emotion as each member of the **management** team was keen to avoid seeing their face on any wasted World-Corp dollar **bills in the** future.

As they caught up following the meeting with the VP and his team, they realised that something else was needed.

"I think that we should hold a workshop with those who will be responsible for implementing the ideas," Jane suggested, thinking back to what she'd done with her own extended team. "I'd be happy to coordinate this, and I'm sure that I can get the manager who helped me last time to help again."

"Great idea Jane," Angela announced.

"I'd be happy to help," the manager replied to Jane's request, "but only on one condition: you have to facilitate this, with my support."

Jane was horrified at the suggestion.

"But I haven't even been here a year," Jane replied, feeling sick at the thought of standing in front of all those people.

"Jane, you just have to be yourself," the manager explained. "You have a great personality and you know the content inside out, so all I need to do is help you with the process. You've seen me do it, and at a basic level it's really not that hard. All you need to do is draw out the answers from the people in the room."

Jane, still not fully convinced, agreed that she would do it only if the manager were in the room to help her. The entire day before the workshop Jane felt sick with nerves.

"What if I screw this up?" Jane said to her newly-proclaimed American boyfriend when he called that night.

"You're thinking about this the wrong way, babe," he said in his New York accent.

"We all get nervous," he continued. "I bet that even your friend the manager gets nervous before something like this. But you need to focus on how great it will feel at the end of the day when it has all gone right."

"Close your eyes," he then said. "Now picture yourself in front of all those people getting them engaged and excited about what you could really achieve here. Trust me, they want to believe in what's possible, after all they are human. Think about how you're standing and moving around the room. Think about what you're saying and how you're feeling. Think about the likely questions they will be asking you."

He continued as Jane visualised her success.

As they finished the call, Jane's nerves had all but drifted away.

"Thank you so much," Jane said, softening her tone. "You're so great. I guess that's why I love you."

As it slipped out, Jane realised what she had just said. *Oh God* she thought, *we've only been together a little while. What have I just said?*

After a second or two of silence, his voice came back over the line.

"I love you too," he said, meaning every word. "Now you knock 'em dead tomorrow, gorgeous, and let me know how it goes."

As she hung up, Jane's faced beamed with a smile from ear to ear and that night she slept soundly.

During the workshop the next day, Jane facilitated. Although her nerves had returned, she kept focused on the Problem/Opportunity, Outcome, Options and Action process they had chosen to follow. She'd even written this on a piece of flipchart paper and put it on the wall in front of everyone.

With the manager and her colleagues' assistance, Jane then used everything she had learnt to draw out what those in the room considered to be a fantastic plan with clear targets and actions, responsibilities and timelines. In the final part of the workshop, the manager supporting Jane then took the group through some ideas on how those involved could help 'lead the change', as she referred to it. The manager drew a picture on the board of what she called the 'change curve'.

CHANGE CURVE

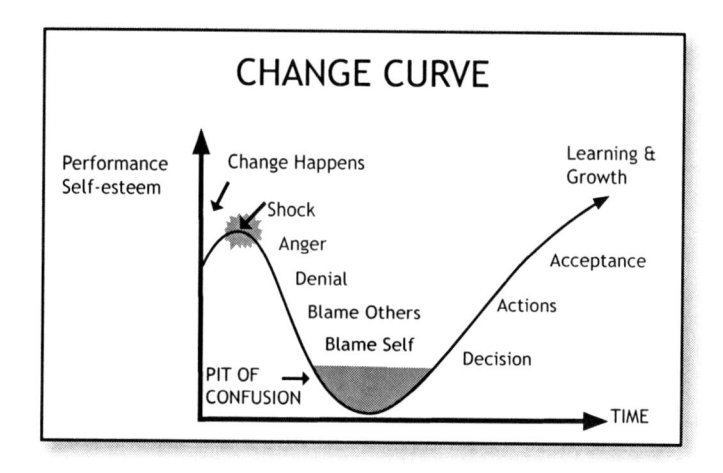

Performance Self-esteem — Change Happens — Shock — Anger — Denial — Blame Others — Blame Self — PIT OF CONFUSION — Decision — Actions — Acceptance — Learning & Growth — TIME

Directing everyone's attention to the picture, the manager went on to explain what it meant.

"Whenever you seek to improve or fix things there is almost always an inevitable change to what people do day to day. For some people this change could be quite minor, but for others it may be quite scary, especially if they're used to a certain way of doing things. A person called Elisabeth Kubler-Ross said that when people realise that they are going to be affected by change, they will experience a range of emotions as shown in the picture."

She paused to allow people to look at the picture.

"Now, different people will experience different emotions at different times," the manager continued. "But when you're seeking to make change happen, you need to be conscious of where individuals are on the change curve so that you can help manage those emotions and come through to acceptance, learning and growth.

If you don't help people manage their emotions during change, then you are likely to experience resistance. What I've found to be the best way to help them through this emotion and remove resistance is to get them involved, hence take action with others. Just remember that it's better to have people inside your tent pissing out rather than outside pissing in."

Laughter erupted around the room.

For the team, as they listened to the manager they each hurriedly took notes, only occasionally pausing to smile at each other realising how well things were going. Just as the manager finished talking about the change curve, she was asked a question about the best way to let people know what was going on.

"Through telling stories," the manager responded enthusiastically.

The manager then went on to draw on another sheet of paper.

> **Communicate Change: Story Telling**
>
> **Purpose**
> Why is the change needed?
>
> **Picture**
> What will things look like when the change is implemented? and, What's in it for them?
>
> **Plan**
> What is the plan to implement the change?
>
> **Part to Play**
> What we need them to do

"A guy called William Bridges created this simple way of structuring stories," she said, referring to the notes she'd written. "The key is to create a consistent story that you can tailor to each audience that will help them understand quickly what you're seeking to achieve and what part they need to play."

"As an exercise, why don't you each now create a story that you can use to tell to those people who were both affected by and also interested in the plans that you're proposing?" the manager suggested.

Each of the people in the room, including the VP, sought to do exactly that and then practised telling their story to the others.

After the workshop everyone involved headed out to celebrate. Throughout the evening, many of the managers who had attended congratulated Jane on doing such a fantastic job of facilitating. One of them, who'd been in the business for over ten years, even said that he couldn't have done what Jane had done.

Feeling the euphoria of her achievement, Jane called her boyfriend in America as soon as she got home that night.

"I couldn't have done it without you," Jane said as she began to calm herself.

"It was all you," the voice replied from the other end of the line. "It was just you being you."

Continue Evolving with Purpose

Following the resounding success of the workshop, action was well under way within each team that was responsible for implementing the changes proposed. Simon, Jane, Angela and Steve all continued to support the implementation teams to make things happen. This involved helping them achieve quick wins by focusing on easy-to-improve areas first, and then helping them to build momentum by celebrating success when targets were hit.

After the workshop, Taylor had seemingly dropped off the radar.

"I think that things are really getting worse for Taylor," Simon told the others when they caught up. "He let it slip to me that he's got no hope of hitting his sales targets and he was still trying to get back together with his ex-girlfriend."

"Poor Taylor," Jane responded. "I only wish he'd let us help."

At the end of August, the day came for them to meet up with Alex. Knowing that Alex was a busy man, they'd prepared a brief presentation on the key things they'd done but, once the meeting commenced, they realised quickly that Alex knew everything already.

"So I hear it's been a huge success," Alex remarked as soon as he entered the room.

How does he know that? they all thought as Alex retold their story.

They then presented Alex with a pack outlining the story and a summary of the key principles for 'Know where to Focus' and 'Take Action with Others'.

"This is great, guys," Alex beamed. "You've all really outdone yourselves."

"But we're struggling on the third point – Continue Evolving with Purpose," Simon admitted, feeling a slight sense of disappointment.

Upon hearing this admission, Alex laughed.

"Continuing to evolve with purpose is definitely the trickiest one," he commented with a smile. "That's why we in World-Corp are focusing so heavily on it at the moment."

"What I've come to realise over the last six months is that success breeds complacency," Alex admitted. "See, we in World-Corp have had some real successes over the last five, even ten years. But because of this, you might say, we became lazy and started resting on our laurels, hence why Tom has started focusing us all on it so heavily."

"But, how do you avoid complacency?" Jane asked.

"Good question, what do you think?" Alex fired the question right back at Jane.

Jane, taken aback, stammered slightly before being rescued by Angela.

"I think that constant monitoring is a good way to keep focused," Angela stated confidently. "You know, always measuring your performance and also measuring yourself against other companies."

"Sounds good," Alex replied nodding.

"That will also help you to raise your game," Simon continued, "I mean, by constantly monitoring your performance and asking what's working well, what's not working well and what could we do differently, you can always look for things to fix or improve."

"That's right," Jane added, feeling ready to join the conversation. "And when looking for things to fix you can focus on what to improve, reduce, create or increase."

"Exactly," Alex said, smiling at Jane, as he stood up and drew a picture on the board.

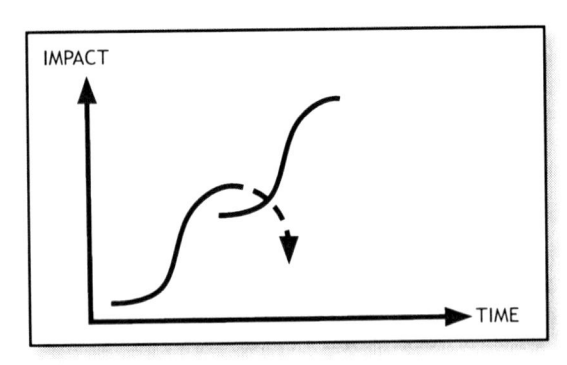

"I think that continuing to evolve with purpose also means knowing when you're at the top of your S curve," Alex thought out loud.

The rest of them waited patiently for him to continue as he gathered his thoughts.

"What I mean is that when you make a difference the intent is to create real and sustainable impact – you leave a footprint, if you know what I mean. This is easy to do when you're new to a position because you have a fresh set of eyes and you can see things objectively, much the same as you have. But as you stay there for longer, it is easy to get comfortable and take things for granted, which means that you risk losing your impact through being complacent," he added, pointing to the dotted line at the top of the first S curve.

"Therefore, the key is to continually refresh your impact through either moving on once you know you've given all you can, or through bringing in new sets of eyes to help you see things differently," Alex continued, taking a moment at the end to draw breath.

"So I guess that continuing to evolve with purpose means recognising that success breeds complacency, constantly monitoring how you're performing, and recognising when you have maximised your impact," Simon summarised.

"Exactly," Alex said excitedly as he pointed a finger at Simon.

"So against all of this, what could go wrong?" Alex asked, deciding to avoid embarrassing Simon any longer.

"You don't understand the issues you need to resolve well enough, hence you focus on the wrong thing," Angela replied instantly.

"You don't involve the right people, creating resistance once you start to try and change things," Steve quickly followed with.

"And you don't make the change stick, meaning that once you leave, things revert back to the way they were," Jane added without thinking what she was saying.

"You guys are good," Alex said softly, giving them all an approving nod.

As the meeting finished, Alex could not contain his excitement. He announced that he would take this straight to Tom and seek to get it implemented right across the business.

Once Alex had left, they all collapsed back into their chairs.

Liz looked at each of them, feeling an overwhelming sense of pride in what they had done. *These new guys,* she thought to herself as a smile came to her face, *are changing the face of our company.*

Just as they were about to leave the room so they could celebrate their latest success, Jane said what the others were thinking.

"It's a shame Taylor couldn't be here today."

PRINCIPLES TO REMEMBER

There is a 'Right Way' to make a Difference

Know where to Focus
Identify what needs attention through Positive Dissatisfaction.

Define what business you are in – *drills or holes?*

Talk to people to find out what's working,
what's not working and what can be done differently.

Identify the root causes of key issues.

Pick only the most critical issues to fix (80/20 rule).

Take Action With Others
Test your theories with others – *present a straw man.*

Gain commitment from key sponsors – *encourage emotional commitment.*

Develop your plan with those who will implement it.

Lead the change – *get people involved to reduce resistance.*

Tell a story to communicate the plan – *Purpose, Picture, Plan and Part to Plan.*

Build momentum – *focus on quick wins and celebrate success.*

Continue Evolving with Purpose
Recognise that success breeds complacency – *never rest on your laurels.*

Constantly monitor your performance – *always
look for areas to improve, reduce, create or increase.*

Recognise when you've maximised your impact –
never say 'it's always been done this way'.

TASKS FOR THE READER

There is a 'Right Way' to make a Difference

Through positive dissatisfaction and positive impact you can make a real difference in your area. Making a difference requires a considered approach so that you gain the maximum results from your effort.

Task 1: Know where to focus

Knowing where to focus is the first step in seeking to make a difference. The secret to knowing where to focus is to identify the root causes of issues, so that you deal with causes and not symptoms.

What areas at work do you believe need improving? *(Remember positive dissatisfaction)*

What do you believe is the root cause behind the issue(s) you've identified?

What would be the impact on the bottom line, customers or people if you dealt with this issue(s)? (Try to be specific about targets)

Task 2: Take Action with Others

Taking action with others requires that you get others – your key stakeholders – involved in seeking to make a difference. The first step in taking action with others is to identify who else needs to be involved in building and implementing the plan.

Who else do you need to involve in building and implementing the plan to make a difference?

Who?	Why does this person need to be involved?	How and when will you engage them?

Task 3: Take Action to Make a Difference

To make a real difference you have to commit to taking action. You must also secure the right sponsor. A sponsor is someone who will help provide you with the support you need. They must be sufficiently enthusiastic about the change you are proposing and sufficiently senior to help make it happen.

Who can you approach to sponsor you to make a difference? How and when will you approach them?

What action will you take next to make a difference?

Action?	By when?

Part 2

Who Are You?
Why Are You Here?

6.
Your Future...*Really Now Starts Here!*

No Longer the New Joiners

"Name?" Simon asked the next person in the queue.

The guy, who looked as though he had been daydreaming, quickly realised that he'd just reached the front of the line.

"Um, um, Josh," the guy blurted out as his cheeks went red.

"Sorry, I meant surname," Simon said, feeling a strange sense of *déjà* vu and sympathy towards the new guy.

"Oh," he said apologetically, "it's Brown, Josh Brown."

"Great, here you are Josh," Simon said, picking a name tag and handing it to him. "People are just assembling at the bottom of the stairs. Help yourself to tea or coffee and welcome to World-Corp."

"Thanks," Josh replied, taking the tag and walking away towards the stairs.

As Simon continued handing out name tags to the new joiners who seemed to be arriving by the dozen, Angela appeared out of nowhere.

"Everything OK?" she asked Simon with a sense of urgency in her voice.

"No problems so far," Simon replied.

"That's a double negative, Mr Trimble. Remember we must be setting the right example for these new joiners," Angela said with a slight tone of authority mixed with anxiousness.

Simon immediately stood upright and snapped his heels together.

"Yes Miss. Sorry Miss. It won't happen again Miss," he blurted out and then gave her a wink.

"Sorry," Angela said, "I can't believe it's a year and we're no longer the new joiners."

"I know," Simon replied, returning his attention back to the name tags.

"And I can't believe you volunteered us to help out at induction," he continued, shooting a quick glance at Angela who was already thinking about the next thing she must check on.

"You agreed," Angela responded, realising what he'd just said.

"I'm only joking Ang. Now why don't you go and see what the others are doing? I wouldn't be surprised if that lazy boyfriend of yours is just drinking coffee and eating cake!"

Angela looked at Simon and smiled. *I'd best go check on Steve*, she then thought to herself. As Angela retraced the same steps they had all walked into the reception area a year ago, all she could see were people. Within the room there was the same growing hum of voices, as it filled with the next round of 350 new joiners. Hanging in the air and across all the faces in the crowd, Angela could see and feel the unmistakable sense of uncertainty and anticipation that she, too, had felt last year on her first day.

Stopping just above the bottom of the stairs, Angela could see that a few groups had started to form. As she looked a little more closely, she saw that smack in the middle of what seemed to be the noisiest group was Steve doing his best to entertain the crowd. It appeared that he was re-enacting his first day and how he'd spilt coffee on himself and then sought to wash it out of his shirt in the bathroom. She also noticed that Taylor had found himself a group to entertain; however he appeared to be far more subdued. Jane was wandering around the edge of the group, seeking to ease the nerves of the few stray individuals who were distracting themselves with their mobile phones or sipping at their drinks.

Standing there looking across the mass of people, the same thoughts re-entered Angela's mind: *I can't believe we're a year on and no longer the new joiners. Where did last year go?*

Looking up from the crowd, Jane saw Angela standing there as if in a daze.

"Hey Ang, everything all right?" Jane asked as she reached the bottom of the stairs.

"Yeh," Angela replied, being drawn out of her own thoughts, "I think they're just about all here. What's the time?"

"9:50," Jane responded. "We must be just about ready to go."

Cutting over the last word of her sentence, the same voice that had made the announcement the year before came over the loudspeakers.

"Could all new joiners please make their way into the auditorium and take their seats according to the seating plan," the well-spoken lady's voice requested.

"Here we go," Jane said to Angela before taking a deep breath.

"Yes, here we go," Angela replied, taking a deep breath as well.

Just like the year before, upon hearing the announcement the mass of people started their migration towards the main entrance like a herd of wild animals. Once the last few stragglers were rounded up and shown to their tables, Simon, Steve and Taylor walked over to where Jane and Angela were standing.

"All right chaps?" Steve broke the silence, putting on the most posh English accent he could muster.

"All right," they all replied with a smile.

"Tally ho, think we best get all this cleaned up then, eh wot," Steve continued with his fake accent now faltering as he realised he was volunteering them to do some more work.

Just Surviving Isn't Enough

For the remainder of the day, Steve, Angela, Taylor, Jane and Simon ensured that things ran as smoothly as possible. Following their induction, they'd recommended some improvements so that this year's intake got a better start then they did, especially in making sure the new joiners' project managers were ready for them.

Steve had arranged for welcome drinks to be held in the pub across the road after the induction. In the pub, Angela, Steve, Simon, Jane, Taylor and others from their intake mingled amongst the new joiners, answering any questions they were asked. They each also did their best to pass on the key tips they had learnt during their first year.

By 8:30 p.m. the group of new joiners had started to thin out as people thought about needing to be fresh for the next day. Simon, feeling responsible, wandered around to those who remained making sure they were all OK and that they still knew where their new equipment was. Once he'd done the rounds, he joined the others who were standing with Liz by the bar.

"Fancy a bite to eat?" Simon asked.

"Absolutely," Jane responded. "Any ideas where?"

"How about Jim's?" Taylor responded, thinking back to the steak that he'd had there last time.

"Jim's it is then," Simon announced as everyone nodded in agreement.

Once in Jim's Wine Bar, they made their way to the same table in the back corner and proceeded to get themselves settled.

"Ah, my lovely ladies," the same Italian waiter announced as he appeared out of nowhere.

Jane and Angela looked at each other and smiled as they wondered how he could have remembered them from so long ago.

Without wanting to delay, Taylor ordered as soon as the waiter was ready, prompting all the others to do the same. Whilst waiting for their drinks to arrive, an uncomfortable silence descended on the group. It seemed that each of them, exhausted from the day's events, was half reminiscing about the last year and half wondering what the next year had in store. Once the waiter had brought their drinks and disappeared, Liz decided to break the silence.

"So...you've survived your first year," she said with a proud tone in her voice.

"Survived is about right," Taylor responded with a slight slur and having already had his first gulp of wine. "Yeh, I've survived but only just."

Taylor paused to gather his thoughts.

"I mean, I've done OK," he continued, realising that the last statement just slipped out, "but I'm not quite sure I'm where I should be. That's it. I think I should be doing something else so that I can really show people what I'm capable of. People just haven't seen the real me yet."

Everyone stared at Taylor, waiting for him to continue, but instead he just stopped. Once they realised he wasn't going to carry on, Jane spoke up.

"Well, I think I've survived too," she said. "In fact I think I've done a little more than survive. You know, talking to the new guys today has really made me realise how far I've come and how much I've learnt. But I'm not sure that surviving is enough."

"I agree," Simon butted in, "I had to stop myself a couple of times as I got carried away with trying to tell them everything tonight, but I still feel there has to be more than this."

They all nodded, except for Taylor who appeared to be daydreaming.

"I guess if I'm really honest," Jane added, "I'm still not sure exactly whether I should be here or not."

Each of them stared at Jane following her admission.

"I mean, I really love World-Corp," she continued, "and I have learnt so much over the last year, but I just don't know if this is what I want to be doing for the rest of my career."

Steve, feeling exactly the same as Jane, decided to jump in.

"I know where you're coming from, sister," he said, trying to lighten the mood, "I'm amazed at how far I've come as well. But as I imagine myself in 20, maybe 30 years time, do I see myself as a senior executive here? Probably not. Actually, do I see myself as a senior exec at all? I'm not sure."

As Steve finished, he glanced at Angela and then looked towards Liz, hoping that he hadn't said anything that he shouldn't have. Simon, realising that Steve was feeling out on a limb decided to add his opinion.

"I have to agree, Steve, I'm not sure I see myself here in 20 or 30 years time either. But, as I say that, I'm not sure where I see myself."

"I second that," Angela burst in. "There are just so many possibilities and options for the future, how do you know which is the right one? Every time I speak to someone or see something new I think, *wow that would be great*, which takes me off in another direction."

"That's right," Simon added, "I've had some great conversations lately and each one produces another idea on what I could, or even should do with my life. Whilst I know it's great to have opportunities, I just don't know which ones to pick or even how I should make my decisions. Every day I go home and talk about different things and it just makes me more confused than before. I hate to say this, but sometimes I even wish I just didn't care and therefore would be happy doing anything…but not caring is just not me."

They all paused, realising that Simon had just described what they were all thinking.

"So whilst it feels like I've come a long way," Jane continued almost unconsciously, "it doesn't actually feel like I'm any further forward then where I was this time last year. And what's worse, I feel like the year has disappeared so fast and I've wasted time because I'm wondering where it's gone. I mean, where has last year gone?"

"I actually feel like I've gone backwards," Taylor added before finishing his first glass of wine and pouring himself another from which he proceeded to take a large sip.

As Taylor did this, Simon watched him carefully and then glanced casually at Steve who was also looking concerned.

"You all right, mate?" Simon asked Taylor, realising that something wasn't right.

"Yeh, couldn't be better," replied Taylor just before his Blackberry that was on the table erupted with the latest UK number-one ring-tone.

"Yep," Taylor said as he picked it up and left the table.

"Is he all right?" Liz asked, looking concerned.

"I don't know," Jane replied. "I think he's been having some real problems at work and at home. I've asked him a couple of times, but he just won't talk to anyone about it."

"I've tried too," Simon followed with, "but all I get is a few closed comments and not much else. I'm worried for the guy. He just doesn't seem to be all there at the moment."

Before Simon could add any more, Taylor returned to the table and unceremoniously threw £20 down before finishing his wine and announcing that he had to rush off to deal with an emergency. Being completely startled, they sat there in silence until he was out of sight.

"Liz, it might be good if you had a chat with him," Angela suggested.

"Mmm, I think you might be right," she replied.

They sat there for a few more moments wondering what Taylor might be dealing with, only to be interrupted by the food being delivered by the waiter who now seemed fixated with Jane.

"And the chicken is for the angel from heaven," the waiter said softly as he placed Jane's plate down.

"Thank you," Jane said, trying to hide her embarrassment.

Deciding that it might be best to change the attention away from the dilemma with Taylor, Liz focused back on the previous topic.

"It's amazing how easy it is to be distracted away from some of the bigger issues you face when you're busy," Liz announced to the others' surprise.

"What do you mean?" Steve asked.

"Well, when you first arrive in this new world you have big dreams and ideas about what it will be like and how you can have an impact. I know that I definitely did. I thought I was going to change the world. But then you get busier and busier and those ideas slip into the background as you focus on how to just get by, or even just survive."

Each of them had now stopped eating and had focused their attention on Liz.

"That's why, when you get some time to think about things, or 'head space' as I've heard it called, you start to wonder again where this is all going. See, what you guys have done through all you've learnt last year is figure out how to work in the professional world more effectively. And, as a result, you've got some head space back. That's time and space to think about who you are and why you're here."

They each stayed silent, still looking at Liz.

"When you get this head space back, your big dreams and ideas start to creep back in and you realise that you've lost time to achieve them. I think that I even wondered whether those dreams are worth me trying to pursue, which made me feel even more lost. And, as Jane said, it's very easy to start to feel this false sense of urgency as time flies by and you feel like you just need to be doing something, rather than the right thing," Liz continued.

"Wow," Angela said, trying to collect her thoughts. "I think that's how I feel. I mean last year some of my dreams just disappeared as I focused on how to do well here. But now we're not the new joiners any more, I feel like they've all flooded back, and the challenge I face is knowing which are the right choices to make."

"So what next?" Steve asked, hoping for an easy answer so they could get on to a lighter topic of conversation.

"Well, I have an idea now you've each got some head space back." Liz started. "It's a bit out of left field, so you might have to work with me, but it is something, or someone, who has really helped me who might be interesting for you to meet."

They all sat there, wondering who the person was that Liz was referring to.

"His name is Mark," Liz replied as if reading their minds, "and he's my current mentor."

"I'll drink to that," Steve announced raising his glass, "and to my fair queen, the queen of World-Corp."

They all erupted in laughter as Angela stood to give a royal curtsy.

Using Head Space

First thing the next morning they all logged on to their computers to find an email from Liz.

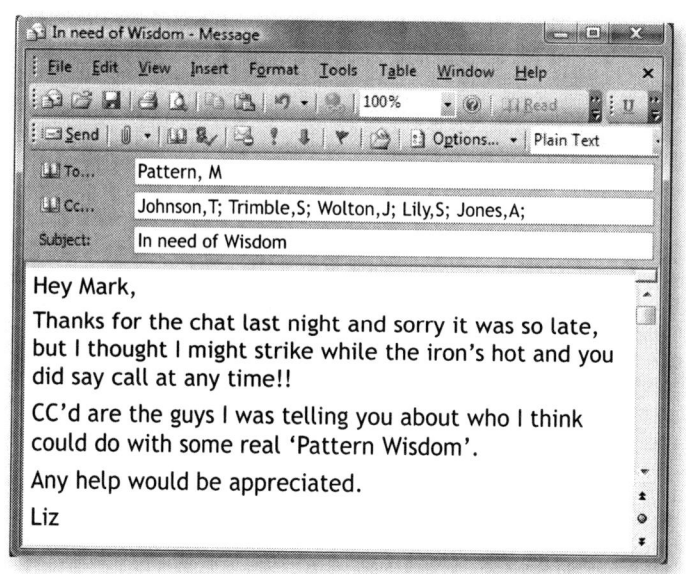

```
In need of Wisdom - Message
File  Edit  View  Insert  Format  Tools  Table  Window  Help

To...    Pattern, M
Cc...    Johnson,T; Trimble,S; Wolton,J; Lily,S; Jones,A;
Subject: In need of Wisdom

Hey Mark,

Thanks for the chat last night and sorry it was so late, but I thought I might strike while the iron's hot and you did say call at any time!!

CC'd are the guys I was telling you about who I think could do with some real 'Pattern Wisdom'.

Any help would be appreciated.
Liz
```

Taylor, being Taylor, looked up on the directory to see who Mark Pattern was and then announced to the others that he was actually a Vice President of Finance. This created even greater anticipation within the group as they all wondered why Liz would be putting them in touch with such an important person.

Later that day an email invitation hit their inboxes simultaneously.

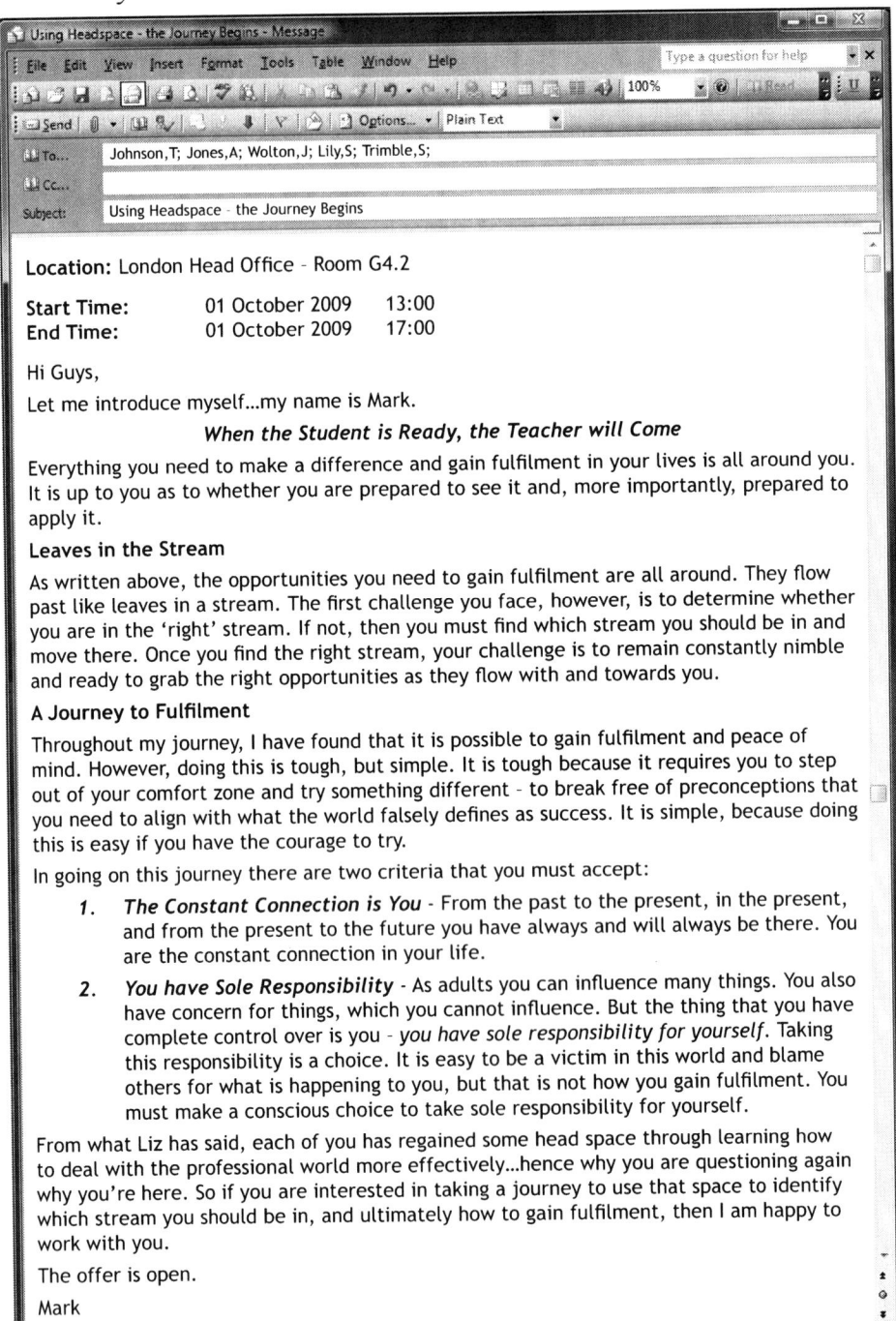

Subject: Using Headspace - the Journey Begins

To: Johnson,T; Jones,A; Wolton,J; Lily,S; Trimble,S;

Location: London Head Office - Room G4.2
Start Time: 01 October 2009   13:00
End Time: 01 October 2009   17:00

Hi Guys,

Let me introduce myself...my name is Mark.

When the Student is Ready, the Teacher will Come

Everything you need to make a difference and gain fulfilment in your lives is all around you. It is up to you as to whether you are prepared to see it and, more importantly, prepared to apply it.

Leaves in the Stream

As written above, the opportunities you need to gain fulfilment are all around. They flow past like leaves in a stream. The first challenge you face, however, is to determine whether you are in the 'right' stream. If not, then you must find which stream you should be in and move there. Once you find the right stream, your challenge is to remain constantly nimble and ready to grab the right opportunities as they flow with and towards you.

A Journey to Fulfilment

Throughout my journey, I have found that it is possible to gain fulfilment and peace of mind. However, doing this is tough, but simple. It is tough because it requires you to step out of your comfort zone and try something different - to break free of preconceptions that you need to align with what the world falsely defines as success. It is simple, because doing this is easy if you have the courage to try.

In going on this journey there are two criteria that you must accept:

1. **The Constant Connection is You** - From the past to the present, in the present, and from the present to the future you have always and will always be there. You are the constant connection in your life.

2. **You have Sole Responsibility** - As adults you can influence many things. You also have concern for things, which you cannot influence. But the thing that you have complete control over is you - *you have sole responsibility for yourself*. Taking this responsibility is a choice. It is easy to be a victim in this world and blame others for what is happening to you, but that is not how you gain fulfilment. You must make a conscious choice to take sole responsibility for yourself.

From what Liz has said, each of you has regained some head space through learning how to deal with the professional world more effectively...hence why you are questioning again why you're here. So if you are interested in taking a journey to use that space to identify which stream you should be in, and ultimately how to gain fulfilment, then I am happy to work with you.

The offer is open.

Mark

Upon reading the email, each of them sat there in amazement. *Who is this guy?* they all thought. *Why is a VP talking about streams and leaves?*

Although they were all surprised at getting such an email, they were intrigued as to where this journey would go to. So, one by one, they accepted eagerly. Even Taylor, who scoffed initially at the invitation, decided to take up the offer, especially considering it was from someone so senior.

"What do you think about Mark's email?" Jane asked Simon over coffee on the day they received the invitation.

"I don't know, but I have to say that I'm curious. I mean, I understand the constant connection and sole responsibility stuff, but streams and leaves…what does that mean?" Simon replied, looking puzzled.

"Well, I'm keen to find out. After all, he is a VP in Finance so he must be doing something right," Jane responded, wondering what Liz had got them into.

PRINCIPLES TO REMEMBER
Your Future…Really Now Starts Here!

Head Space

Time and space to consider who you are and why you are here; *what you really want from your life.*

Once you regain some head space it is important to use it consciously and positively.

When the Student is ready, the Teacher will come

The lessons and knowledge you need to make a difference and gain fulfilment in your lives are all around you.

It is up to you whether you are prepared to see them and whether you are prepared to apply them.

The Constant Connection is You

As an individual you are the one constant throughout your life.

From the past to the present, in the present, and from the present to future, you have always and will always be there.

You have Sole Responsibility

The one thing you have complete control over is you – *you have sole responsibility for yourself.*

You can choose what you think and feel.

7.
Recognise the Crisis

Nervous Anticipation

They all arranged to meet in the first floor café shortly before their session at 1:00 p.m. with Mark. Each of them felt slightly nervous about what they were getting into so they had decided to meet beforehand and go to the room together.

"Ready?" Simon asked, looking at his watch and realising that it was 12:55.

"Yep, wouldn't want to be late," Steve replied, trying to hide his nerves. "After all, I'd hate for all those streams to dry up."

As they approached the room, they saw the door was slightly ajar. Angela, who was in the lead, looked at Steve who was beside her but his eyes were fixed on their destination as his nerves were getting the better of him. *Get a grip*, Angela thought to herself, *Mark is only human after all*. With that thought, she strode forward and knocked confidently on the door before entering.

The remainder of the group, all relieved that Angela had taken the initiative, followed quickly a pace or two behind her. Immediately upon entering the room, Angela saw a figure at the far end of the table. The figure looked up slowly from his notes and then proceeded to stand up, reaching out to shake Angela's hand.

"Hi I'm Angela, and you must be Mark," Angela said, trying to get on the front foot to hide her nerves.

"Pleasure to meet you," Mark replied with a firm handshake.

The rest of the team now in the room also sought to introduce themselves before standing politely behind their chairs as if back in school.

"Please, grab a seat," Mark said enthusiastically.

Jane had noticed that Mark was not as tall as she thought he would be. She also noticed that, while well-groomed, there was also a ruggedness about him that seemed quite attractive. *He looks a little like a young George Clooney*, Jane thought as she looked him up and down for a second time.

"Thanks for your time," Mark said as they all sat there patiently. "Liz has told me so much about you, and I have to say I've been incredibly impressed with what I've heard."

They all looked at each other quickly, feeling slightly embarrassed by such a compliment.

"It was nothing, all in a day's work as they say," Steve blurted out before he could stop himself.

"Yes, I've heard all about what you've been up to, especially you Steve," Mark said playfully.

"Mmm, I'd best be quiet then," Steve replied, realising that Mark had the measure of him.

"So I bet you're all thinking *Who is this guy and why is he talking about streams?*" Mark announced as if he had listened in on all their previous conversations.

"It had crossed my mind," Angela admitted cautiously.

"Well, let me tell you why I offered to help after Liz's call the other night," Mark continued. "You may not believe this but when I was in your position I was considered by many to be a complete no-hoper. Yes I'd done university and yes I'd got a job, but I had no idea who I was or where I wanted to be. And what was worse, I never had anyone as fantastic as Liz to help me. As a result, for my first year or so at work I struggled to find my feet. I didn't feel like I wanted to be there and so I didn't try that hard.

Seeing this, my bosses never gave me the opportunity to prove myself, which meant I never tried; a self-fulfilling prophecy you might say. Anyway, this spiral continued until one day, about 18 months after joining, I missed a critical deadline. My boss exploded and immediately involved HR. Yes, I was about to be sacked from my first real professional job. Not a good outcome."

The group was mesmerised by the story and completely astonished that Mark had started his career in this way.

"So what happened?" Jane blurted out.

"Well," Mark continued, "it came to the day of my formal hearing with HR. I was told to bring a senior manager to represent me. The only problem was that I didn't know anyone who I thought wouldn't want to see me out of the business. So I decided to represent myself. *How hard could it be?* I remember thinking.

Just as I sat down ready for the hearing to commence, in walked this manager who I had met only a couple of days earlier by a photocopier. When I met him, the guy looked like he was in a real hurry whilst struggling to deal with a paper jam. As he looked so stressed I offered to help out. He initially just stared at me and then asked if I could finish his copying and bring it to the CEO's PA for a board meeting which was starting in five minutes. '*No problem*' I said. After all, fixing the photocopier was one of the things I'd become good at.

Anyway, I dropped off all the stuff that the manager requested and then didn't think any more of it. But then, as I sat there in the room about to do my best impersonation of a lawyer, using quotes from Tom Cruise in A Few Good Men yes, *'you want the truth you can't handle the truth'* and all that, the door opened and in strode the same manager. He then proceeded to defend me during the hearing by suggesting that he take me into his team for a trial period of three months. HR could do nothing but agree, especially when the manager said that if I didn't pick up my game he would escort me out of the building."

"Wow, who was he?" Simon asked.

"He turned out to be the Head of Manufacturing and the reason he decided to get involved was that, without prompting, I had offered to help him," Mark explained. "After our impromptu meeting at the photocopier, the manager made some enquiries about me, only to be told that my career was about to be cut short. He later told me that he thought I had potential and that all potential should be drawn out. At the time I just thought it was something to do with karma, you know, one good turn deserves another."

They all sat there thinking about how lucky Mark was that he'd met the manager that day and that the manager had offered to help him.

Luck or Synchronicity

"But I don't get how that all made you decide to help us. I mean you must be a mega-busy man," Simon said, intrigued by the story.

"Well, you might think that I was just lucky that I managed to meet the guy at the photocopier that day or that he'd chosen to help me. Luck may have something to do with it, but later that manager explained to me the idea of synchronicity," Mark continued.

"Synchronicity?" Angela exclaimed.

"Yes, synchronicity," Mark stated. "See, what I didn't understand then, but I do now is that there are things happening all around us all of the time. Much like what is meant by the saying *When the student is ready the teacher will come*. It just so happened that, on this day, there was an opportunity to do something for someone else that would later benefit me in more ways then I could ever have imagined."

"But you didn't know that helping that person was going to result in them helping you," Taylor stated, as if cheapening what Mark was saying.

"That's right, but what I realise now is that because in my mind I'd accepted that I was getting the sack, I unconsciously eased up on my attitude and instead just sought to be myself. So when I saw someone who needed help, that's exactly what I did: I helped him as I would normally. Whilst that event in isolation means nothing, what happened as a result was that another flow of energy, if you like, was set in motion that saw the manager wanting to help me. This is what I mean by synchronicity: a meaningful coincidence of two or more events, where something other than the probability of chance is involved. They're Carl Jung the Swiss psychologist's words, not mine."

They all sat there trying to make sense of what Mark was saying, while still wondering where this was leading.

"So because I'd changed my attitude, I was more aware of what was going on around me which allowed synchronicity to occur. That is, I helped the manager who later took me under his wing, which helped me understand who I was and who I wanted to be. And because he had done that for me all those years ago, I can only return the favour by passing on the same knowledge to others," Mark stated.

Crisis – What Crisis?

"So what happened next?" Taylor asked impatiently.

Before responding, Mark stared directly Taylor for a few seconds. He then shifted his eyes to the others and continued.

"Well, believe it or not, once the hearing was over the manager just rushed out of the room before I could thank him. I then returned to my desk wondering what exactly had just happened, only to find an appointment in my inbox for the whole of the next day. In the appointment the manager told me to take the rest of the day off and then to meet him in the front entrance of the building at 9:00 a.m. sharp the next morning. He also requested that I wear a suit and a tie, polish my shoes and also make sure that my shirt was well-ironed. So that's exactly what I did."

"How bizarre," Steve announced.

"That's what I thought," Mark replied with a smile, noticing that Steve had, all of a sudden, become self-conscious about his clothes. "So at 9:00 a.m. sharp the manager appeared and escorted me out of the building and to a waiting taxi. The driver took us to Hyde Park Corner where we jumped out and then made our way through the park and towards the café by the lake. As we walked through the main gates, the manager asked me a question that I can still remember as if it were yesterday: *'So what's the story?'* Whilst I knew exactly what he was asking, I still responded with *'What do you mean?'* To that he said, *'You seem like a smart guy, but somehow you've managed to end up in front of HR in your very first professional job, so there must be a story, and I'd like to hear it'*.

We walked along in silence for a minute or two as I tried to collect my thoughts so I could paint a rosy picture proving that the world was against me. But instead I decided to tell him the truth. I told him how I'd taken the job at the company because I didn't know what I wanted to do and because all my other mates were taking corporate jobs. But once I got in, I felt completely lost and like nothing I did was right, which meant that my bosses didn't trust me etc., etc. Throughout my story, and even when we ordered coffee, the manager gave me his full attention. I think that because of this I just kept talking, revealing all sorts of things about myself. Without knowing it, I think I ended up talking for over two hours."

"Wow, that's amazing," Angela exclaimed as Mark paused. "Weren't you worried that the manager would judge you?"

"Part of me did, Angela," Mark replied, "but ultimately I thought what the hell, this guy asked so I'll tell him."

Mark paused again before continuing.

"Anyway, at the end of my story the manager said, *'Son, I think that you're in the middle of a crisis'*. When I asked him what he meant, he went on to talk about how the mid-life crisis as we know it is now coming forward for the current generations, a quarter-life crisis, he called it. And this crisis was fuelled by greater choice in education, employment and lifestyle, which led to greater uncertainty for those who were entering the world of work.

See, I loved university. It was a place where I was allowed to define and be me. But once I got to work, I felt that being me just didn't seem to fit. This meant that I questioned who I was and who I should try to be, and I put on a mask to try to be the person I thought others expected. This mask led me to be miserable and ultimately to fail. And whilst I didn't grow a pony-tail and buy a sports car, my manager was right; I was going through a crisis, a quarter-life crisis. The final thing I said at the end of my story was that this is not who I want to be, and this is not what I want to do with the rest of my life."

Mark then paused again, only to have the silence broken by Jane.

"A quarter-life crisis, that makes so much sense. But what did the manager tell you to do?"

"Now that's the interesting part," Mark replied as the group looked at each other wondering how much more interesting it could get. "As I made my final statement, the manager just asked me *'Well, who do you want to be and what do you want to do with the rest of your life?'* To that I just blurted out that I had no idea."

Fighting, versus Flowing with Purpose

"Wow," Angela remarked. "So what did the manager say to do?"

Without saying anything, Mark stood up and wrote some words on the board.

> **Fighting**
> versus
> **Flowing with Purpose**

"This, ladies and gentlemen, is what the manager told me was the secret to dealing with my crisis. He said, *'Son, what you've got to realise is that you can't fight against the energy of the universe, instead you've got to flow with that energy, but flow with purpose'*."

Looking around the room he saw a familiar look on all of their faces.

"Exactly what I thought," Mark continued. "It took him over half an hour to explain what he meant. But the long and the short of that explanation was that there's a theory suggesting that energy just flows through the universe and that we, people, are a part of that flow. And, instead of fighting that flow what we should do is go with it, but do so with purpose.

In other words, rather than try to force our lives in this world through being in such a hurry all the time, we should relax and we should define what the purpose of our lives is and flow with that purpose. It is by doing this that synchronicity happens. Let me give you an example; who plays sport?"

All five of them nodded.

"When playing your sport did you ever have a game where things just worked for you. You were in your zone, unstoppable?"

"Absolutely," Simon jumped in. "Last week I had an absolute blinder and scored three goals. After the game a couple of the lads asked me how I got past some of the opposition and I just couldn't remember, it was if it just happened without me thinking."

"That's it," Mark remarked, looking at Simon, "that is what we mean by flow. Things just happen, you are not forcing it or trying too hard, but it's just flowing. Now what I learnt from that first manager was that if you define who you are and what you believe the purpose of your life to be, then you can just relax and allow yourself to flow with purpose."

"I'm still not sure I get it, sorry Mark." Steve stated.

"Well, imagine that you're floating down a stream. Now imagine that the stream represents the channel of energy that aligns with the purpose of your life. That is, it has banks which represent the limits of your journey towards your purpose. For example, what you won't do to fulfil your purpose sits on the banks of the stream, like robbing someone etc. The water represents the energy flow that is taking you towards your purpose. And within that water are all sorts of turbulence and challenges, just like life, but it's still flowing. And the things floating along with you down that stream represent opportunities for you. Now at any stage you can choose to stop floating and stand still against the current, trying to fight its natural flow. But by doing this you remain static and do not progress towards fulfilling your purpose."

Jane, now fully engrossed in the idea of the stream, butted in.

"But if you're just floating with the current of the stream, or flowing as you put it, surely that's not with purpose."

"Good point Jane," Mark replied. "To flow with purpose takes two things. The first is to make sure you're in the right stream. There are many different flows of energy, some join together and some do not. To find the right stream involves defining what your purpose is. The second point is that once you find yourself in the right stream, you must remain nimble and ready to take the opportunities that come to you, or to avoid the traps or perils that may be present. For example, by remaining nimble it could be that by flowing with your stream towards your purpose you have the opportunity to meet someone significant who can help you. But if you are not aware, nimble and ready, then you may miss this opportunity altogether."

"So how do we do all of this?" Steve asked.

"Well," Mark said with a smile, "if you are interested I will take you on the same journey as the one that manager took me on many years ago. He helped me define my purpose and get in the right stream. And he did all this through just helping me to define and then be myself."

"I'm in," Angela erupted, not wanting to miss the opportunity of a lifetime.

Around the table, all the others followed suit quickly, except for Taylor.

"I don't know," Taylor stated, "I mean I really appreciate your time today Mark, but I'm very busy and just not sure that I would get anything out of it. I know who I am and where I'm going, so I just don't see that it would be a worthwhile use of my time."

"Mmm," Mark responded, "I guess I'd challenge that, Taylor. See I also thought I knew who I was and where I was going, but when I got into work those things went out the window as I struggled to even survive. But it is your choice."

Taylor nodded without saying anything.

By this point it was 2:00 p.m. so Mark decided to call a break.

"Stretch your legs and grab a coffee," Mark announced, looking at the clock in the room, "and I'll have a peppermint tea, whoever's buying."

They all wandered out of the room in silence until out of earshot of Mark.

"Well, that isn't exactly what I had expected," Taylor stated a little too loudly for the others' liking.

"Me neither," Jane added, almost whispering to lower the volume.

"Yeh, fancy him almost getting sacked from his first job," Steve stated.

"Well, I wonder where to next?" Simon asked.

Achieving Alignment

Once back in the room with their own drinks and the peppermint tea, they sat down patiently waiting for Mark to return. As they sat there in silence, they all contemplated the story they'd just heard.

"So what's next?" Angela asked as keen as ever, as soon as Mark came in the room.

"Let me tell you a bit more of the story," Mark replied, "and then I'll explain the journey that I followed."

They all, except for Taylor, nodded enthusiastically.

"Well, when we had finished our coffee by the lake it was 12:30 and the manager suggested that we should go for a business lunch. As we wandered back to get a taxi, the manager told me a little about himself, like where he came from, that fact that he was married with two children etc. He said, *'It's always important to get to know people as people'*, which has stuck with me ever since.

Once we had jumped into a taxi, the manager directed the driver to what he called his favourite restaurant. *'Why is it your favourite?'* I asked him. *'Because of the food and the atmosphere'*, the manager told me. *'It is authentic'* I remember him saying. In the restaurant we were taken to a table from where we could see the whole place. The food was a real mix of different things, and so too were the people who were eating there. It seemed that there was everyone from business people to hippies.

As I picked up the menu at our table, out of nowhere walked the owner who greeted the manager with a huge smile and a hug. I was then introduced to him before he disappeared back into the kitchen. *'The reason I brought you here'*, the manager told me, *'was to show you what is possible when you achieve alignment between work and life – to show you what is possible when you fulfil your purpose'*. He then proceeded to draw this picture," Mark said as he stood up and re-drew the same picture that the manager had drawn for him.

Achieving Alignment

- LIFE | WORK — 1. life & work as separate
- LIFE | **WORK** — 2. live to work
- **LIFE** | WORK — 3. work to live
- LIFE | WORK (merged) — 4. alignment through fulfilling your purpose

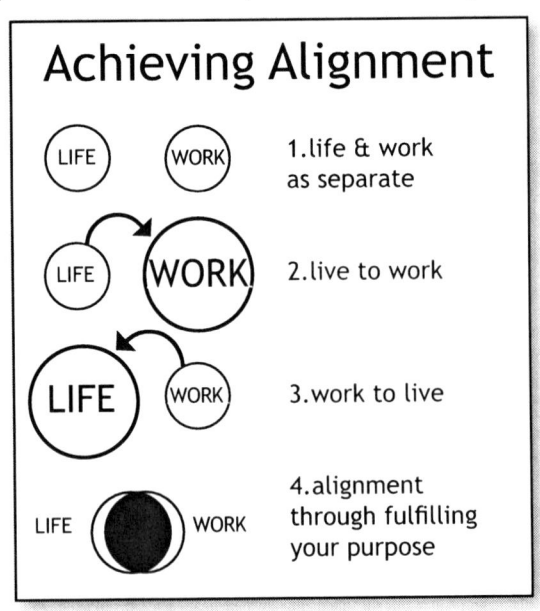

Mark took his seat as he went on to explain the picture.

"The manager said that, as in Picture 1, too many people see life and work as separate. He said that we see work as the eight-plus hours we spend there every day and we see life as all the time outside of work. He then said that creating this separation resulted in people choosing to either live to work, or work to live, where living to work means that your life outside of work is squeezed to insignificance. Or, if you live to work, your attention to work is less significant as you see it as just a means to an end."

Each of them stared at the picture.

"What the manager then said," Mark continued, "was that if you seek to define your purpose and then if you seek to get into the right stream to flow towards that purpose, the artificial separation between life and work disappears. This is because they are both aligned to your purpose. What I realised from gaining this alignment myself is that this is what's meant by living - true synergy that comes from aligning the aspects of your existence through fulfilling your purpose."

"Wow, that's deep," Steve said softly.

"But what if work is your purpose?" Taylor asked, challenging Mark's philosophy.

"Work cannot be your purpose, Taylor. It can only be a mechanism for you to fulfil your purpose. If you believe work to be your purpose, then I would suggest that all you are really doing is using work, through living to work, as a crutch to hide away from something else. After all, would you really want people at your funeral to say that you came to work diligently every day?" Mark replied.

"What if you like where you work, but you still see it as just a way to pay the bills?" Jane butted in without giving Taylor a chance to respond. "Don't get me wrong, I'm not just doing the bare minimum, but I'm not sure that being here is helping me to fulfil my purpose."

"And I would suggest that is because you do not fully know what your purpose is," Mark responded with a smile.

Starting Your Journey Toward Fulfilment

They all sat there for a few more moments trying to process what they'd heard.

Streams, purpose, alignment, Angela thought to herself, *where is all this going?*

"So," Mark stated, breaking their individual trains of thought. "What I would like to suggest, if you are keen, is to help you to start your journey toward fulfilment. To help you define who you are and what your purpose is."

Each of them, including Taylor, nodded before Mark continued.

"At the end of lunch that day with the manager, he told me that the owner was an old friend of his. His passion in life and his purpose was bringing people together and helping people through food. That is why his work as a chef or through the various charities and other activities he did were all focused in helping him fulfil that purpose. He had done many things from teaching people about nutrition, through to setting up kitchens to feed the homeless or those affected by disasters etc. For this person there was no separation between life and work, there was only the fulfilment of his purpose."

As Mark paused they all sat there imagining the person he spoke about.

"As I said," Mark concluded, "if you are keen to go on the journey that the manager took me on, then I'm happy to take you. There is no pressure, but I guarantee you'll find it interesting to say the least!"

"Where do I sign?" Steve said excitedly as he volunteered first.

PRINCIPLES TO REMEMBER
Recognise The Crisis

Synchronicity
A meaningful coincidence of two or more events, where something other than the probability of chance is involved (Carl Jung).

Fighting versus Flowing with Purpose
You can't fight against the energy of the universe; instead you've got to flow with that energy, but flow with purpose.

Achieving Alignment
Make a choice between living to work, working to live, or gaining alignment through fulfilling your purpose.

TASKS FOR THE READER

Seeking Alignment

The crisis we often have is when misalignment between the elements of our existence occurs. The first step to regaining alignment is to recognise when misalignment is present.

Circle whether you believe you are: living to work, working to live or if you have achieved alignment.

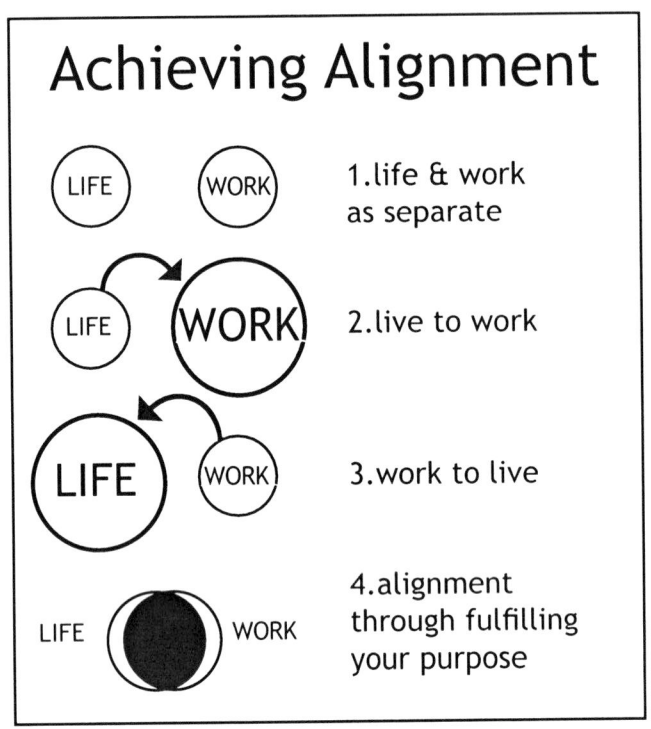

Achieving Alignment

LIFE WORK — 1. life & work as separate

LIFE **WORK** — 2. live to work

LIFE WORK — 3. work to live

LIFE ⬤ WORK — 4. alignment through fulfilling your purpose

Why did you circle this choice?

What would you prefer instead? And what would this look and feel like for you to achieve this?

8.
Acknowledge Where You've Come From

Product of the Past

"So what do you think about 'the journey'?" Jane asked Simon as they caught up a couple of days after they'd met with Mark.

"I'm not sure," Simon replied, "but I think I'll go with it and see what happens. I guess I know what I think he's saying, especially with the quarter-life crisis stuff. As soon as he said that I thought, *that's definitely me, I'm definitely in the middle of that right now.*"

"Me too," Jane responded. "But now I recognise it, I'm not sure what to do about it. So I guess the journey sounds like as good an idea as any at the moment."

"Mmm, I know what you mean. How's Captain America going?" Simon asked.

"Really good," Jane responded with a smile. "It's a bit tough with him being all the way in New York though. I always said that I'd avoid long-distance relationships, but with him I think it's worth it."

"I guess when you know, you know," Simon replied with a smile, "plus with all his super powers why doesn't he just fly over more frequently?"

Jane smiled and then slapped Simon playfully on the arm.

Two weeks after their meeting with Mark, he had arranged for them to visit the Natural History Museum. Once they arrived, however, Mark sent an apologetic text message saying he'd be an hour late. He also suggested that they visit some of the exhibits, especially the one titled 'Early Man'.

"This place is great, isn't it?" Mark stated once he arrived to join the group as they assembled in the main foyer.

"Fantastic," Angela said, marvelling at all she'd seen, "I haven't been here for years."

Mark then escorted them through to the main café where he invited them to take a seat around a large rectangular table. The area they sat in was full of the noise of chairs being dragged across a tiled floor and the screech of excited children who insisted on doing their best dinosaur impersonations.

"What I love about this place," Mark said once they were seated, "is that it gives us a real glimpse of where we've come from."

As they sat there, a little boy who was only about three years old ran up to the table and let out the loudest roar he could. Mark swivelled around in his chair quickly made claws with his hands and roared back at the small child. Standing momentarily stunned, the boy then proceeded to erupt with laughter before running off towards his mother.

"So, as I was saying," Mark said composing himself and returning his attention to the team, "what I love about this place is what it teaches us about who we are and where we've come from. This is the first step in your journey towards defining and fulfilling your purpose."

Each of them sat silent, amazed at what they'd seen.

"So we should look at dinosaurs and ape men?" Steve asked, snapping himself out of the trance.

"Not quite, Steve," Mark replied with a smile. "Let's fast-forward through evolution a bit rather than looking so far back, shall we?"

Steve looked down at the table to hide his embarrassment.

"So what do you mean?" Angela asked, seeking to help save Steve.

"Well the first part of the journey is about recognising where you've come from and, before anyone asks, I don't mean about the birds and the bees. What I mean is what in your past has contributed to you being the person you are today."

"Ah," Steve exclaimed.

"So we need to think about why we are who we are?" Taylor asked.

"That's right," Mark replied. "It isn't until you understand why you are who you are that you can really start to define who you want to be and what your purpose is. This is because we are all a product of our past. We've each had experiences that shaped us into the people we are today. For the majority of people, however, they've never considered what things in their past have really impacted on them."

"I'm still not sure I follow," Simon admitted.

"That makes sense," Jane said before Mark could continue. "If I look back through my past I can see quite a few key events and people which have shaped me into who I am today. I have to say that not all have been positive, but they've still had an impact on how I think and behave."

Recognising the Impact

"That's right Jane," Mark continued. "And for each of those experiences, events or people, it is critical to recognise what the impact has been."

"But on one of our training courses we were told not to dwell on the past," Taylor added, challenging Mark's statement.

"Who said I told you to dwell on it?" Mark replied. "What you were told is absolutely right.

What I'm proposing is that you really seek to recognise the impact of events and people from your past, and learn how that impact has shaped who you are today."

Looking around the table, Mark could still see that they were looking a little confused.

"Let me give you an example," Mark continued. "When I was ten years old I had a maths teacher who I really struggled to understand. When I told her I couldn't keep up, she seemed to take a dislike to me because she then ignored me in class. The impact of this was I fell behind and ultimately believed that I was rubbish at maths and numbers."

"How's that possible when you're a VP in finance?" Taylor exploded.

"Good point, Taylor," Mark responded with a smile. "Well, I continued with that belief for the rest of my time through school and university and once I started work I avoided anything to do with numbers, especially finance. But when I went to work with that manager, the first task he gave me was to work out where we could save money across manufacturing. Can you imagine my dread? Especially when the task was accompanied by reams of spreadsheets to analyse. For the first two days I sat there wanting to burst into tears, not even knowing where I should start. Then I snapped out of it and decided to speak to one of the people the manager had told me to talk to. As it turned out, this person was the CFO, and he spent a whole two hours slowly talking me through all aspects of how money flowed around the company. He then gave me names of some more people to talk to. Within the week, my fear of numbers had all but disappeared and over the next month I ended up saving the company over £20m."

"Wow, that's amazing," Angela burst out with. "£20m - I bet your manager was delighted."

"He was, and both he and the CFO took me out for dinner to their favourite restaurant to celebrate," Mark replied.

They sat there amazed that Mark had gone from being almost fired to saving the company so much money.

"So the moral of the story is to understand what key experiences, events and people have had an impact on your life, and understand how that impact has helped to shape who you are today. If you think about the manager who helped me, he also had an impact on me and a pretty amazing one at that," Mark concluded.

Understand and Learn

"So once we've identified the impact of all those experiences, events and people, what do we do?" Steve asked politely.

"Well, the key is to understand the impact and then seek to learn from it," Mark responded.

"What do you mean?" Simon asked seeking more clarification.

"Taking my example of the maths teacher, I understood later that the impact she had on me was making me become scared of numbers. As I looked deeper, however, I realised that it wasn't just numbers she was making me scared of, but also of asking others for help. If you think about it, because of the way she had dismissed me so easily, I became fearful of moving out of my comfort zone and seeking assistance. Therefore, when I got into work I refused to ever ask for help or do anything I wasn't comfortable with, which resulted in photocopying being my core capability. Now, what I learned from meeting the manager was that I was actually capable of stepping right out of my comfort zone and by asking for help I could achieve some great things. This then gave me further confidence to keep doing more and more."

"Don't you resent that first teacher?" Taylor asked.

"Not at all," Mark responded. "Initially I did. But I'm now an adult and I can make a choice as to how I respond. So I could easily dwell on the fact that the teacher had that impact, especially in helping to create my beliefs but ultimately the past is just that, the past. So rather than dwell on it, I sought to understand and then learn from the experience. Then I sought to use what I learned to develop myself into who I am today."

"I'm not sure I could do that," Taylor snapped, "I mean that teacher failed to do her job. I would be tempted to go and find her and tell her the impact she had."

"Mmm," Mark replied, considering his response, "I could have done that easily, but what would it have achieved? As I said, the past is just the past so why dwell on it? And rather than using my energy to hunt down that old teacher, why don't I invest it into improving myself and, more importantly, improving the impact I have day to day. After all, whilst I may never forget about that teacher, I can forgive her."

"That's all very noble, but really?" Taylor snapped again, sarcastically.

"Yes really," Mark replied calmly, still choosing not to rise to Taylor's challenge. "See, as I thought about it, yes the teacher was being paid to do a job and yes she did fail me in doing that job. But I'm not perfect either. Even today I make mistakes, as I'm still human. So as I look back, I remember there were 30 incredibly rowdy children in the class, all of whom wanted her time and attention. I'm sure she was doing the best she could, so why would I not forgive her?"

"That's amazing, Mark," Jane said softly, "but surely you didn't just start doing that one day?"

"No, not at all," Mark replied. "It did take me a while to get there through my journey, but where I started was right here in the Natural History Museum with that manager many, many years ago."

Everyone sat there in silence, realising the irony of the situation.

Your Past

"So here is my task for you," Mark announced as he handed a sheet of paper to each of them.

<u>**RECOGNISING WHERE I HAVE COME FROM**</u>

Age	Experience, Event or Person	What impact that had on me

What have I learned about who I am today?

"What I want each of you to do is to consider where you have come from," Mark said referring to the papers in front of them.

"Start by mapping out the key experiences that you recall throughout your life. They need not be in chronological order, but for each one I want you to include your age at the time, what or who the experience, event or person was, and finally what you believe the impact was on who you are today. Once you've done this, and it will take some time, I want you to summarise at the bottom what you've learned about how those events have shaped you into the person you are today."

Each of them stared at the sheet of paper in front of them, trying to think about what they would include once they started writing. Mark yet again broke their train of thought with his final instruction.

"The last thing I want you to do once you have captured all you can is to explain it to one of your esteemed colleagues."

All of them, apart from Taylor, shot each other a quick glance, realising they would have to reveal something about themselves to the others. Taylor, who hadn't lifted his eyes from the table, was beginning to feel sick at the thought of letting others into his world.

"So...um...when you do you need this by?" Taylor stammered, looking slowly in Mark's direction.

"How about in one month?" Mark replied. "That way, it gives you plenty of time to really think about your past and to discuss it with each other. It will also mean that you can avoid rushing it and lessening what you learn."

"Right," they all agreed, except for Taylor who was still dreading the thought of showing any level of vulnerability to the others.

Simon and Steve

After a couple of weeks of some deep reflection, Steve dropped Simon a note asking if he wanted to catch up over a beer one evening after work. Simon, who was thinking the same, agreed.

"So, how'd you go with the exercises from Mark?" Steve asked as they settled themselves at one of the tables after buying a couple of beers.

"All right, I think," Simon responded after taking his first sip. "I mean, it was pretty tough at first, but as I started thinking about it the more I started to realise."

"Me too," Steve replied, feeling relieved that Simon had taken it seriously as well.

"It was funny that, when I started, my first focus was on my younger sister and my mum," Simon continued.

"What do you mean?" Steve asked while Simon took another sip of his beer.

"Well, I never really thought about it, but I think that for my entire life I've been looking out for both of them. See, there's only me and my sister and my old man was away a lot with work, so I seemed to take on the role of man about the house. And what I realised from this was that I have a real protective streak in me that means I will try to look after people whenever I can. It also means that, whilst I don't mind mucking around, I have a strong sense of responsibility when it comes to others."

"Wow," Steve replied, "what else did you come up with?"

"I captured heaps of different events, such as birthdays, starting at the football club and starting at university. I also had a few events where others were getting picked on so I stood up for them. All of this taught me that I really like my independence but I still need to be around people, especially to help others."

"What about key people?" Steve continued.

"Well, that was easy. There were quite a few people who had a real impact on me, mostly for positive reasons, but there were also some for negative reasons. The first person on the list was definitely my mum. I think that she really helped me be who I am today. I know that my girlfriend always tells Mum that she did a good job raising me in terms of helping me know how to look after myself and others. The second person was my dad; he wasn't around as much as I'd have liked, but he always spent time with me when he could, either playing football or making sure I got involved in the right things. I guess he taught me how to really make decisions and consider things properly. On the flip-side, though, I think that not having him around meant that I didn't always have someone to ask questions of."

"Anyone else?" Steve asked.

"One of the other people I put down was an early football coach that I had. He taught me patience and persistence. He'd always say *'If you want to make it in anything you must be patient and you must persist.'* Don't give up too easily, was his motto."

Simon paused to take another drink.

"What about yourself, what did you come up with?" he then asked Steve.

"If I'm honest, mate, I found this really tough. I've spoken briefly to Ang about it, but I haven't told her the whole story." Steve replied softly. "See, like you I started the task by capturing my family experience, which wasn't great at all. I was the youngest of three with two older sisters. My old man walked out on my mum just after I was born so I never really got to meet him. I've often asked Mum about him and she said that he was a good man, but just couldn't deal with all the responsibility of having a family."

"Bloody hell," Simon exclaimed as Steve paused to take a sip of his beer.

"So I was thinking about what impact this experience had on me. Now, my mum and sisters were great, they did everything for me and whilst we never had a lot, we never went without either. But I think that by doing that, I just became lazy as they'd always help me with everything, including homework. Mum married again when I was about 14, which was tough because then there was another man in the house. It was OK, because I got along with him, but he wasn't my dad if you know what I mean. So as I got older, rather than working with him to keep the peace, I just rebelled. If I'm honest, as I look back I feel real sorry for the guy because he was trying his best. But ultimately I just became lazier and more rebellious against any form of authority."

"But you couldn't have done all that badly," Simon stated, "otherwise you wouldn't have ended up here."

"Well that comes down to some key people who I captured," Steve continued. "The first was one of my sixth-form teachers to whom I gave a particularly hard time. One day this teacher kept me back after class and said, 'Steve it doesn't bother me that you want to waste your life just clowning around. It doesn't even bother me that you're a slob who doesn't care about your future. But it does bother me that you're not prepared to be a man and take responsibility for yourself or for those around you. See whilst you think it's funny to be the joker and muck around, all you're doing is hurting yourself and others. Now if this is the man you want to be, then please do, but don't take others with you'."

"Wow, how did you respond to that?" Simon asked.

"Not well. At the time I just strode out of the classroom thinking I was a real hero. But when I got outside I realised that there was no-one waiting for me. I was all alone. As I walked home cursing all of my so-called friends, those words take responsibility just kept ringing in my head. I think that what the teacher had helped me realise was, although I had never met the guy, I was becoming just like my father."

As he finished his admission, Steve took a slow drink from his beer. Simon sat there silently just watching Steve who was clearly upset but trying his best not to show it.

"Harden up, mate," Simon said, punching Steve in the shoulder in an attempt to lighten the mood.

"Ha, you should talk," Steve responded punching him back.

"So did you have anyone else on the list?" Simon asked, realising that Steve had not quite finished.

"Yeh, there were a few." Steve replied. "Another person who's had quite an impact on me is Liz."

"Liz?"

"Yeh, Liz," Steve continued. "Remember when I was having all those problems on my first project. Well it was Liz who really helped me out. I don't exactly know what she did, but I think it was similar to the teacher that day. I think she also gave me a bit of a kick up the arse to take responsibility for myself, but she also helped me to understand how to take responsibility as well. I reckon that if it wasn't for Liz I wouldn't still be here."

"In World-Corp?" Simon asked feeling concerned.

"Yeh...in World-Corp," Steve replied.

"Another beer?" Simon asked, looking at Steve's empty glass.

"Is the Pope a Catholic?" Steve responded with a huge smile.

Jane and Angela

A couple of days later, Jane and Angela also decided to catch up. As it had been a tough few weeks for both of them at work, they decided that over dinner would be the best time for a chat. And an ego boost from an Italian waiter also seemed to be a good idea, so they chose Jim's Wine Bar.

As they sat down and prepared themselves for their first dose of compliments, a different waiter appeared.

"Hey ladies, what can I get you?" the obviously English waiter asked politely.

"Oh," Angela replied, disappointed not to hear the Italian accent.

"How about a bottle of this one," she said pointing to her choice.

As the waiter left, Angela immediately spun round to face Jane.

"So, before we get into the past and all that, how is Captain America?"

"Well, Tod - which is his real name - is just fine, thank you for asking," Jane responded politely.

"Just fine…you're going to have to do better than that," Angela responded.

"Well, if you must know," Jane started rolling her eyes, "Tod is great. He is so sweet and lovely that I just can't get enough of him, except for the fact that he is over 3000 miles away."

"I just don't know how you do it, Janey," Angela replied as the waiter re-appeared.

"It's really tough," Jane continued. "We're getting to see each other about every two months but that is nowhere near enough."

"Have either of you thought about moving?"

"Well, as a matter of fact," Jane replied as her eyes lit up, "Tod is going to transfer to the UK."

"Wow, that's fantastic Jane."

"I know, but I'm also nervous because it's a pretty big move."

"Yes, but what's meant to be is meant to be," Angela responded. "Just remember it's all about flow and synchronicity. Now we'd best order."

They both looked through the menu and gave their order to the waiter who still wasn't anywhere near as charming as his Italian colleague.

"So how did you go with Mark's task?" Jane asked as the waiter disappeared from view.

"Good, I think." Angela responded as she took a sheet of paper from her bag. "I actually found it really interesting to do. I mean, I don't think that I discovered anything I didn't already know, but it was interesting to consider the various things that shaped me into who I am today."

"What were some of those things?" Jane asked.

"Well, for starters my parents were really supportive of me doing heaps of different things as a child. So as the oldest of three girls I was always doing something new, and I think this helped me be the type of person who would get into doing anything and everything. However, I think that because I did so many different things I have never really found what I'm good at. So because I like to try everything, I always feel confused about what I want to do. In terms of people, I think there have been many who've had an impact, but the one who really sticks out is Steve."

"Steve?" Jane gasped.

"I know Jane. I'm sure that you wonder what I see in him. But I can tell you that he's helped me to learn to really lighten up. I mean, when I first got to World-Corp I had a clear plan of where I wanted to go and I was wound up like a spring. But since I've been with Steve I've realised that some things just aren't as important. I still want to get somewhere in my career, but not at all costs and definitely not at the expense of life, if you know what I mean."

"Well Ang, I have to say that you've definitely relaxed since starting with Steve, which I think is great, and I think that you guys are a great couple," Jane replied with a smile.

"What about you? How did you go with the task?" Angela asked, deciding it was Jane's turn.

"Well, I found it really tough. I mean it was easy to map out the things that I've experienced and identify people who've had an impact. But I really didn't enjoy looking at myself. I constantly found that I was being negative about who I am," Jane replied sheepishly.

"What do you mean 'negative'?" Angela asked.

"Well, I started to realise that some of the experiences I've had haven't been that positive and, as a result, the impact is that I've ended up being quite a shy person who doesn't push herself forward enough. I also really doubt what I'm capable of, which means that I definitely don't want to put myself forward any further than I have to," Jane admitted.

"But you've done some great things, Jane, and Tod is fantastic," Angela responded.

"I know I have surprised myself a few times over the last year but I guess that what this task has done is help me realise that I doubt myself too much. I even wonder sometimes why Tod's with me, which I know is stupid. But I do still wonder sometimes."

Angela looked at Jane and then leant over the corner of the table to give her a hug.

"Well, Jane, all I can say is the past is just the past, so let's both seek to understand and learn."

Just at that moment their meals arrived.

Taylor and Jane

Two days before their next meeting with Mark, Taylor called Jane asking if they could have a chat through the task they'd been set. Jane, although feeling concerned for Taylor, didn't want to spend too much time with him alone. Despite this, she still agreed to a meeting in the office café.

"Thanks for your time Jane," Taylor stated professionally as they both sat down.

As Taylor searched for his notes in the massive pile of papers in his laptop bag, Jane couldn't help but notice how different Taylor looked from the first day they had met. Whilst he was still wearing a suit with a tie, he looked scruffy. His shirt wasn't fully tucked in, his hair was a mess and he hadn't shaved that morning

"Taylor, are you OK?" Jane asked as Taylor continued shuffling papers in the bag.

"They're here somewhere, Jane," Taylor responded without lifting his eyes.

"Ah, here they are," he announced suddenly.

"So what did you come up with, Taylor?" Jane asked, hoping to make the session quick.

"Well, there were many great experiences that shaped who I am today and many great people, including my father and my brother," Taylor stated as a matter of fact.

"Why am I surprised?" Jane said rolling her eyes.

"What does that mean?" Taylor asked sharply.

"Taylor, everything is always great with you. Or at least that's how you tell it. But I can tell you we all know the truth. We all know that you're struggling. You only have to look at you to see that. So why don't you cut the crap and start looking at things a little more objectively?" Jane responded, deciding that it was about time that Taylor got some tough love.

Taylor stared straight at Jane, not knowing how to respond. But as he sat there, a tear appeared in the corner of his right eye. On seeing this, Jane realised that she might have gone too far.

"Taylor," she started in a softer tone, "we all think you're a good guy and we want to help you. I want to help you, but you just make it so hard to."

Taylor had now hung his head, hoping to hide the fact that he was clearly upset.

"Why don't we get out of here and go for a walk through the park across the road?" Jane asked.

Taylor nodded as they both stood up and made for the side exit out of the office. Once in the park, Jane and Taylor walked slowly down a small path away from the main road. As they approached a bench out of public view, Jane motioned for Taylor to sit down.

"It's just I always feel like I have to live up to them," Taylor blurted out, no longer trying to hold back the tears. "I mean both of them are fantastic surgeons. At home all they talk about is medicine and how great each other is and all they see me as is another manager type."

"I'm sure they see you as more than that," Jane added, putting her arm around him.

"No they don't," Taylor continued. "They know I'm not as good as them and they know I never will be. I'm just the mistake."

"A mistake?" Jane gasped, "What do you mean by 'mistake'?"

"That's right, I'm seven years younger than my brother; a mistake!"

"Hey," Jane said, now squeezing Taylor a little tighter.

"I'm sure that they don't think you're a mistake; an accident perhaps but not a mistake," Jane continued with a slight laugh, trying to ease the mood.

"And just remember, Taylor, whilst all these things have an impact on us, it is up to us how we respond. And I'm sure your dad and brother don't actually know how to be or say anything different, so whilst you can't ignore or forget their attitude to you, you can forgive it."

Taylor sat back in his seat as Jane moved her arm. He then took out a tissue from his pocket to wipe his eyes and blow his nose.

"What do you mean?" Taylor asked.

"Well, you think about it," Jane continued, trying to think what Mark or Liz would say. "Your dad and brother are comfortable in each other's company because it's what they know, it's what makes them feel safe. And whilst I'm sure your dad is proud of you and does want you to know that, I'd guess that what you do is just a bit foreign to him. And to admit that he doesn't understand what you do would mean showing vulnerability, which I'm sure famous surgeons aren't very good at."

"You can say that again," Taylor said.

"What I'm saying, Taylor, is that whilst you can't ignore or forget what your father does, you can understand him and you can seek to forgive him for it. And I think that if you do that you can stop trying to prove how great you are, and just start being how great you are."

Taylor spun around to face Jane.

"So from this moment," Jane continued, "I want you to stop trying to prove yourself to everyone and start just being you. People will respond to that and people will like you."

"I guess that's just the problem, Jane," Taylor turned his head to gaze back the way he was facing, "I don't actually know who I am."

"Well, I'm sure that our journey with Mark is going to help you with that one," Jane responded with a smile.

PRINCIPLES TO REMEMBER
Acknowledge Where You've Come From

Product of the Past
We are all a product of our past.

The experiences you've had and the people you've met over time all helped to shape you into who you are today.

Recognise the Impact
It is important to recognise the impact of your experiences to see exactly how they influenced what you think and feel today.

Understand and Learn
By acknowledging your past you can understand the impact that your experiences have had on you, and you can then seek to learn from them.

TASKS FOR THE READER

Acknowledge Where You've Come From

By acknowledging the experiences you've had throughout your life and the people you've met, you can understand their impact in shaping who you are today. As you embark on this task be sure to take your time, as it isn't until you start thinking where you've come from that you realise how big an impact certain things have had on you.

Task 1: Mapping your Past

Use the table below to capture the key experiences, events or people who have had an impact on shaping who you are today.

Age	Experience, Event or Person	What impact that had on me

From mapping your past, what are the key things you have learnt about who you are today?

9.
Build Who You Are

Sharing the Learning

"So what is the one key thing that each of you learned about yourselves?" Mark asked once they had all settled ready for their third meeting.

This time Mark had chosen another interesting venue for their meeting. The location was a small meeting room within the Tate Modern art gallery in London. All of them had been to the gallery before, but they were still fascinated to know Mark's reason behind this choice.

"How about you go first, Angela?" Mark suggested. "Nothing too in-depth, just one key thing you learned would be good."

"OK," Angela replied as she looked around the rather stark white meeting room.

"Well, the key thing I learned was that I've always been in too much of a hurry and have sometimes failed to enjoy the moment. So I've learned that I need to slow down to enjoy the moment," Angela continued.

"That's great Angela," Mark replied, delighted to get some real honestly. "What about you Simon, what did you learn?"

"The key thing I learned is that I have a real compassionate streak that comes from feeling from an early age that I needed to look after others," Simon explained.

"Thanks Simon," Mark replied with a smile. "What about you, Steve?"

"Mmm," Steve mumbled as he slowly worked up the courage to say what he'd learned. "I think that what I learned was that I really resented my father who I've never actually met. And to avoid being like him I need to look in the mirror a lot more and take responsibility for the man I see."

"Wow," Mark exclaimed. "It sounds like you've gone on quite a journey through looking at your past."

"A journey, you can say that again," Steve remarked, "but I feel better for it. I think that it was good to actually stop and think about the things that have shaped me."

"Excellent," Mark replied yet again. "What about you, Jane, what have you learned?"

"Um, well if I'm really honest, what I learned is that I don't believe in myself enough and, because of that, I put myself down too much. So I think I need to be more conscious when negative thoughts enter my head so I can control them," Jane said quietly.

"That's great Jane. Being conscious about what you're thinking is definitely the first step to doing something about it. So you're already halfway there," Mark replied, giving Jane's shoulder a quick pat of reassurance.

"So last, but not least, we have Taylor. What did you learn?" Mark asked, wondering how Taylor would respond.

Rather than bursting out with an over-confident response in 'old Taylor' style, he sat and paused for a moment. Looking at the sheet of paper in front of him, he took a deep nervous breath as he tried to compose himself.

Just get a grip, Taylor thought as he worked out what he was going to say.

"Um, um, well," Taylor stammered very quietly. "I realised that I'm living in my father and brother's shadow," he continued, still looking down.

"And...I learned that I just want to make my father proud of me," he gasped as the tears started rolling freely down his cheeks. Taylor dared not look up for fear of showing the others that he was crying, but they all knew.

The others, including Mark, sat there in silence all wondering what they should do next. Then, as if out of nowhere, Steve leaped from his seat and ran round to the other side of the small room. Taylor almost jumped out of his skin as he saw Steve approaching, arms outstretched. Just as he was almost on top of him, Steve burst out with "Come here big fella," as he threw his arms around Taylor to give him a big bear hug.

Jane, who was sitting to the right of Taylor, also spun around in her chair and threw her arms around the now seemingly-joined Taylor and Steve. The rest, almost in tears, just looked on in amazement at what was going on.

After what seemed like a few minutes, Taylor broke the silence, still smothered by Steve and Jane.

"Thanks guys," Taylor mumbled, "I really appreciate it."

Both Jane and Steve slowly loosened their grip and moved back to their original positions. As Steve walked back to his chair, Angela touched his hand and looked up lovingly to thank him for what he'd done. Once Steve was in his seat, Mark decided to break the silence.

"Thank you Taylor, that couldn't have been easy, even amongst friends. If I can reinforce anything, it is that, as each of you is discovering, this is a journey and it won't always be easy. But we're all here to help, me included. And sometimes feeling the pain or dissatisfaction of being where you are is what is needed to move forward. If you're not dissatisfied with where you are, why would you change?"

They all nodded, knowing that Mark was right.

"Today," Mark continued quickly, "we are going to focus on the areas of building your core person and building your self-beliefs. But first, who knows why I picked the Tate Modern for this location?"

"Because you like modern art," Steve blurted out the first thing that came into his mind.

"Not quite, Steve," Mark replied, smiling and shaking his head. "Any other thoughts?"

Everyone sat in silence not really knowing the answer.

"Well," Mark said, breaking the suspense, "I think that modern art is all about people expressing who they are in a considered way. Obviously some stuff here some of you will like and others will not, but ultimately each piece is different and each piece is an expression of something different. And this is what I want to talk about today."

Building your Core Person

"So what do you think I mean by your core person?" Mark asked as if starting a lesson.

"Is it who you really are as a person?" Angela jumped in as soon as Mark had finished.

"That's part of it," Mark replied.

"Is it who others see you as?" Steve included, hoping to show off his intelligence.

"That's part of it too," Mark replied.

They all paused to think of the correct answer.

"Let me put you out of your misery," Mark said as he took a piece of paper and drew a picture.

Your Core Person

who I = who others = who I
want to be   see me as   really am

Building Your Core Person means Gaining Congruency

"Have you ever heard the statement that there are really six people in every conversation?"

They all shook their heads.

"Well, there is who you want to be, who you really are, and also who the other person sees you as, and vice-versa for the other person," Mark explained. "And your core person is the combination of each of these three factors, so building your core person involves gaining congruency across them."

"Sorry Mark, I'm not sure I follow," Simon butted in quite unceremoniously.

"Yes, that makes sense," Angela jumped in before Mark could answer. "So who I want to be is what I portray against who I want people to see me as. But who others see me as is their belief of who I am as a person, based on the perceptions they create about me. And who I really am is just that: the person that I am when I'm naturally me and not trying to be anything different."

"OK," Simon replied cautiously.

"So that must mean," Angela continued, feeling like she was on a bit of a roll, "that building my core person is when I am really who I want to be, and I'm not trying to be someone different, and that people see me for who I really am."

"Bingo," Mark announced, "give that girl a gold star!"

"But surely these things are always equal, aren't they?" Simon asked.

"No, not necessarily," Mark replied, enjoying the questions. "It could be that you don't know who you are trying to be. For example, it could be that you unconsciously put on a mask each day. And by doing so, you think that you are creating a certain perception, which is different from what people see."

"I know that feeling," Jane butted in, thinking back over her first six months in World-Corp. "When I first got here I constantly felt like I was putting on a mask to be a far more confident and forthright person. But one day I was given feedback that I just needed to relax because occasionally I came across as quite rude, which is not who I thought I really was."

"Right, I think that makes sense," Simon replied slowly. "But I don't understand how you fix that, or how you get congruency as you call it, Mark."

"That's a really great point Simon, so let me tell you a story about what happened with me," Mark replied, shifting his gaze towards the others.

"When I was first given this exercise by that manager, I thought exactly as you did, Simon, that surely all of these things were equal. But what the manager asked me to do was capture exactly what I thought against each of the three things: who I thought I wanted to be, who I thought I really was and who I thought others saw me as."

Mark paused for a moment before continuing.

"I started with who I really wanted to be, which was very much someone who was stable and who enjoyed life, and someone who was seen as a professional that others could rely or to whom they would go for assistance. I then captured who I believed I really was in terms of who I saw when I honestly looked in the mirror. I have to say that this was really tough and a little painful. What I discovered when I looked in the mirror was that I had become someone who had lost all his confidence and zest for life. I was miserable, meaning others saw me as a real energy-drainer, which helped me realise why I was starting to lose some of my friends. As you can imagine, when I was really honest with myself I didn't see a pretty picture."

"How did others see you?" Jane butted in.

"Well, unfortunately many saw me as that negative person who they really couldn't trust, which was not good at all," Mark replied, softening his voice.

"Wow, what did you do to fix it?" Jane asked quickly, hoping for an answer.

"Now that's the interesting part," Mark responded with a smile as he leant forward in his chair. "What the manager then made me do were two things. The first was to test how others saw me using friends, family, colleagues etc. In testing this I had to get their absolutely honest opinions on this and also on who they thought I could be. Astonishingly, when I asked different people this question about who they thought I could be, it came out very similar to who I wanted to be."

"That's amazing," Angela remarked.

"At the time I thought so too," Mark replied, "but ultimately it made sense. They all saw my potential and obviously believed that I could be the person I wanted to be. But it was me who was not making the right conscious choices to be that person. I was focusing too much on putting on a mask to be someone else, you might say, rather than just being the real me."

"So what did you do?" Jane asked again.

"When I presented it back to the manager, he looked at both who I wanted to be and who others thought I could be. He then asked me a couple of simple questions: *'Is that who you think you can really be? Is that who Mark Pattern is?'* My instant response was yes to both, to which he replied, *'Well you just need to be conscious about being yourself then.'* As soon as he said this it made perfect sense. See, what I realised was that the person I wanted to be was actually the real me, but I had just become buried under a pile of negativity and fear. So to build my core person all I had to do was get back to being me, to being myself. To help me do this the manager gave me the second task which was to identify three simple things I could do each day to be myself."

"And what were those things?" Simon asked, feeling fascinated by Mark's story.

"Well, they were really basic, but the first was to dress like a professional each day because when I dressed like a professional I felt like a professional. Adopting the right image was something I learned that first day I went to lunch with the manager. The second was to make a choice about always being positive when talking to people. So no longer saying *'I'm not too bad'* or that things weren't good. But instead I chose to see the glass as half-full. And the third was to look at how I could really help others, both in my personal life and at work."

"That's what you did?" Simon exclaimed, realising how simple each of those actions was.

"That's it," Mark replied. "Now don't get me wrong, whilst they are simple things to do, it was quite tough at the start to do them. It meant that I really had to change the way I thought and behaved. But as I became more conscious, it became easier until ultimately it didn't take any effort at all."

They all paused, amazed at Mark's story.

"So I bet you can't guess what I'm going to ask you to do next?" Mark asked with a smile as he reached in and pulled some sheets of paper out of his folder.

BUILDING YOUR CORE PERSON

Who do you want to be?	Who do others see you as?		Who do you believe you really are?
	name	who do they see you as?	
	Who do others see that you can be?		
	name	who do they see you as?	

"What I want each of you to do," Mark said as he handed out the sheets of paper, "is to go away and complete the questions on the sheet. First capture who you want to be. Then I want you to identify some people to speak to and ask them who they honestly see you as, and then who they believe you can be. Finally, I want to you to be honest with identifying who you believe you really are. Once you've done all of this, I want you to once again work with one of your colleagues to identify what simple actions you can do every day to build your core person."

They each looked down at the sheet of paper and then back at each other as they thought about what they would capture. Once again, they all felt that sense of uncertainty about opening up and getting others' opinions of them. Seeing that they needed a few moments to digest what they'd just heard, Mark suggested they take a short break. As the others left the room, Jane lagged behind, hoping to have a quick chat with Mark.

"Mark, did this really help you?" Jane asked, hoping to ease her uncertainty.

Mark stood still and looked Jane directly in the eyes.

"Absolutely," he said confidently. "I have no idea where I would be today if it weren't for that manager taking me through this. And if you guys get half of what I did from this process then you'll be amazed at how far you will go as well."

"Thanks Mark," Jane replied sincerely. "I hope you know how much we appreciate this."

Mark gave her a smile and a quick nod of his head as he motioned for them to follow the others.

Building the Right Beliefs

Once back in the room, they settled in their seats with their collection of drinks and snacks from the canteen laid out in front of them.

"So what's next?" Angela asked eagerly as she put her Coke can back on the table.

"What indeed?" Mark replied with a smile. "Next I want to talk about beliefs. What do you think I mean when I say beliefs?"

"They're what you believe in," Steve once again blurted out the very first thing that came to mind.

"Thank you Steve, very insightful," Mark replied with a huge smile, "would you like to expand on that?"

"Why, of course my good fellow, I'd be delighted to," Steve replied playfully in his fake posh English accent.

"I'm sure what you mean in this context, my good chap, is what you believe about yourself," Steve continued.

"Perfect," Mark replied, now with an even bigger smile that was mirrored by the others.

"You see, we all have beliefs about ourselves, and these beliefs come from all the various experiences that we have had throughout our lives. Now the reason for us focusing on these is that some of the beliefs that we hold are actually empowering and some disempowering."

"What do you mean by empowering and disempowering?" Jane asked before Mark could continue.

"What I mean by empowering is that they are positive beliefs about yourself that help you achieve the goals you have. What I mean by disempowering beliefs is that they are things you believe about yourself that actually hold you back, or stop you from reaching your potential. For example, if you think back to my belief about numbers, that was a disempowering belief. I believed that I was no good at numbers, which meant that I avoided them at all costs and this meant I never got any good at them – a self-fulfilling prophecy," Mark replied before pausing.

"The key with disempowering beliefs is to identify them and then use your empowering beliefs to overcome them," Mark added. "To continue with my example, my disempowering belief was that I was no good with numbers. But with the help of the manager I identified that one of my empowering beliefs was that I was a reasonably smart guy who, if supported, could actually learn new things. So as I started to develop my empowering belief, I created a new self-fulfilling prophecy that actually saw me succeed rather than fail."

"That makes sense," Jane replied quietly. "I think I've got heaps of disempowering beliefs and I know what you mean by self-fulfilling prophecies, because when I don't try to overcome them, they always seem to come true."

"Me too," Steve jumped in. "I think that coming to World-Corp has really helped me realise what my disempowering beliefs are and I think that I've hidden behind them a fair bit and acted as a victim, where I blame the world rather than just taking control."

"Thanks Steve, it is very easy to do, I definitely know I did," Mark replied before pulling more sheets of paper out of his folder and handing one to each of them.

BUILDING YOUR BELIEFS

My Disempowering Beliefs	My Empowering Beliefs	My New Beliefs about Myself
What beliefs do you have about yourself that are holding you back?	What beliefs do you have about yourself that are helping you succeed?	What new beliefs will you develop about yourself to overcome your disempowering beliefs?
Disempowering belief no.1:	Empowering belief no.1:	New belief no.1:
Disempowering belief no.2:	Empowering belief no.2:	New belief no.2:
Disempowering belief no.3:	Empowering belief no.3:	New belief no.3:

"So, what I want each of you to do is to think about what beliefs you hold about yourselves, firstly in the context of yourselves as professionals, and secondly about yourselves in general. I want you to start by identifying your disempowering beliefs – what you think is limiting you as a person. Then I want you to consider the empowering beliefs that you have – what is helping you to succeed. Finally, I want you to look at your disempowering beliefs and consider what new beliefs you will develop about yourself that will help you succeed. The best way to do this is to look at how you can use your empowering beliefs to overcome your disempowering ones. As you do this, focus only on the top three. Just remember the Pareto principle."

Taylor, after having remained quiet for the entire time, sat there and reflected on Mark's last statement before he decided to ask his question.

"But how do we really start to believe in these new beliefs?" Taylor asked tentatively.

"Good question," Mark replied. "Any thoughts?"

"Well," Taylor said, "I guess there is a lot to be said for being conscious and honest with ourselves about our beliefs. I know that with my disempowering beliefs, as you call them, it is very easy to believe and reinforce them unconsciously. For example, I believed that this client didn't like me and hence I think I was scared to go and talk to him and then, when I did, I just went over the top which reinforced my belief."

"So I guess," Taylor continued, building momentum, "in that instance, my new belief could be that they didn't like how I was approaching them, rather than them not liking me and that way, with my new belief, I can just change how I approach them in the future."

"That's right, Taylor," Mark said with a smile of pride that Taylor was now starting to get it, "and you can base this new belief on your empowering belief that you are a likeable guy."

"But, it can't be that easy," Jane butted in. "I mean, I think I know what my disempowering beliefs are, but I think I will find it hard to build new beliefs to overcome them."

"That's probably because to reinforce your disempowering beliefs, you argue with yourself," Mark replied directly but with a sympathetic tone.

"I what?" Jane blurted out, looking puzzled.

"Well, there is a guy called Eckhart Tolle who has written that we are all plagued by a dreadful affliction of not being able to stop thinking. Hence our minds are filled with constant noise and I think that a lot of this noise comes from us arguing with ourselves," Mark stated.

"Who here has ever caught themselves replaying a tough situation after the event? You know, where you're replaying who said what, and what you should have said but perhaps didn't," Mark asked as they all nodded.

"Well, often when we have a certain belief about ourselves, especially a disempowering belief, that voice inside our heads continues to reinforce it. So what Eckhart Tolle recommends is to not continue arguing with that voice in your head, but to just consciously listen to it and, by listening to it consciously, it will cease to exist."

Jane started smiling as if having an epiphany.

"I would also suggest," Mark continued, "that when you feel you have a certain disempowering belief, write it down and consider what real evidence you have to support it. I have often found that, as with Taylor's example, my beliefs were based on my own subjective perception of the situation rather than reality. So I suggest that you start to look at your own beliefs, especially the disempowering ones, then consider what evidence you have to support them as this will help you identify your new beliefs to overcome those which limit you."

They all looked at Mark as he finished and then, almost simultaneously, down at the paper in front of them.

"So my task for you is to consider your disempowering beliefs, your empowering beliefs and then identify new beliefs to overcome those which limit you," Mark stated, giving them their second task. "And, you guessed it, I want you to discuss this with one of your colleagues as well."

Steve and Jane

"Hey Jane, you got any time this week for a chat over Mark's latest onslaught of work?" Steve asked as Jane answered his call.

"Actually, I'm free right now for a couple of hours if you like," Jane said.

"Great, let's head out to the café over the road. I'll meet you in the front foyer in five," Steve responded.

"See you then."

Once settled in the comfy chairs of the café, Steve decided to get on the front foot with the conversation.

"Well, I have to say that Mark has outdone himself this time. I found that these latest tasks were even tougher than the last ones."

"Me too," Jane replied. "I found it hard to focus on creating new beliefs, especially ones that helped me get over some of my limiting ones. And the core person task was challenging as well."

"Mmm, I know what you mean." Steve replied. "When I started this I was really hard on myself in the 'who I really am' part and with the disempowering beliefs. A lot of what I captured was about not being professional enough and being too relaxed because I'm hiding my fear about whether I'm good enough to be here. This is why I think I play the fool so much in groups. I guess it's also why I haven't cared about how I look at work."

"So, who do you want to be?" Jane asked, realising that Steve was focusing solely on the negatives.

Steve looked up at Jane as he snapped out of his negative mindset.

"Well, that was interesting. I really liked some of the stuff that Mark said about being relaxed, but what I want people to think about me is that I am fun to be around, and that I'm really positive. I want them to think that whilst I'm a professional and I do what I say I will, I am also relaxed but not in a lazy way. I guess one thing that I also want people to see me as is someone who comes up with lots of ideas and who is good to go to for a different perspective on things."

"And what new beliefs did you identify that would help with this?" Jane asked, hoping to keep the positive momentum going.

"Well, some of my empowering beliefs are that I am really good with people and that I'm fun to be around. I also realised that I am an ideas person, although I have to watch that I don't always just say exactly what's on my mind. So, my new beliefs are: one, that I have something to offer in terms of a fresh perspective for people to tap into; two, that I am a professional who can make a real difference to a company and to others; and three, that I am in complete control of me."

"That's great," Jane burst out with pride as she reached over to touch Steve's arm.

"I know," Steve said with a smile. "It actually felt really good identifying those new beliefs and I have to say that I've decided that I'm going to start to dress a bit sharper in order to create the right image to reinforce them."

"That's so fantastic," Jane remarked. "That person you described is exactly who I see you could be. I'm constantly amazed at the things you come up with and I think that working on your image will definitely help people to take you more seriously, if you don't mind me saying so."

"Not at all," Steve replied. "I think I've always played the slobbish fool just to hide from really having to take responsibility. So it's nice to get some honest feedback."

They both sat there for a moment just taking a few seconds to reflect on what had been said.

"So what about you? How did you go with it?" Steve asked.

Jane felt a sudden weight on her chest as the euphoria of Steve's lessons evaporated and she considered some of what she had written.

"Umm...well," Jane stammered. "As I said, I really struggled with this and I think that I could do with some help. I mean, I think that I also focused heavily on the negatives that just seemed to block me from even considering some empowering beliefs or even new beliefs. And I found it really hard to consider who I want to be."

Steve stopped for a moment just looking at Jane as her eyes lifted slowly from the half-completed sheets of paper she had in front of her.

"Well, let me tell you what I think of you," Steve announced, much to Jane's surprise. "I think that you are an incredibly intelligent and gifted person. I'm constantly surprised at how you understand things that I have no clue about and how you are prepared to get in there and try things out. Think back to how you facilitated the group that day; there is no way I would have tried that. And how you stuck it to those idiots who were giving you a hard time about your uncle being CEO, now that was something. Simon and I still laugh about that."

Jane sat there amazed at what she was hearing.

"You also have this way about you that you really seem to care about people and you show it through what you do for them. And you always deliver, no matter what."

"You really think all those things about me?" Jane asked, feeling herself beginning to blush.

"Absolutely," Steve replied. "So my question is 'Now how do you want others to see you?'"

Jane, feeling almost empowered by Steve's words, sat a little more upright in her chair.

"Well, I want people to see me as someone they can turn to for help or assistance, and I want to be seen as someone who does what they say they will, as you said. I guess I also want others so see me as someone they can really rely on. But I don't want to be seen as a push-over; I want to help people to help themselves, if you know what I mean."

"I sure do," Steve replied. "So what beliefs do you have that support being that person?"

"Well," Jane considered for a moment, "I believe that I'm actually quite smart or intelligent as you said. I tend to be able to understand most things and see how they work, and also how they can be improved. I seem to understand people and where they're coming from, which is why I think that I can often help them. And I guess I believe that I can make things happen. There have been quite a few times where I've surprised myself in doing things, like facilitating that day."

"That's fantastic," Steve replied, throwing himself back into his chair.

"Thank you," Jane replied modestly.

"However," Steve added with a serious tone, "I think, Jane, that what you really need to focus on is reinforcing those empowering beliefs because we all see how great you are. I do, Ang does, Simon does, and I'm sure even Taylor does. Hell, that's why Captain America is so head-over-heels for you. But you need to believe in yourself. So every time you catch that doubt entering your mind or allowing your thoughts to run away, I want you to think about what we all think and know about you."

Steve then paused as he looked into Jane's eyes.

"And who knows, Jane, perhaps even one day you and Tod could become the king and queen of World-Corp."

Jane erupted with laughter as Steve pretended to take off his crown and hand it to Jane.

"Thank you Steve, I really appreciate it."

"Hey, we're on the same side and I think that you're a fantastic person and we're all amazed when we see you being the real you!" Steve replied softly with a smile.

Angela and Simon

A couple of days after Jane and Steve met up, Angela dropped Simon a note over instant messenger.

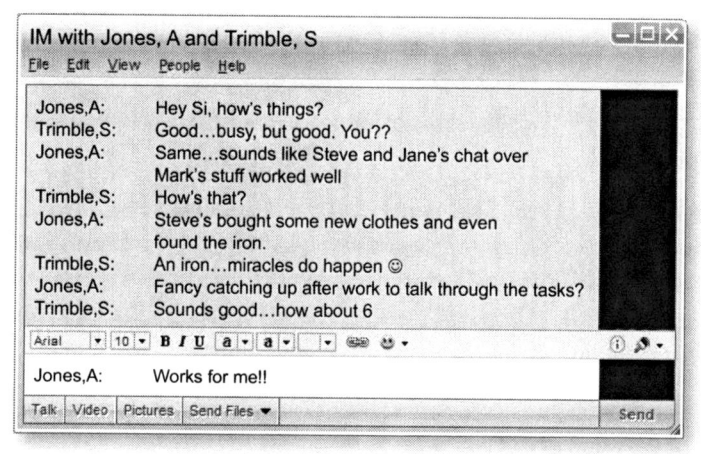

```
IM with Jones, A and Trimble, S
File  Edit  View  People  Help

Jones,A:     Hey Si, how's things?
Trimble,S:   Good...busy, but good. You??
Jones,A:     Same...sounds like Steve and Jane's chat over
             Mark's stuff worked well
Trimble,S:   How's that?
Jones,A:     Steve's bought some new clothes and even
             found the iron.
Trimble,S:   An iron...miracles do happen ☺
Jones,A:     Fancy catching up after work to talk through the tasks?
Trimble,S:   Sounds good...how about 6

Jones,A:     Works for me!!
```

At 6:00 p.m. Angela and Simon met in the foyer of the World-Corp head office and walked to the same café where Jane and Steve had met.

"So how did you go with it?" Angela asked once they were settled.

"Good, I think," Simon responded. "It was tough, but a real eye-opener. Much like the last task, I guess."

"So what were some of the things you discovered?" Angel asked.

"The first thing I discovered was that I think I am largely who I am, who others see me as and who I want to be. I mean there are a few things that I want to develop further, like sharpening up my image for example and being better at dealing with senior people, but largely I'm happy with who I am."

"So who do you think others see you as?" Angela continued.

"I think people see me as a person who's always happy to help others and who is able to make a difference to others," Simon replied.

"What do you mean by difference?"

"Well, helping people achieve what they want to achieve," Simon replied confidently. "I mean I find that a lot of people come to me with things they need to get done and I'm always able to provide a slightly different way of looking at it. And what I've focused on lately is helping them to solve their own problems rather than me doing it for them. This means that I tend to try to keep an open mind to what people tell me and then I ask a lot of questions of them to see what their outcome is etc. Just like the Problem/Opportunity, Outcome, Options and Action process."

"That's great Simon, what about beliefs?" Angela asked, not being surprised that Simon had this under control.

"Well, I think that I have a few disempowering beliefs, especially when it comes to senior people. I think that I feel like I am below them and that I have to act as their subordinate. And I think this comes from a slight belief or question as to whether I really deserve to be here," Simon responded thoughtfully.

"I know what you mean," Angela replied. "So what new beliefs have you identified to help you overcome them?"

"Well, I spoke to my current boss about being a subordinate and he said that what he always does when he feels slightly insecure around senior people are two things. Firstly he reminds himself that they are just humans too and that they are, therefore, not likely to be perfect. And secondly he asks himself whether he will be as good as them when he is their age or in their position."

"Wow," Angela remarked.

"Yeh, that's what I thought," Simon replied. "What my boss said about the second question was that often we feel insecure around senior people because we are making the wrong comparison. He said that we compare ourselves as who we are today to who they are today, which is wrong because they have obviously had far more experience than we've had. He said that by using those questions you can avoid feeling insecure and really focus on what you can learn from them instead."

"That's great! I'm definitely going to use that in future as well," Angela replied as she hurriedly wrote down the two questions.

"And with my second disempowering belief, I've just focused on the fact that they've given me the job and haven't sacked me yet, and I've done some really good things in World-Corp which means I deserve to be here as much as the next person," Simon concluded.

"Simon, that's all great."

"As I said, it was an eye-opener and I do have a few things to work on which has helped," Simon replied, ready to move the conversation on. "So what did you come up with, Ang?"

"I came up with similar stuff to you," Angela started. "I think that a couple of the key disempowering beliefs I have is that I believe that I need to be the best at everything, and that I have to get to the top to be successful."

"OK," Simon said slowly. "How exactly are those disempowering?"

"Well, with the first one I find that I tend to throw myself at far too many things and often really do more work than is required to achieve what I need to achieve. Let's just say I go beyond the Pareto Principle if you know what I mean. And I think that this means that I try to do far too much, which then means I either burn myself out or eventually miss things. So my new belief is that I just need to do the vital things really well and I need to focus on identifying what they are before I take action."

"That makes sense," Simon replied. "What about the second belief?"

"Well, I think that I'm starting to redefine what success means. For some reason, I always thought that success was related to position, but now I'm not so sure. So my new belief here, and I think this will evolve with Mark's work, is that success isn't about what level you are, but it is about what impact you have."

"Right," Simon stated, trying to grasp what she was saying. "But what do you mean by impact?"

"Well, I think about impact in terms of impact on the business and impact on people. You see, I really want to be seen as someone who makes a positive impact in terms of whatever the business or people are trying to achieve. And I guess this is what I have to offer."

"That really does make sense, Ang," Simon replied. "I always see you as a really focused person who can and does have a really great impact. In fact I wouldn't be surprised if I saw myself working for you one day."

"Ha," Ang laughed. "Simon, I think that we'd make a great team!"

Taylor and Liz

Rather than pairing up with one of the others, Taylor had decided to take Liz up on the offer of a chat following his disappearance on the new joiner induction night. Seeking to retrace their steps, Liz had arranged for them to meet in Jim's Wine Bar.

"Hi Taylor, great to see you," Liz said as Taylor approached the old wooden table that she was sitting behind.

"Hi Liz, thanks for agreeing to catch up," he replied as he sat down opposite her.

"So how are things going, Taylor?" Liz asked in a soft tone.

"Well, not all that great," Taylor replied as a waiter appeared to take their order.

"Just a coffee for me, thanks," Taylor said to the waiter.

"I've decided to quit drinking for a while," he then remarked to Liz.

"I'll have a tea, thanks," Liz said to the waiter.

"So, what do you mean by not great?" Liz asked as the waiter walked off to fetch their drinks.

"Well, I'm really struggling with the targets and my boss is riding me non-stop at the moment. I also think that my clients don't like me at all, which means that I just hate going to see them for fear of the next battering they dish out."

Taylor paused as he looked to see Liz's reaction, but she just stared directly into his eyes as if completely tuned in to what he was saying.

"The exercises Mark has been giving us have also been interesting," Taylor continued, feeling slightly wary of opening up too much.

"Mark is a bit like that," Liz replied with a smile to reassure Taylor. "What do you mean by interesting?"

Taylor described what had happened in his conversation with Jane and how he felt like he was living in a shadow. He then went on to describe how he felt constantly inadequate and like he needed to prove himself.

"So whilst it looks like I really believe in myself and how great I am, it's not true. In fact, it is quite the opposite. I tend to believe that I'm not good enough and that I never will be," Taylor concluded without looking up from the table.

"Who would you really like to be?" Liz asked, deciding to see if she could get Taylor to consider a different approach.

"I don't know," he replied quickly before pausing to gather his thoughts. "I guess I do want to be a professional and I want to be someone that people admire for who I am and what I do."

"And what would you like people to admire you for in terms of who you are?" Liz continued with a question.

"Well, I want people to see me as a sharp professional, who dresses and acts like one. But I also want people to see me as a real person who they can talk to about personal things. It always feels at the moment that all people talk to me about is work and that's usually in the form of complaints."

"OK, what about what you would like people to admire you for in terms of what you do?" Liz asked.

"I want to be seen as someone who fixes things and makes things better. I want my clients to see me as someone who really helps them rather than just a person who sells them stuff, or who tries to anyway!"

"So, let's think about what might help people to do that. What sort of things do you need to believe about yourself?"

Taylor thought for a moment and then looked up slowly at Liz. She could see from his face that this wasn't easy for him. Liz could also see that he was fighting internally against years of programming that had helped to build and reinforce those disempowering beliefs within him.

"I think I need to ease up on myself," Taylor remarked slowly and carefully.

"What do you mean?" Liz asked another question.

"I guess I need to believe that I actually am a good person and that people do like me. And that means that I need to stop trying so hard to prove myself and, as you say, just be myself."

"And how can you do that?" Liz continued.

"I think that I really need to slow down and not be in so much of a hurry, and that way I can take the time to get to know people," Taylor replied.

"I always feel like I've got to get to the top so that my dad will recognise me and be proud of me," Taylor continued, looking down at the table. "But I guess I just need to stop worrying about that and just focus on being me. I do think that I am a good person and others have said that before. But I get carried away a lot trying to be someone I think I should be and not who I want to be."

"So what's the one thing you're going to do differently from today to do that?" Liz asked.

Taylor thought for a moment and then replied.

"Just slow down I think. If I believe that I am a good person and that people like me, then I need to give them the chance to. And this means that I need to slow down and get to know them, so that they can get to know me."

"I think that sounds great, Taylor, and how will you know it's been a success?"

"Well, my clients might actually want to talk to me for a start," Taylor stated with a slight smile, "and others will want to spend more time with me."

"That sounds really great, Taylor, and if I can help you in any way, just let me know." Liz replied as she reached out and touched Taylor's hand reassuringly.

Taylor paused yet again and then looked up at Liz.

"Liz, I really want to thank you for all your help. I really do appreciate it, and I know I've never said this, but thank you."

PRINCIPLES TO REMEMBER

Build Who You Are

Building your Core Person

Your core person consists of who you want to be, who you really are, and also who other people see you as.

Building your core person involves achieving congruency – you are one person – who you are, is who you want to be, is who others see you as!

Building the Right Beliefs

The beliefs we hold about ourselves, whether conscious or unconscious, create self-fulfilling prophecies.

For those beliefs which are disempowering it is essential to replace them with new beliefs that help you fulfil your potential.

TASKS FOR THE READER

Build Who You Are

Building your core person and building the right beliefs helps you be the person you want to be. As for the last task, be sure to take your time. Building who you want to be in terms of your core person and your beliefs will not happen overnight. But it will happen with focused effort each and every day.

Task 1: Build your Core Person

Use the table below to define who you want to be, who others see you as, who others see that you can be and, ultimately, who you believe you really are.

Who do you want to be?	Who do others see you that could be?	Who do you really believe you are?

What three simple things will you do each day to build your core person by being the person you want to be?

1.

2.

3.

Task 2: Build Your Beliefs

Your beliefs influence what you think and feel, and also what you say and do. They therefore influence what impact you have in seeking to make a difference and gain fulfilment.

Use the table below to understand what your disempowering and empowering beliefs are. Also identify what new beliefs you will develop about yourself to overcome your disempowering beliefs.

My Disempowering Beliefs	My Empowering Beliefs	My New Beliefs about myself
What beliefs to you have about yourself that are holding you back?	What beliefs do you have about yourself that are helping you succeed?	What new beliefs will you develop about yourself to overcome your disempowering beliefs?
Disempowering Belief No.1:	Empowering Belief No.1:	New Belief No.1:
Disempowering Belief No.2:	Empowering Belief No.2:	New Belief No.2:
Disempowering Belief No.3:	Empowering Belief No.2:	New Belief No.2:

How will you ensure you develop your new beliefs?

10.
Define What's Important… *To You*

What is Important…

"It's amazing how quickly time is disappearing at the moment," Simon remarked as they all sat down for lunch in the World-Corp head office cafeteria prior to their next meeting with Mark.

"You can say that again," Steve replied as he lifted the lid on his salad.

"Going healthy are you Steve?" Jane asked.

"You got it. It's all part of the 'new Steve' image," he replied as he straightened the collar of his well-pressed shirt.

"Yes, doesn't he look handsome," Angela remarked as she put her arm around his shoulder.

"Just watch the threads, babe," Steve said jokingly as he then pretended to dust off his new suit jacket sleeve.

Each of them could see that the others had started to sharpen their image, even just slightly, in line with Mark's last activity. Even Taylor had returned to his former professional self, in his slick-looking suit with a tie.

"So you've learned how to use a razor," Taylor said with a smile as he slapped Simon on the back.

They all laughed as Simon ran his hand across his smooth chin, not knowing how to respond.

"How's aligning to your new beliefs going?" Taylor asked openly, trying to stimulate some conversation.

Jane looked up at Taylor, recognising that this wasn't like him to start taking an interest in others. On his face she could see that he was really trying to get involved so she decided to respond first.

"It's been quite hard if I'm honest. I keep drifting into this pit of worry and reinforcement of the 'old Jane' way of thinking, but then I just keep bringing myself back to being conscious about who I really want to be."

"Me too," Steve added. "Every time I feel like I'm slipping back a bit I keep thinking about

Jane's question of 'Who do I want to be?' and then I focus on that. And, if I may say, I'm looking pretty sharp as I do it."

Steve straightened his collar yet again to reinforce to the others that he had learned how to use an iron.

"How about you, Taylor, how'd you go with it?" Steve returned the question to Taylor as if he were just another one of the group.

"Very similar," Taylor replied. "I think I'm learning a great deal about myself which I have to say has been pretty uncomfortable. I never really realised how much baggage I was carrying around but it feels nice to finally off-load some of it."

"You can say that again," Steve replied with a nod.

Following lunch they all proceeded up to the room where they had met Mark initially. Like the first time they'd met him, Mark was already in the room, sitting in the same seat at the far end of the table.

"Wow!" Mark exclaimed, watching them walk into the room. "Don't we all look smart?"

Each of them immediately felt self-conscious about what they were wearing and how they'd groomed themselves that morning.

"I'm guessing it must feel great. I know that when I worked on my image in line with building my core person and beliefs, I immediately started walking taller both in and out of the office, and people noticed," he continued as they all started to relax feeling their confidence return.

"So I can see straight away that each of you has gained some insight from the last activity. And just from looking at you I can tell that your new beliefs are kicking in."

They all nodded as they looked at each other and saw what Mark was referring to.

"What I want to talk to you about today is defining what's important to you. Everything you've done up to this point has really been about helping you to create a foundation for you to define and then fulfil your purpose. And this purpose is based on understanding what is most important to you in your lives."

They all sat still in silence waiting for Mark to continue.

"So what we're going to consider is what your values are and then I'll give you some things to think about to help you start to identify your purpose. Now, I must add that neither of these activities is easy as they will both require some very serious thought about who you are and then what you plan to do with the remainder of your time on earth. I should also add that the second thing we'll consider, your purpose, is the most critical aspect of your journey because it will help define the stream that you choose to be in. Now that doesn't mean that once you answer the questions I give you all will remain fixed; that is impossible. But it does mean that your answers will form the foundation that you can use to focus your thinking as you progress with your life."

Mark paused for a moment.

"Any questions?" he asked.

Each of them around the table shook their heads, not wanting to disrupt Mark's flow.

Define your Values

"So let's start with talking about your values," Mark announced. "Why do you think values are important?"

"I think that your values tell you what's right and wrong in this world," Jane replied confidently.

"OK, what else?" Mark responded to Jane with an approving nod of his head.

"Well, your values help you make decisions," Angela added, "especially when the decisions are tough."

"Absolutely," Mark replied, looking at both Angela and Jane. "I believe that your values represent your guiding principles, they are where the line in the sand sits for you when you need to make decisions."

"Now, although very few people ever articulate their values," he continued as he turned his attention to the others, "most people will know when they are being breached. For example, one of my values is honesty and that means being honest with yourself and with others. Now I know when people are not being honest with me and I know how much it affects me when I find this out. But I also know when I'm not being honest with others and I know how that makes me feel. So as a result I always try to align with this value."

Mark then took some paper from his folder and handed a sheet to each of them.

DEFINING YOUR VALUES

Who have you met over your life who you have really respected?	What was it about this person that you respected?	What value do you believe they displayed?

Who have you met over your life for whom you have had little or no respect?	What was it about this person that caused you not to respect them?	What value in you do you believe triggered you not to respect this other person?

What rules in your life will you absolutely not break?	Why is this important to you?

"To define your values I want you to consider three things. The first is to consider people who you've met throughout your life who you have really respected. For these people I want you to consider what specifically it was about the person that you really respected and then consider what value, or values, you believe they displayed. For example, I really respected the manager who helped me, and one of the things I most respected about him was his willingness to help others, especially if they were prepared to help themselves. This revealed to me that he was selfless and this value is something that I have sought to adopt for myself."

They all nodded as they considered people they had met who they respected.

"The second thing I want you to do is the same exercise but for people for whom you have had little or no respect. For example, when I first started working after university I had a manager who always seemed to be more interested in himself and his own career than in the company. As a result he would often do things to the detriment of the company or others just to better himself. This infuriated me, and I later understood that this was because integrity, or doing what is right regardless of the consequences, was my most important value. And finally, the third thing I want you to consider is what rules in life you absolutely won't break and why."

Mark paused for a moment.

"Once you've done all of that I want you to capture what you believe your values to be on a separate sheet of paper."

As Mark finished, they all set about capturing whatever they could on to the template that he'd provided. As they each got into the exercise, they found it easier to complete and after 30 minutes they were ready for the next set of instructions.

"So tell me some of your examples," Mark requested, seeing people were ready to share.

"Well, I had a friend once, or rather an acquaintance," Angela volunteered first, "who used to drive me insane with her lies. It seemed that she was just incapable of telling the truth even on the simplest of issues. So that tells me that honesty is high up on my list."

"Thanks Angela," Mark responded. "Does that mean that you never lie yourself?"

"Well…not exactly," Angela replied cautiously as she began to feel like a bit of a hypocrite.

"And that's the thing about values," Mark jumped in before Angela felt too bad. "Just because we have values, it doesn't always mean that we ourselves don't breach them occasionally. But what it does mean is that when we do breach them we know that we are, and we are doing it consciously."

"Exactly," said Angela, feeling a slight sense of reprieve.

"Integrity is a big one for me." Simon announced before any further questions were asked.

"I cannot stand people who are just in it for themselves and I've seen a few people here in World-Corp who would do well to adopt that value."

"Thanks Simon," Mark replied. "Unfortunately I have to say that I agree with you. But just to let you know, one thing that I've come to learn throughout my career is that integrity always wins above all else. So rest assured, even if they look like they're benefiting now, in the long run they don't," he continued, giving Simon a reassuring wink.

"Professionalism is one for me," Taylor jumped in. "Whilst my father and brother, I realise, have their flaws, I really admire their professionalism and desire to do things properly all the time."

"I guess you'd hope so, being that they are surgeons and all," Steve added cheekily, resulting in an eruption of laughter from all around the table, including from Mark and Taylor.

Once the laughter subsided, Mark reached down and took off the floor an A3 laminated card. He then placed it in the middle of the table for all to see.

MARK PATTERN - MY VALUES

INTEGRITY
'I will do what I believe is right in all situations regardless of the consequences'

POSITIVENESS
'I will see the world as a fantastic place that is full of opportunities'

OWNERSHIP
'I will take conscious ownership of my thoughts, feelings and actions'

SELFLESSNESS
'I will remain aware of and focus on others in the world'

HONESTY
'I will tell the truth at all times'

PROFESSIONALISM
'I will achieve excellence in all that I do'

FUN
'I will bring a sense of joy and excitement in everything I do'

LOYALTY
'I will show commitment to those around me'

"These are my values," Mark announced as he directed everyone's attention to the card on the table, "and they are in priority order. I keep this on the wall in my office so that all who come in know who they are dealing with and I can remind myself about who I am."

They all studied the card, reading every word.

"Positiveness, now that's an interesting one," Jane remarked. "Why is that there?"

"Mmm, well that came from me realising one day that my outlook on life was very negative. See, my father was an incredibly negative man. It seemed that no matter what happened he would always see the worst of it, and because I grew up in that environment I too learned to look at the world in that way. So when I met that manager and went through this process, I realised that I wanted to be seen as a person who was positive, and the only way I could do that was to take ownership of my thoughts, feelings and actions," Mark replied.

"That's amazing," Jane responded in a half-whisper as she realised just how far Mark had come in his life.

"So what I encourage you to do is really define what your values are, capture them and then display them somewhere to remind yourself as well," Mark suggested. "That way you can keep them at the front of your mind and ensure that you are living by what you consider important."

They all nodded yet again in agreement to Mark's suggestion.

Mark looked at the clock on the opposite wall and saw that it was 3:00 p.m.

"Shall we have a quick break?" he asked.

Angela, Steve, Simon and Jane all stood up and headed for the door. Taylor, on the other hand, stayed behind to grab a few quiet minutes with Mark.

"How's things, Taylor?" Mark asked, noticing that Taylor obviously had something to say.

"Good, thanks Mark. I just wanted to say thank you for all this and to say sorry for being such an arse over the last few months," Taylor responded.

"What do you mean?"

"Well, I think you've really helped me realise how important it is to look in the mirror sometimes and be honest with yourself about what you see. And I have to say that I haven't been too happy with what I've seen, which I guess is why I finally want to do something about it, forgive not forget and all that."

"I'm glad to hear it, Taylor. I think you're a good guy and you've got a lot to offer the world. But as hopefully you've all picked up, the key is to get out of the shadows and flow, with purpose, as yourself. And you can only do this if you first define who you are and why you are here," Mark replied, patting Taylor on the shoulder as he followed him out of the room.

Define your Purpose

Once they were all settled back in the room, Mark started without waiting to be prompted.

"Right, so we've covered your values. Now with each of those I encourage you to constantly review them. It's important to make sure that they really fit and define who you are and what guiding principles you live your life by."

They all nodded in agreement.

"So here comes the hard part – defining your purpose," Mark continued. "Now who believes that there is a purpose to their life?"

They all sat there silently for a few minutes, none of them really wanting to expose themselves to potentially looking silly for such a serious question.

"I guess it depends," Angela responded, breaking the silence. "I would like to think that I'm here for some reason, but I don't know what that reason is."

"OK," Mark replied, "what do the others think?"

"I'd tend to agree with Ang," Steve added. "I'd like to think there is a reason, but I guess it all depends what you believe in."

"That's true," Mark replied. "So let me tell you what I believe, based on what I've learned over time both through working on myself and with others. Each of us is on this earth for up to 90+ years and maybe more if we've looked after ourselves. Now, if we are able to make conscious choices about what we think and feel, and what we say and do, then we should be able to decide consciously what we do with the time we have available on earth."

"But what about flowing with the energy of the universe?" Taylor asked.

"That still applies," Mark replied politely, "but we flow with purpose rather than just letting the world happen around us."

They all sat there for a moment trying to contemplate exactly what Mark was saying.

"So are you saying that we can define our purpose through deciding how we will spend our time on earth?" Jane asked.

"Absolutely," Mark replied, sounding excited. "You are adults and you can decide how you spend your time and, as a result, you can define your purpose. This will allow you to get in the right stream, as I've described it, which will mean that you can then seek to fulfil that purpose through allowing the right flow of energy to work in your favour."

Simon and Steve shot each other questioning glances wondering where this was going.

"Just work with me for a bit," Mark suggested.

"But how do we do that?" Angela asked. "How do we define our purpose?"

"Well, can I suggest that you fast-forward your lives a little and start with thinking about what you would like people to say about you at your funeral?" Mark responded.

"You what?" Simon exclaimed.

"Right, everyone, close your eyes," Mark instructed as they all did what they were told.

"With your eyes closed, imagine that it is 80 years from now. Each of you has had a pretty good innings and made it past 100, but you have finally passed on. Now imagine that it is your funeral. In the room there is a lectern in front of long rows of seats. To the left of the lectern if you were standing behind it is a coffin that holds your body. The room is full of people. Now imagine yourself floating up in the top front corner of that room looking over the events. Imagine looking over the faces of those you can see. There are people there you recognise and there are people that you don't. Now imagine that different people take turns to get up and speak and imagine that they are going to tell the truth about you. What I want you to consider is what you want those people to say about you. I want you to imagine what sort of person you would like them to describe you as. Then I want you to imagine what you would like them to say about what has been most important to you throughout your lives. And finally, I want you to imagine what you would like those people to say are your greatest achievements."

On finishing the last sentence, Mark let silence engulf the room. They all sat there fully swept up in their own imagination.

"Now open your eyes and start to think about what those people were saying," Mark said softly.

He then handed out yet another sheet of paper to each of them.

DEFINING YOUR PURPOSE

Imagine yourself at your own funeral and consider the following:

What sort of person would you like others to describe you as?

What would you like others to say has been most important to you - what were you passionate about?

What would you like others to say are your greatest achievements - what has been your contribution to the world?

"Now I want you to capture what you imagined. Then I want you to take this sheet away and consider the questions some more, as it is these questions that will help you define what your purpose is," Mark continued as they each started capturing what they had imagined on the sheet of paper.

"But how does this turn into our purpose?" Simon asked, taking a break from writing.

"Well, as you consider these questions over time, you will ultimately find some common themes emerging and it is the consolidation of these themes that contribute to defining your purpose," Mark replied, still with a soft tone to his voice.

"The key here though is to not try and force this. It is not a university essay, it is something that will emerge and evolve as both your conscious and your subconscious mind work at it," Mark explained.

Steve looked up, rather confused at the last statement. Without waiting for the question, Mark continued with his explanation.

"Do you ever have the experience where you can't remember something at a pivotal moment, but then it comes to you when you're doing something completely unrelated?"

"Absolutely," Steve responded, "all the time."

"Well, that is your subconscious mind working for you. And I would suggest that by considering these questions and then leaving them for a few days, your subconscious mind will do the same for this activity. Once you have a greater level of thought and detail for each of the questions, you can then start to refine your answers and identify some common themes. This will then help you start to distil what you believe your purpose to be."

"So once we figure it out, then we have our purpose?" Taylor asked, still slightly unsure.

"Not exactly," Mark responded. "You will have the start of something that will continue to evolve and be refined as you consider it further and as you grow throughout your careers and life. But by considering these questions now, the answers will give you a sense of focus that will help your subconscious mind work more effectively in your favour."

They all nodded cautiously, still not convinced at the precise process they needed to follow to define their purpose. Seeing this, Mark continued with his instructions.

"So what I want you to do is take this away and consider it for the next couple of days and then forget about it. As you do this, you will see what your subconscious mind comes up with. Then, by the end of the month I want you to have built on the answers you have already captured and started to look for the common themes that you can distil into the first definition of your purpose."

Simon looked at Mark, then at the papers in front of him and then at Mark again.

"Right, I'll give it a go," Simon responded as the others nodded.

A Purpose Emerges

Three weeks after their meeting with Mark, each of the team, including Liz, received an invitation from Taylor for a Christmas party. They all accepted the invitation and were pleased that they could get together before the holidays started.

"Great pad," Steve announced as Taylor greeted Steve and Angela at the door.

"It's my folks'. Not bad, hey?" Taylor replied as he ushered them into the warmth of the house.

Simon and his fiancée, as well as Jane, Tod and Liz, had already arrived and were chatting together in the corner. After the group had swapped a few pleasantries, Taylor did the introductions to the other people who were there, including some friends from his basketball team. In all, there were about 20 people at the party. As the festivities got under way, Steve kept people entertained with his antics, especially with his coronation ceremony crowning Tod and Jane as the new king and queen of World-Corp. Liz just rolled her eyes as she was instructed by Steve to announce that the new king and queen were now in power.

As the crowd filtered out towards the end of the night, only the group and their partners remained. They positioned themselves on the sofas in the front room.

"So, Liz," Tod broke the silence in his strong accent, "it sounds like Mark has been taking these guys on quite a journey."

"Yeh, he has a way of doing that," Liz responded with a smile.

"How have you done with your purpose questions?" Angela asked openly.

"Well, I've found that Mark was right about the subconscious mind thing he talked about," Simon responded first. "I left it for a couple of weeks and, as soon as I did, all sorts of answers to the questions were coming to mind."

"Me too," Jane added. "I found that side of it worked really well, but I'm struggling to refine it all."

"Mmm, I think I'm having that problem as well," Taylor responded.

"I guess the difficulty with this task relative to the others," Liz stated, deciding to get involved in the conversation, "is that there is no real definitive short-term answer."

"What do you mean?" Simon asked.

"Well, I'm going through this process as well, thanks to Mark, and what I'm finding is that there are a couple of themes in my answers. So some of the things I would like people to say about me are that I was a loving parent, a loving friend and that I was someone who helped others fulfil their potential. And I guess this is why I take certain things like being a buddy or being a boss so seriously."

Each of her team looked at Liz, recognising how great a buddy she had been to them.

"So whilst this doesn't have some catchy vision-statement or slogan attached to it, I think that my purpose is really around helping others to fulfil their potential, and this is something that I can do both in and outside of work." Liz concluded.

"That makes a lot of sense," Taylor replied as he contemplated the answers he had captured.

"Mmm…it's going to take a bit more thinking I reckon," Steve added. "And cheers to a great party, Taylor."

PRINCIPLES TO REMEMBER

Define What's Important... *To You*

Define your Values

Understand what your guiding principles are for the decisions you make.

Display your values to keep them at the front of your mind.

Define your Purpose

Define your purpose to understand which stream you wish to flow in.

The common themes within your answers lead to the definition of your purpose.

Your purpose will evolve as you allow your conscious
and subconscious mind to consider it.

TASKS FOR THE READER

Define What's Important... *To You*

Understanding what's important to you helps you focus your energy and time on the right areas. Defining your purpose allows you to flow, with purpose, as yourself on the journey through your life. Do not rush this task. Defining what's important to you takes time and evolves as both your conscious and subconscious minds go to work. Therefore, be prepared to capture your initial thoughts and then let them grow and become clearer over time.

Task I: Define your Values

Use the table below to identify the values which are most important to you.

Who have you met over your life who you have really respected?	What was it about this person that you respected?	What value do you believe they displayed?
Who have you met over your life for whom you have had little or no respect?	What was it about this person that caused you not to respect them?	What value in you do you believe triggered you not to respect this other person?

What rules in your life will you absolutely not break?	Why is this important to you?

My Values

Task 2: Define your Purpose

Defining your purpose starts with imagining yourself 80+ years from now at your own funeral. Use the table below to consider what you would like others to say about you, so you can begin building the foundation for defining your purpose. Remember to take your time with this task and use both your conscious and subconscious minds to consider the questions proposed. It is unlikely that your definition of your purpose will come to you in a blinding flash, but it will evolve and become clear as you think about it further.

At your funeral…

What sort of person would you like others to describe you as?

What would you like others to say has been most important to you - what were you passionate about?

What would you like others to say are your greatest achievements - what has been your contribution to the world?

Refine your answers to identify the themes that will define your purpose

My Purpose

II.
Take Considered Action

Life is too Short

"Hey Liz," Jane said as she answered her mobile after seeing Liz's name flash up on the display.

"Hi Jane, I'm really sorry to tell you this, but I've just been told that Taylor was in a serious accident last night and is in hospital," Liz replied, sounding anxious.

Jane stopped moving, trying to comprehend what she was hearing.

"Oh God, is he OK?"

"I'm not sure Jane, it doesn't sound good though. Can you get Angela and Steve to meet me in the café in 20 minutes? I'll find Simon," Liz continued with a sound of urgency in her voice.

"Sure," Jane replied, still not believing the situation. "I'll see you soon."

Jane grabbed Angela and Steve as instructed and they assembled in the café waiting for Liz to arrive with Simon. As Liz approached, Jane could see that she was clearly upset.

"What's happened?" Steve asked, wanting to hear every detail. "I mean, is he OK?"

"I'm not sure what really happened," Liz replied, "but what I can tell you is that HR called me just before I got hold of Jane. They said that Taylor was in a car accident last night and that he is in a serious but stable condition in hospital. I've since managed to get hold of his brother who is at the hospital with his parents. His brother said that Taylor had a big fight with their father last night and then jumped in his dad's car and took off. He wasn't sure what happened after this other than them getting a phone call to tell them that Taylor was at the hospital."

"Is he going to be all right?" Simon asked.

"From what his brother said, I think so," Liz replied, "but apparently he isn't in good shape and he's had a lot of surgery during the night."

"Oh no...poor Taylor," Jane said as she burst into tears.

Simon stepped over and threw his arms around Jane, as did Angela who was also crying. Steve stared at Liz who was managing to hold it together, although he could see that she too was almost in tears.

"Can we go and see him?" Steve asked, now staring through Liz as if she were a ghost.

"His brother said to wait until later today to give him time to recover from the surgery. So how about we head over to the hospital after work?" Liz replied as she pulled a tissue from her pocket and wiped her eyes.

"We'll be there," Angela replied for each of them as Steve handed her his hankie.

After what felt like the longest day of their lives, as soon as they could after work they made their way to the hospital. As they walked into the reception, they were all struck by the strong smell of disinfectant. They could also hear the squeak of people's shoes as they moved swiftly across the lino surface that covered the floor. Before they reached the reception desk, they heard a strong male voice from behind them.

"You must be Taylor's friends," the voice announced.

Immediately, they all spun round to see an almost mirror-image of their friend standing there. Although the likeness was uncanny, as they looked closer they could see that the person was a few years older than Taylor and he had obviously not slept for the entire night.

"I'm Taylor's brother," he stated, breaking their concentration. "Thank you so much for coming. I know it will mean a lot to him to have you here. Taylor has told us a lot about you and about how close you are to him."

They each felt a slight sense of shame as they thought back to times when they could have done more for him.

"How is he?" Jane asked.

"We think he's coming through," Taylor's brother replied as he directed them towards the lifts. "He's had some pretty severe head and internal injuries and also quite a few broken bones. All the tests are showing that there shouldn't be long-term damage, but we won't know until he is fully conscious. I have to say that it has been touch and go for the last 12 hours and we're very lucky that he's alive."

As they entered the lift, Simon saw that this was too much for Jane so he put his arm around her.

"But how did this happen?" Steve asked.

"We're not sure," Taylor's brother replied as he pushed the button for the sixth floor. "What we know is that he was found in the car which was upside down in a large ditch by the side of the road. The police seemed to think that speed was involved and that he may have been using his Blackberry at the time. The hospital also detected alcohol in his blood, although he wasn't over the limit."

They all stood in silence trying to comprehend what they had heard. Once at the sixth floor, the lift stopped with a sudden jolt and the doors opened. Directly outside the lift was the reception to the intensive care ward. Taylor's brother directed them to the right of the reception and down a corridor that had doors on either side of it. As they approached the door with the number 612 on it, Taylor's brother slowed to a stop. With his hand on the door handle, he then swung around slowly to face the others.

"We are going to have to be really quiet and it's likely that he may not be conscious. If he is, please talk really slowly and don't do anything that might excite him," Taylor's brother instructed in little more than a whisper.

"So no rap-dancing then?" Steve whispered back, trying to make light of an awful situation.

Angela elbowed Steve in the ribs as the others just glared at him.

Taylor's brother then opened the door and they entered slowly. Immediately, they saw an almost mummy-like figure in the bed, wrapped in bandages and attached to what seemed to be every machine in the hospital. Each of them stared in amazement that this was their friend, Taylor. Their once energetic and confident colleague now lay motionless, wrapped in bandages and prevented from moving by a series of braces that held his broken bones in place.

"Thank you for coming," a lady's voice spoke softly from the side of the room. "I know it will mean a great deal to Taylor that you have managed to come along."

They all looked over to see an immaculately-dressed lady rise from her seat beside the bed. To her left was a man who they figured was Taylor's father. He looked up briefly but returned his concentration back to Taylor and the many machines that were sustaining his life.

"Father," Taylor's brother started in a loud whisper, "these are Taylor's friends from World-Corp."

Taylor's father snapped out of his focus on the machines and looked at the group. As he did so, they could see the hollowness in his eyes as if the life had been drained from them. He then proceeded to stand up slowly and make his way towards them in an almost shuffle-like motion. They could clearly see that he had not left Taylor's side since he had arrived at the hospital.

Standing directly in front of them, Taylor's father, who was a tall and seemingly-dominant man, looked each of them in the eyes, one by one.

"I am so sorry," Taylor's father said, clearly shaking as tears started rolling down his cheeks. "What have I done?"

Jane, finding it too much to bear, burst into tears as she stepped forward to grab hold of this man who seemed lost in his own emotions. Taylor's father, not knowing what to do, just stood there and slowly returned the embrace.

For a few moments they all stood in silence, only to be interrupted by a nurse entering the room.

"I'm afraid visiting time is over now," the nurse said softly, slightly startled at the number of people in the room.

"I'm not leaving," Taylor's father replied.

"I'm sorry Dr. Johnson, but you know the rules. Your son is in good care with us," the nurse stated, recognising the challenge being set.

"Dad, you know how this works and it is best if we leave Taylor to rest," Taylor's brother added in support of the nurse.

Taylor's father looked at his son and then shuffled back over to Taylor's side. With tears still rolling down his face, he did a final check of each of the machines and then led the others out of the room. Once outside, they all stood in the corridor motionless not knowing what to do next.

"Thank you," Taylor's father said softly. "I know how much you mean to my son and I cannot thank you enough for making the time to come along."

"We'll be back tomorrow," Liz said as she reached out and touched Taylor's father's still shaking hand.

As the group walked back towards the lift, no-one dared speak about what they had just experienced. Each of them was still in shock from seeing their friend in such a dire state and from seeing a grown man and world-renowned surgeon express his emotions so shamelessly.

The sudden jolt of the lift reaching the ground floor broke them from their trance. As they waited for the doors to open, Simon broke the silence.

"Life's just too short to take it for granted," he said, still staring forwards.

"You can say that again," Angela responded as the others nodded.

For the next week, they established a ritual to visit the hospital to see how Taylor was. Although he hadn't regained consciousness, Taylor's father and brother, who were now taking turns at being by his bedside, told them that his condition was improving. Their only sense that this was true was that there were now fewer machines in the room, which they assumed had to be a good sign. Mark had also paid Taylor a visit, leaving a pile of World-Corp merchandise to remind Taylor to return to work as soon as possible. He explained to Taylor's father that Taylor was a real asset to the company and that there was no way we wanted to lose him.

On the Saturday, five days after the accident, they had decided to go for lunch first and then visit the hospital. After following the same familiar footsteps they had walked every day that week, they noticed something different when they approached the door: this time it was open. As they got closer, they noticed that inside the room there appeared to be a controlled commotion of doctors and nurses standing around Taylor's bed.

"Oh no, what's happened?" Jane burst out with as she saw Taylor's brother looking concerned as he watched the medical staff in action.

"It's OK Jane," he replied in a calm voice. "Taylor's just regained consciousness and they are checking him to see if he is OK."

"He's conscious?" Simon asked as he peered around the door frame to see what was going on.

"Yes, isn't it great?" Taylor's father announced as he appeared from behind them.

"Could you please come back in say 30 minutes as we don't want too much excitement for him now that he has just regained consciousness?" one of the doctors asked, seeing the number of people in the doorway.

They all nodded and proceeded to move away from the door. As they did so, Angela saw a flicker in the eyes of the 'mummy' who was surrounded by people in uniform.

"I think he's going to be OK," Angela said as they made their way down the corridor.

"How do you know that?" Steve asked.

"I don't know, but I think I just saw one of those Taylor looks when I got a glimpse in his eyes," Angela responded, trying to explain something she couldn't understand.

A good 45 minutes later, and ten minutes before visiting time ended, they walked back up to Taylor's room. As they entered the room, they could now see him bandageless, still lying in the bed supported by the variety of braces holding him motionless. His hair had been completely shaved and his face and upper body were still showing the sign of severe bruising that was now starting to subside. The brace from his shoulders to his head, whilst preventing him from moving his neck, did not stop his eyes from following them as they walked across to either side of the bed. A slight smile even appeared on his face.

"Bloody hell, you look gorgeous," Steve announced without knowing what he should say.

Jane and Angela both glared at Steve, wondering how he could be so insensitive. But Taylor's smile grew even larger as he felt pleased that they had come back to his room.

"Glad you're still with us, mate," Simon said as Taylor's eyes caught his.

"Unfortunately he still can't speak because of his neck brace," Taylor's brother informed them.

"So Taylor can't speak," Jane started as she moved her attention to look affectionately towards him.

"That must be a first," she then continued, giving him a wink.

A Direction for Action

Over the coming week, Taylor steadily got better, although his reliance on pain-relieving drugs was high and his inability to speak was causing him immense frustration. When they visited, Liz, Steve, Angela, Simon and Jane spent most of the time talking through stories of what they were up to and developed a way of communicating, with Taylor using only blinks and winks to reply. On the Wednesday, two weeks after the accident, Mark arranged a meeting for the team in Taylor's hospital room.

"So, whilst I know that you're unable to speak, Taylor, what I wanted to do is continue from where we left off before Christmas. I hope you don't mind me saying this but it seems that you've given us all a reminder of our own mortality and hence there is no time like the present to think about our purpose and to set a direction for action," Mark started as the others settled in their chairs around Taylor's bed.

"So how did you find the activity on defining your purpose?" Mark asked, looking at Simon with the hope that he would volunteer to share first.

"Umm...well," Simon started, realising that he didn't have a choice. "I found it quite tough and I'm not sure that I've really defined my purpose. I'm also not sure that I focused overly heavily on work."

"That's not such a bad thing," Mark said as Simon paused to think.

"What I captured against the questions you set was that I really want people at my funeral to say that I was a compassionate person who really cared for other people. And against this I want them to say that whilst I cared, I was also challenging which helped them achieve what they wanted in their lives. It means that I wasn't just a push-over who would do everything for others, but I would help others fulfil their own goals. In terms of what was important to me, I want people to say that my family was most important, both in terms of providing for them but also helping them to achieve what they wanted in their lives. This is both my girlfriend and also my kids if we have any. I also want people to say that I had a balanced life and what they saw is what they got."

"What do you mean by that last statement?" Mark asked.

"Well, I want people to see me as a complete person wherever they see me, whether it is at work, in the street, or even coaching kids' football. I guess I just want to be one person or my core person as you call it. But I'm still not sure that this helps me define my purpose."

"Well your purpose comes from those themes, so what do you think your key themes are?" Mark asked.

"Good question. I'm not sure." Simon replied.

"What I see," Angela decided to jump in, "is that your purpose is something about helping others to fulfil their goals and to be themselves, or build their core person as you put it."

"What do you mean?" Simon asked, looking at Angela.

"Well it is obvious that your compassionate streak is a big driver for you to help people, but you're not prepared to do it all for them as that is not actually helping them. Therefore, as you think it is so important to have a strong core person, your purpose sounds like something to do with helping others to fulfil their goals through building their core person, whether it is at work or outside of work," Angela replied.

"I agree," Mark replied, "they were definitely the strong themes for me."

"Thanks Ang," Simon responded slowly. "I think you might be right you know, but I'm not sure how that influences what I do at work."

"We'll get on to that," Mark replied quickly, "but I can tell you that your purpose defines how you do what you do, as well as what you do, if that makes sense. So as you define your purpose, through every interaction you have or activity you undertake you can seek to fulfil it."

"I guess that makes sense," Simon replied, still thinking. "So now that I've volunteered to coach kids' football is exactly me seeking to fulfil my purpose."

"Exactly," Mark said with a smile as he paused to contemplate Simon's latest activity.

"So who's next?" he then asked, looking across the faces of the others.

"Well, I also struggled," Jane replied not wanting Mark to volunteer her. "But now hearing what you're saying makes sense. What I want people to say is that I was a confident person who was prepared to try and get involved in things without being forced. I want them to say that I helped people build their confidence in themselves so they overcame the same fears that are holding them back. I also want them to say that I was a great friend and daughter etc., but at this stage I think that I can really help people to overcome their fears."

"That's great Jane, and from what I've experienced of you that also makes a lot of sense," Mark replied, smiling at Jane.

"I'll go next," Angela responded not wanting to be left out. "I really want people to say that I helped people make the most out of their opportunities, whether it was individuals or groups of people in a team or company. I want people to say that I always did what I said I would and what I did made a difference to people and organisations. I also want people to say that I was never afraid of trying new things or getting my hands dirty when needed. But most of all I want people to say that I was a loving wife, mother, daughter and friend as I think that with all that has gone on lately I realise how important those things are above all else."

Angela paused as they all remembered where they were and Taylor's predicament.

"So I guess my purpose is to make a real difference to the lives of people through what I do in life, and this difference is helping them make the most of their opportunities," Angela concluded.

"Thanks Angela," Mark stated. "How about you, Steve?"

"Well, I guess what I want people to say about me is that I helped people to feel good about themselves. I mean, I've always been the one at parties who entertains others, and I would like people to say that doing this made a difference to them, even if only for a moment. Like the others said, I also want people to say that my friends and family were most important to me."

Steve paused for a moment.

"And," he started again, "I would really love people to say that I was a great dad who always took responsibility."

They all looked at Steve, realising how important that last statement was for him.

"Thank you Steve," Mark replied, "and with a statement like that I've no doubt you will be."

After a brief pause, they all looked up to Taylor whose eyes were darting between them.

"Don't worry Taylor," Mark added, realising that people were feeling disappointed that he could not replay his realisations, "there will be plenty of time for you to tell us everything when you're ready."

They all nodded as Taylor blinked out his version of 'thank you'.

"So the idea of answering those questions is to get you thinking about how you will shape your journey, to help you start to find the right stream to get into. I'm guessing that none of you found the answers in a blinding flash and instead each of you had to let your subconscious mind do the work to come up with what you have. Now if I can encourage you to do anything, it is to not stop that thought process. The definition of your purpose is not a one-off activity, but it is an ongoing task where your purpose will evolve and become clearer as you become more conscious about what it means. It is a matter of being conscious about it and refining your answers, and then leaving it to allow your subconscious mind to work, and then again being conscious about it, and so on. So please keep your purpose and your answers to these questions visible so you are constantly triggering your conscious and subconscious minds to consider what your true purpose is."

"But I'm still not quite sure how all of this turns into helping me with the constant choices I have to make," Angela said directly.

"Good point Angela," Mark replied. "As your purpose evolves it will help guide you in your decision-making through bringing new things into your consciousness and shifting non-relevant things out. And, along with your values, it will also help you decide on the things you won't do. For example, I found that part of my purpose is about making a difference to the lives of people - many people if I can. And I defined that difference as helping people to live a prosperous life and fulfil their purpose. So each new opportunity I've had throughout my life I assess against this."

"But how does that relate to being in finance?" Steve asked.

"Well, if I do my job properly I can help ensure that World-Corp is a strong and profitable company that delivers the best for our shareholders, for our customers and, most of all, for our employees. So by doing my job well I can help contribute to the prosperity of the lives of each of those groups of people. That's some reach! Also, by doing things like this work with people like yourselves, and then encouraging you to continue spreading the message, I can also help people define and fulfil their purpose."

They all stopped and thought about what Mark was saying.

"I guess that makes sense," Angela remarked, "but that could still apply to any job you do."

"That's true," Mark replied, "but the next part of your purpose is to find the media in which to fulfil your purpose."

"Sorry Mark, I'm not following." Simon stated.

"Well, as I progressed on my journey I found that, despite my earlier programming, one of my loves was numbers. I found that I was actually really good at finance and by doing it well in a big company I could make a difference to more people. So, much like an artist discovers his media to be canvas, or a pianist a piano, I found that my media was numbers in the corporate world. Believe it or not, I really love numbers, but despite that I would only do this role if by doing what I love I am fulfilling my purpose. The other thing to add is that as you find out what you love, or your media, look for others who also share that passion. As you find these people, you will have the help you need to fulfil your purpose."

"So what you're saying is that we need to recognise what we really love doing, our media, and then seek to fulfil our purpose through that," Jane said tentatively.

"That's right Jane," Mark replied. "So what I encourage each of you to do whenever you're making a decision is to consider the parameters that define what you really love doing, and use them to make your decisions."

"How would we consider the parameters?" said Simon, feeling confused.

"Well, whenever I'm making a decision about the future I always look into what I've learned from my past. For example, when considering my current role I knew it had to involve managing a team, managing the numbers and I had to be able to make a tangible positive difference to the business and to people. But to understand this what I did was look at what I've really enjoyed about roles in the past and define my parameters about what I love doing to influence my decisions about the future. This way I avoid re-learning things that I don't have to."

"That makes perfect sense," Angela said excitedly. "I always think about what I've enjoyed in the past and try to match that. But I never really considered it before in terms of setting some parameters or against my purpose, so I just know that will help me."

"The other thing I would say is don't be afraid of regular change," said Mark. "As humans, we undergo constant change, even if only in the fact that we are getting older each day. So don't be afraid to move around a bit or to change roles. That's how the world works and that's how you grow and develop and, more importantly, how you find and fulfil your purpose."

"So I guess that these parameters, along with our purpose, represent a direction for our action?" Steve asked as if thinking aloud.

"That's right Steve," Mark replied. "If you constantly and consciously consider them when making decisions you will make sure you are in the right stream. And once in the right stream you will be more consciously aware of the opportunities available to you. Just remember, when you flow with purpose synchronicity occurs!"

For each of them, including Taylor, things were starting to make sense. They realised that their desire for a specific and unambiguous answer was no longer there, as the vision of finding and flowing with purpose as themselves in the right stream filled their thoughts.

"Sorry, visiting time is now over," a nurse announced as she popped her head around the door.

"Already!" Mark exclaimed. "Well Taylor, we will see you tomorrow then."

They all then said their farewells and left the room.

The Need for a Plan

As they went towards the lift, Steve walked closely alongside Mark.

"Mark, all of this with Taylor has really got me thinking about my own life," Steve started.

"How so?" Mark replied.

"Well, I've always really drifted through life, not really caring and thinking that I was invincible. But I think that seeing Taylor like this, and also going through this journey with you has really got me thinking about getting some more structure to my life. But I just don't know where to start."

"It sounds to me, Steve, that you've identified the need for a plan," Mark replied, patting Steve on the back.

"How about tomorrow?" Mark continued. "I'll take you all through that my manager taught me about planning. He gave me some really great techniques that helped me take considered action in fulfilling my purpose; to flow with purpose if you like."

"That sounds great, Mark, I think we'd all really appreciate that," Steve replied as they reached the lift.

The next day they all arrived at Taylor's room only to discover that Taylor wasn't there.

"Excuse me, nurse," Simon approached the first person he saw, "do you know where Taylor Johnson is?"

"Yes, he's getting some scans done," the nurse replied politely.

"Scans, what sort of scans?" Steve asked, feeling himself becoming concerned.

"I'm afraid I can't tell you as you're not family," the nurse replied, still being polite.

"Do you know when he might be back?" Steve asked, getting frustrated.

"I'm afraid I'm not sure," the nurse replied. "It could be anything from a few minutes to a few hours. Can I suggest you come back tomorrow and I'll let him know you visited?"

"That would be great," Mark butted in. "Could you please tell him that his World-Corp family came to see him?"

"I can do that for you," the nurse replied with a smile.

Wandering to the lift, they all felt a sense of concern and dejection that Taylor wasn't there. *Scans, what scans? That doesn't sound good at all*, Steve thought to himself.

Once in the lift, Mark made a suggestion.

"I know a great little old English pub around the corner from here, why don't we head over there and discuss planning? I can always bring Taylor up to speed when he's good and ready."

"Great idea," Angela replied, realising the group's sense of disappointment.

Once settled in the pub, Mark decided to share a story.

"So, how I know about this place is because my mother fell sick and was treated in that very hospital a few years ago," Mark announced, drawing the others in. "At the time, I was totally distraught and felt completely helpless, but I knew I had to put on a brave front for both her and my family. It was really tough, but what it taught me was that we have a choice, no matter what the situation. I didn't choose for my mother to fall sick, as much as we didn't choose for Taylor to be in the position he is in. But we can choose how we deal with it and by making that choice we can each make a difference in the situation."

"You're right Mark. It's just hard sometimes. I mean I'm really worried about Taylor. I can guess why he has all those braces on him and if he's also having scans that could be a really bad thing. I mean, what if he can't walk or even leave his bed any more?" Steve said.

"True," Mark replied, "but we don't know the full details, so we're at risk of making up what we don't know, which will not help anyone. We also cannot influence Taylor's condition, at least not in medical terms. So whilst we are concerned about it, we cannot influence it so we should not expend energy worrying about it."

Mark paused for a moment to think about Taylor.

"I know this is easier said than done," he then continued, "but by worrying about what we can't influence we are wasting energy that could be better used on what we can influence. So can I suggest we focus on redirecting that energy towards what we can influence? In my view, what we can influence is how we see this situation and how we can help Taylor deal with what he is facing?"

"You're right Mark," Jane replied. "I think that, no matter what, we should be positive around Taylor and really help him focus on the positive. Otherwise we could end up being more of a problem than a solution."

They all nodded in agreement, knowing that it would require a real conscious effort to keep focused on maintaining a positive mindset for their friend.

Alignment through Planning: Who and Where I want to be

"So let's talk about planning," Mark announced as he sought to change the subject.

"Who has a plan?" Mark asked.

Angela's hand shot up as if still in primary school. Everyone else spun their head to stare at her.

"What's in your plan?" Mark directed his attention to Angela.

"I won't go into detail, but it mostly focuses on my finances and how much money I will have in the bank so that I can buy a house and that sort of thing. I also had a career plan that focused on what level I would like to be in a business at what time, but I'm finding that I'm re-evaluating that with the journey we're going on with you."

"Don't throw that out altogether," Mark replied. "Having career goals is not a bad thing as they give you focus. But as you do this, it's important to make sure that your goals align with your purpose."

"For those of you who don't have a plan, can I suggest that you start to create one," Mark continued. "Now, with planning, different people will need different things. Some people will need only a vision to focus on, but others will need a specific list of actions that they can tick off. The key with planning is to understand what matches your preference and what works best for you."

"So how do we create a plan?" Steve asked, knowing that he prompted this discussion.

"What the manager told me, and what I've always used since then, was that planning involves two distinct parts and these are where you want to be, and then who you want to be," Mark started as the others listened.

"Where you want to be is all about your ambition in terms of career level, financial stability, education etc. Who you want to be is all about who you want to see when you look in the mirror. Who you want to be is all about your self-concept," Mark continued.

"So are you saying that in creating a plan we need to focus on both our ambitions and also our self-concept?" Simon asked.

"That's right Simon," Mark replied. "The key to planning is to recognise that how you expend your energy needs to be focused both on attaining the position you desire in this world and also being the person you want to be in this world. Taking action in line with this, guided by your purpose, is how you gain alignment between your work and life, and how you gain fulfilment as a person."

"That kind of makes sense," Simon replied. "I guess I always saw plans as being focused on the position side of things, your ambition as you call it. But I like the idea of also focusing on who I see in the mirror as that will help me be the person I really want to be."

At that point, Mark pulled more sheets from his folder and handed one to each of them.

ESTABLISHING YOUR PLAN

WHO DO I WANT TO BE?	WHERE DO I WANT TO BE?
How do I look? How do I feel about myself? What do I do with my time? What is my attitude toward life? How am I regarded by others?	What is my professional status? What is my financial position? What is my family status? What are my ambitions?
3 Years	3 Years
2 Years	2 Years
1 Year	1 Year
6 Months	6 Months
3 Months	3 Months
1 Month	1 Month

"So the first part of planning involves asking yourself certain questions about who and where you want to be at certain intervals over time. Now these questions are really only prompts to help you get some level of definition for who and where you want to be," Mark continued as they each looked at the paper in front of them.

"What do you mean by intervals?" Steve asked.

"What I mean by intervals," Mark said, drawing their attention to the sheet, "is to focus on who and where you will be in three years, two years, one year, six months, three months and then one month's time. By starting at three or even two years from now you can really set a vision against each of the elements."

"So do we first answer these questions imagining ourselves three years from now?" Jane asked.

"That's right," Mark replied. "You start with a far-off vision, like three years, and then ask 'Who and where would I need to be in two years to achieve that?' And then, 'Who and where would I need to be in one year to achieve that?' and so on. The ultimate result is that you can identify realistically who and where you would like to be in one month to help you get the ball rolling, much like getting some quick wins on the board."

"Wow, that's great," Angela remarked. "I love the idea of breaking it down like this as it gives real focus. I always think about where I'd like to be in five years but never work back to ask what that means for me this month. Which means that I tend to lose focus a lot and drift because five years seems so far off."

"Exactly," Mark replied. "The power of this approach is that it allows you to focus on your immediate actions against a more distant vision, and hence you can put things into place to build momentum."

They each sat and considered what Mark was saying.

Visualisation is the Key

"So what do we write?" Simon asked, feeling confused as he looked at the sheet in front of him.

"Well, the key is to use visualisation," Mark replied.

"What do you mean by visualisation?" Jane asked before Simon had a chance to speak.

"Visualisation is where you fully imagine yourself in terms of who and where you want to be at a given point. As a simple example, what I have put on the 'where I want to be' part of my plan is that I will become the CFO of a multinational company in three years. In putting that statement down I imagine myself running the finance team for a multinational company, where I am responsible for the financial success of that company including being responsible for how money flows through it to make it profitable. I imagine the CEO I'll work for and the team I'll work with. I even imagine what I would do each day. From this clear vision I've then worked back to visualise where I need to be at each key interval before that."

"That's great, I think that's what Tod did with me before I facilitated the workshop that day," Jane replied.

"Wow," Angela remarked, focusing first on Jane and then back to Mark, "is that really true that you visualise about becoming a CFO?"

"Absolutely, and since my manager taught me this technique I use it for everything I need to achieve, including about who I want to be," Mark replied. "But the key is to make sure that you focus on really building your visualisations at intervals and that you focus not only on the destination, but also on the journey itself. If you don't do this, all you do is jump from goal to goal to goal."

They each listened intently as Mark continued.

"And this is where your purpose is paramount. Your purpose is what enables you to make a difference and gain fulfilment through being yourself throughout your journey. Your purpose makes sure that your plans are focused on enabling you to flow in the right stream. So your purpose sets the context for your plans and allows you to gain real fulfilment each day as you progress along your journey."

"But if you're so focused on your plan and your journey, don't you risk missing things?" Steve asked. "I mean if you're so focused on being a CFO, surely you risk dismissing other opportunities that might arise?"

"Good point Steve," Mark replied with a smile. "If you remain too rigid, yes you can miss things and it is easy to become seduced by certain visions. But what I was told once is that, like with a sailing boat, if the sails aren't up then the rudder doesn't work. So what a purpose and plan allow you to do is to start moving. But as you move it is essential that you constantly remain nimble and ready to grab the right opportunities, or use your rudder, provided they fit with your purpose and within the parameters of what you love. That means that while you progress in your plan you should be constantly aware of what is happening around you and then assess each opportunity on its merits."

"I think that really makes sense," Jane replied, almost thinking aloud. "So by flowing with purpose towards the visualisations in your plan, and by being constantly nimble and ready, you will start to see opportunities that you may previously have not seen, hence synchronicity occurs."

"Perfect," Mark announced, pointing a finger at Jane.

They paused for a moment as Jane shied away from Mark's praise. Feeling slightly uncomfortable, Steve decided to break the silence.

"Well I think that my vision for the next two minutes is me relieving my bladder, so excuse me everyone," Steve said as he left the table promptly.

Remaining Accountable

"Mark, I love this and it is exactly what I'm looking for," Jane said after Steve was out of sight, "but I've set plans in the past and never stuck to them."

"Mmm, let's wait until Steve gets back and I'll give you my thoughts. Now would anyone like another drink?" Mark replied as he slid his chair back ready to go to the bar.

Mark returned from the bar with a tray full of drinks. As he approached, he noticed that they were all sitting there in silence, contemplating their journeys and also feeling worried for Taylor.

"So how do you remain accountable to your purpose and your plan, I hear you ask?" Mark joked to break them from their daydreams. "Well, the key again is to make sure that it sits within both your conscious and your unconscious minds."

"Once again, Mark, you've lost me," Simon butted in as he lifted his glass to his lips.

Mark smiled as he raised his glass in Simon's direction.

"What I mean by 'in your conscious mind' is keeping your plan somewhere visible so that you continue to take notice of it. The strength in visualisations is that you remember them and they become so strong that they are inevitable. So you must seek to make sure that you continue to develop and reinforce them. For example, what I do is leave the statement of my purpose and my plan right above my desk in my study at home. That way, whenever I sit down at my desk, the first thing I do see is my purpose and plan."

"That makes sense," Steve replied. "I think part of my problem is that I always create documents and then just forget about them. So putting them up somewhere sounds like a good idea although I'm not sure I'm rich enough to have a study!"

They all gave a quick chuckle as Steve gave Mark a wink to show he was joking.

"The other thing you can do is set aside some time to review your purpose and plan. I usually do this every three months or so. What I do is set aside a good two to three hours to review my purpose and plan and then capture what I have achieved against them both. This allows me to see what I've done to help me fulfil my purpose and then make sure that my actions still align with my plan. It's far from rocket-science, but it works for me and, relative to when I started, I am far less worried about the future."

Mark paused.

"So that's planning," he then concluded.

"That's great Mark," Steve replied. "I think that is exactly what I was looking for. And, now that I'm no longer the king of World-Corp, perhaps my sights should be set on the role of CEO!"

They all looked at Steve and laughed at his vivid imagination.

Angela especially found it funny.

"Yes honey, why don't you do that," she said as she patted Steve on the back.

PRINCIPLES TO REMEMBER

Take Considered Action

A Direction for Action

Your purpose provides a direction for your action.

Much like a painter uses canvas, fulfilling your purpose requires you to identify the media in which you operate at your best – *what do you really love doing?*

Defining the parameters for what you love doing helps you pick the right activities to fulfil your purpose.

Finding other people in the same or similar streams provides energy to focus and continue flowing.

Never be afraid of regular change – *we as humans change constantly.*

Alignment Through Planning

Gaining alignment through planning requires consideration of both **who you want to be** (core person) and **where you want to be** (ambition).

Visualising who and where you want to be at set intervals in time is what enables your plans to become real.

Remaining Accountable

Accountability comes from keeping your purpose and your plan visible and present in both your conscious and subconscious minds.

TASKS FOR THE READER

Take Considered Action

Taking considered action requires that you define parameters to guide your decisions towards what you love doing. It also requires that you build a plan to which you can be accountable, based on clear visualisations of who and where you want to be at set intervals. Be sure to focus on the evolving definition of your purpose as you seek to take considered action, as it is the momentum that you build in taking action which will help you clarify your purpose.

Task I: A Direction for Action

Setting a direction for action involves defining the parameters for what you love doing. Consider the various activities you have undertaken both within and outside of work. What is it about these activities that you have really enjoyed doing, and what is it about them that you haven't enjoyed?

Activity (jobs, hobbies, classes, projects etc.)	What was it about this activity that you really loved doing?	What was it about this activity that you disliked?

What parameters define what you really love doing – *what is the media you love operating in?*

How can you seek to find others who are in the same or similar streams as you in seeking to fulfil their purpose?

Task 2: Alignment through Planning

Gaining alignment through planning requires that you develop strong visualisations of who and where you want to be at set intervals in time.

Create visualisations by considering the following questions at set intervals in time.

Who do I want to be?	Where do I want to be?
How do I look? How do I feel about myself? What do I do with my time? What is my attitude toward life? How am I regarded by others?	What is my professional status? What is my financial position? What is my family status? What are my ambitions?
3 Years	3 Years
2 Years	2 Years
1 Year	1 Year
6 Months	6 Months
3 Months	3 Months
1 Month	1 Month

Task 3: Remaining Accountable

Accountability comes from keeping your purpose and your plan visible and present in both your conscious and subconscious minds.

How will you seek to remain accountable to your plan?

12.
Make It Stick...*Maintain Focus*

Focusing on the Positives

"So it will be great to have you at the ball in September," Jane said to Taylor who was still supported by braces in his hospital bed.

"Like this? How am I supposed to go to a ball like this?" Taylor replied as if offended by Jane's statement.

It had been over two months since the accident, and whilst Taylor had regained enough movement to be able to speak, he still could not move his arms or legs.

"Jane, have you got a minute?" Taylor's father asked as he popped his head around the door to Taylor's room.

"Sure," Jane replied.

"I'll be back in a minute," she said to Taylor as she stood up to follow his father.

Taylor did not watch her leave, but instead focused his eyes on the window on the opposite side of the room to the door. As Jane walked through the door, Taylor's father closed it behind her.

"Let's grab a coffee," Taylor's father suggested as he motioned for her to follow him towards the café.

Once in the café they ordered a drink and then proceeded to find a table with two chairs.

"What's up?" Jane asked, sensing some tension.

"Jane, the damage Taylor suffered is very severe. So severe in fact that they think there is only a 50:50 chance of him being able to use his arms, let alone walk again."

"I know," Jane replied, "Taylor told me."

"So," Taylor's father continued, "I'm not sure that it is wise to be talking about Taylor attending the ball in September, even though it is still six months away."

Jane looked across at Taylor's father. Whilst she could see that the experience over the last couple of months had aged him, he still held himself as a dominant character who commanded respect through what he did and what he knew.

As Jane paused she thought to herself, *why am I intimidated by this man? He's just a human and I think he's jumping too much to the negative here and not the positive.*

"You said a 50:50 chance, right? Well that means that there is a 50% chance of him being able to use his arms and walk again, so I'd prefer to focus on the 50% positive rather than the 50% negative if that's OK."

"And," Jane continued, feeling her confidence grow as she reached out and grabbed his hand, "I think that Taylor would really appreciate you doing the same."

Taylor's father looked across the table at her not sure of what to do next.

Before he could speak, Angela's voice punctured the moment.

"Hey guys, what's up?" she asked.

"Nothing," Jane replied immediately, "we were just talking about how important it is to focus Taylor on getting himself to the ball in September."

"Great idea, I think some visualisation work is needed here for young Taylor. We need him to believe in what is possible," Angela replied as she began developing ideas of what to do next.

All three of them then wandered back up to Taylor's room to find Steve and Simon joking about how lucky Taylor was to be getting sponge baths every day from the rather attractive nurse who had just left.

"You know, if I had her washing me every day I wouldn't be in a hurry to leave here either," Simon joked, noticing a slight smirk come across Taylor's face.

"Well I guess there are some benefits," Steve added, "even if you can't feel it."

The smirk grew larger on Taylor's face as Simon and Steve both laughed at their own jokes. Their laughter then stopped suspiciously as the girls entered the room with Taylor's father. Close behind him came Mark with Liz ready for their next session of the journey.

Need to Maintain Head Space

"So I hear the plan is getting you to the ball in September," Mark announced after overhearing Jane and Angela's conversation when they were in the corridor outside Taylor's room. "I think that's a great idea."

"I'll even save the first dance for you," Liz added with a wink and a smile.

"We'll see," Taylor said, not wanting to show his enthusiasm.

"Let's get started shall we?" Mark stated in a matter of fact way as he motioned for them to take a seat.

"What I want to talk about today is the need to maintain head space. As I believe I indicated in my first note to you, head space is the key to us remaining focused on our purpose and also on our plans."

As Mark started speaking, Taylor's father who was in the room also took a seat, fascinated by what Mark was saying.

"What do you mean by head space?" Taylor's father asked.

"Well," Mark started, looking over towards him, "head space is the time and space for you to consider why you're here on earth and what you're going to do with your time. Or, as I just stated, what your purpose is and what your plans are to make a difference and gain fulfilment through being yourself. Ultimately head space is what allows you to flow, with purpose, as yourself."

"I've never heard of that before," Taylor's father responded, considering what Mark had just said.

"See, the affliction that we all suffer from in the modern world is thinking too much about the wrong things. And the noise this thinking creates stops us from really considering what our purpose is and what our plans are to fulfil it. Therefore, if you never get control over your own thoughts you can easily lose the space altogether and thus live your life without knowing your purpose."

Taylor's father sat mesmerised by Mark's words.

"So," Mark continued, "it is important to recognise that whilst you may regain some head space, it is very easy to be distracted, which results in it evaporating. We all know how busy we can get from the constant pressure of our day-to-day lives. And because of this pressure, we all know how easy it is to revert back to our 'busy but without a purpose' mindset. So the key here is to really focus on making a conscious choice as to how to maintain the head space you need to fulfil your purpose."

"But how do we make that choice when things aren't looking too good?" Taylor butted in, breaking Mark's flow.

"Good question Taylor," Mark responded looking towards him in his bed. "Ultimately it is a conscious choice. Just remember that whilst we can't choose our situation, we can choose how we respond. And although sometimes that choice feels incredibly tough, it is still only a choice that we need to make."

Mark paused to give Taylor an opportunity to respond. But Taylor remained quiet as he looked straight into Mark's eyes, searching for the slightest hint of doubt.

"Taylor, none of us can ever imagine what you're going through and how tough it must be to choose to be positive and we also cannot make that choice for you. But what I can assure you is that we can help you in every way possible to regain the space you need to define and fulfil your purpose, even if the first part of your purpose is focused on getting you to the ball in September."

Taylor continued staring into Mark's eyes for a few moments and then he looked back towards the window opposite the door. None of the others knew exactly what he was thinking but Simon thought he saw a look of steely determination come over Taylor's face.

"But I'm still not sure how we maintain our head space," Angela butted in, realising that she still wanted some answers.

"Well, being conscious is the absolute key. We all know when we feel too busy or we feel as though we are drifting, and the key to being conscious is to recognise this and do something about it. The second tip I have relates to being accountable to your purpose and your plan. If you make sure that you take time out periodically to review your purpose and your plan then it is easier to keep it in your conscious and subconscious mind, and therefore you will be more aware of when you lose your head space to focus on it," Mark replied.

"I like that. I think that making sure you maintain your head space is what will help make your purpose and plans stick, and ultimately help you maintain focus," Simon added just before the door to Taylor's room opened.

Through the door came the nurse that the boys were talking about, along with Taylor's brother and mother.

"It looks as though we are having a party," Taylor's mother said, noticing all the people.

"We were just finishing," Mark replied politely, realising that visiting time was almost over.

They each said their goodbye to Taylor.

"Enjoy those baths," Simon said quietly to Taylor just before leaving, "and keep focused on the September ball."

A small smile appeared on Taylor's face.

As they left the room, Taylor's father followed them out.

"Mark, do you have a few minutes?" Taylor's father asked.

"Sure, let's head downstairs." Mark replied as the others went off ahead of them.

"It's OK, this will only take a few minutes," Taylor's father continued. "What you said in there makes a lot of sense, but I don't think I've heard it before. During my life I've been so focused on achievement after achievement that I never had the head space, as you call it, to consider what is really important to me. Hence I think that I've completely neglected my family and the fight I had with Taylor is why he is here."

Mark listened carefully as Taylor's father opened up.

"I think that this whole thing has given me a big wake-up call, but I'm worried that the damage is already done," his father continued.

"Taylor is a good guy and a strong lad," Mark replied, "and it is never too late to make things better."

They paused for a moment and then Mark pulled out all the same sheets that he had given the group.

"Can I suggest that you use this to think about your purpose and your plan for fulfilling it, as I think that doing this is what will help Taylor the most?" Mark concluded as he handed the sheets of paper over to Taylor's father.

"I think you might be right," he responded. "Thank you, Mark."

Sticky to Stuck – Developing the Right Habits

A month later they all arrived at Taylor's room ready for their final session with Mark. It was now the end of March and the days were getting longer. The winter had now well and truly passed and the signs of spring were starting to show. It felt like a new lease of life had engulfed the group, and even Taylor was looking better. During their many visits to the hospital since the last meeting, they had noticed the colour returning to Taylor's face and, during one meeting, Simon even thought that he'd seen Taylor's fingers move ever so slightly. However, whilst Taylor was now out of his braces, each time they visited he still claimed that he could not move.

"Ready?" Mark asked as he opened the door to Taylor's room.

They all nodded as they followed Mark through the door. Once in the room they immediately saw that Taylor was crying.

"Taylor, what's wrong?" Angela asked as she rushed over to his side.

Taylor looked up, startled that he'd been caught in a moment of weakness.

"Nothing," he said as he rolled his head slightly to one side.

"Taylor, you moved," Jane exploded with.

"Yeh, only my neck," he said, still upset. "What good is that?"

"Taylor, that's fantastic," Simon added. "Remember that three months ago you couldn't move anything, not even your mouth."

Taylor rolled his head back towards Simon. He could see how visibly excited Simon was. He then looked and saw the same sense of excitement on the faces of the others, including Mark.

"It's still a long way from dancing at the ball," Taylor said, still choosing to see the negatives.

"Perhaps," Mark responded strongly, "but it isn't a long way from wiggling your fingers."

They all, including Taylor, stared at Mark.

"See, if you're going to go from sticky to stuck with your purpose and your plans, it is critical to keep it simple."

They all relaxed into their chairs as Mark continued.

"The danger with defining your purpose and your plans is that you create them to be so far-fetched and so detailed that they stifle action."

"What do you mean?" Taylor asked, still looking at Mark.

"Well Taylor, if I can focus on you, your plan at this stage is to be dancing at the ball, which is fantastic. But the danger in focusing only on that is that you forget all the steps in between. See, the reason you're upset is that you see that dancing at the ball is a long way off, especially as you're thinking about making that in one leap."

They all listened intently to Mark, none more so than Taylor.

"So whilst having that vision in mind is a great destination to focus on, it is essential that you work back from that to decide what you need to achieve and by when. For example, you could say that you'd like to be walking by August, and before that you'd like to be using your arms by July, and sitting upright by June, and moving your fingers and hands by May. This approach gives you a time-line of smaller steps you can take to make sure that your bigger step doesn't look so large."

"I've never thought about it like that," Taylor responded feeling a little better. "So what I should really be focusing on is being able to wiggle my fingers in the next few weeks."

"Exactly," Mark said. "Just remember small wins build momentum and for each small win it is important to celebrate. Success breeds success and all that."

"I really like that, Mark," Angela jumped in, not wanting to divert attention from Taylor. "I think that works for Taylor and all of us. I'm assuming that you could even break that down to what you do from day to day as well?"

"Exactly," Mark remarked. "That's where habits come in."

"Habits?" Steve questioned. "What do habits have to do with it?"

"Well, a habit is something that drives your day-to-day behaviour. So the secret is to build in habits that allow your actions each day to achieve your goals."

They all sat there listening, still slightly puzzled at what Mark was referring to.

"Who has a habit?" Mark asked sensing their confusion.

Each of them put their hand up.

"What's one of your habits, Steve?" Mark asked.

"Well, I've got plenty of habits," Steve replied, "and they're not all good. For example, one habit that I really want to kick is feeling like I need a double espresso each morning to wake me up. I know it's not good for me, but each morning I still jump in that queue to get one."

"Excellent," Mark replied, "and all of us have something similar. Now the secret to going from sticky to stuck with your purpose and plans is to recognise the good habits you have, and then replace your bad habits with new ones that reinforce your purpose and plan. A bit like what you did with your beliefs. For example, when I realised all of this during the start of my journey, I established new habits in the form of how I responded to people each morning. Rather than saying 'Not too bad', I would say that I was good or great, depending on the day, and after 25 times of responding in this way, it became a habit."

Mark paused as he reached for more sheets out of his folder. As he found what he was looking for he gave each of them one sheet. Jane held Taylor's in place for him to read it.

STICKY TO STUCK - DEVELOPING THE RIGHT HABITS

What bad habits do I have that may prevent me from fulfilling my purpose?	What good habits to do I have that support me fulfilling my purpose?	What new habits can I develop to replace my bad habits with? What will I do each day to establish this habit?
		habit 1: habit 2: habit 3:

"So against your purpose and your plans I want you to consider what habits you have. First I want you to recognise what bad habits you have and why you think they are bad. Then I want you to recognise what good habits you have and why they are good. And finally, I want you to identify what new habits you will replace your bad habits with. And for these new habits I want you to consider exactly what you will do each day to make it stick."

They all looked at the piece of paper in front of them and started considering what habits they would identify.

As the room fell silent, Simon noticed a faint movement out of the corner of his eye. His head spun around swiftly to look towards where he thought he had seen movement: Taylor's left hand. But there was nothing. The others just looked at him wondering what he was doing. Simon chose to stay silent.

The Challenge of Change

For all of them the journey with Mark was now over. He had imparted all of his lessons. They had focused on recognising where they had come from through mapping out and learning from their past. They had then focused on building their core person through defining how they might ensure congruency between who they wanted to be, who others saw them as and who they really were. Along with this, they had sought to build a new set of beliefs about who they were. They had also defined what was important to them against their values and purpose, and then established a plan with specific habits to support them in making the difference they desired and gaining fulfilment.

To celebrate the end of their journey with Mark, he arranged for a small party in Taylor's hospital room. Whilst none of them could show enough appreciation for the work that Mark had done with them, their enthusiasm to continue their own journey was overshadowed by their concern for Taylor. Aside from his ability to move his head now more freely, they were not seeing any visible improvement beyond this, which allowed an element of doubt to creep into their minds about the ball.

"Do you think he'll make it there?" Simon asked Jane after their celebration with Mark was over.

"I'm not sure," Jane replied, "he seems to be a lot better in himself and I think that each of us being around and reinforcing the positives is really helping."

"I agree, but I think that it's going to be a long road ahead for him," Simon replied.

They both paused as they walked out of the hospital and towards the bus stop on the other side of the road.

"Fancy walking a bit further?" Simon asked, recognising that he didn't want to end the conversation with Jane too quickly.

"Sure," she replied, "after all it is a lovely day."

"So how's Tod going?" Simon asked, seeking to change the subject.

"Great," Jane replied with a big smile. "It's so nice having him around all the time. I mean we see a lot of each other, but we're also careful not to live in each other's pockets if you know what I mean."

"Yeh, I do," Simon replied. "Has he noticed any change in you with all the work we've been doing with Mark?"

Jane, while still walking, looked sideways at Simon.

"He has, actually. In fact we were just talking about it last night. He said that I seem to be a lot more focused and confident, but also more free."

"What do you mean by more free?" Simon asked, looking quizzically back at Jane.

"Well, less worried about things, was how Tod described it. He said that it was as if I were finding my place in this world and hence things had started to make sense for me."

"Wow, that's great. And Tod noticed that?" Simon replied.

"Yeh, he tends to be really good and supportive with that kind of thing. I mean, I'm still quite worried about Taylor, but I'm less worried about my life. I guess he's right; things just feel like they make a lot more sense to me."

Simon smiled, feeling really pleased for Jane and how things were working out for her and Tod.

At that moment, Simon's concentration was broken by the sound of his mobile phone going off in his pocket. He quickly found it and answered.

"Hey Ang," he started. "You're where? Right behind us?"

Simon spun round to look through the window of a pizza restaurant they had just passed. Inside he could see Angela and Steve waving and smiling.

"We'll be right in," Simon replied as he hung up.

"Fancy a feed?" he then asked Jane as she realised who was waving them into the restaurant.

Jane and Simon sat down at the table with Steve and Angela.

"We've only just ordered," Angela said, waving for the waiter to return.

Simon and Jane made their selection quickly.

"I reckon he'll make it," Steve announced as if out of nowhere.

"Who, Taylor?" Simon asked.

"Yeh, I don't know what's telling me this, but I reckon he will. Even his old man has started to change his attitude after Mark weaved his magic on him," Steve continued.

"I hope so," Jane responded, looking out of the window.

They all paused to think about Taylor.

"So here's to the next chapter of the journey," Steve said as he raised his glass for the others to follow.

"The next chapter of the journey," they all said in unison to the sound of clinking glasses.

"So do you feel like you've changed, Steve?" Simon asked after his conversation with

Jane.

"Absolutely," he replied. "I mean it's been a real challenge changing who I am, especially in the sense of taking responsibility for me. But I have to say that when I look in the mirror now I really like what I see. I guess I feel more comfortable in my own skin you might say."

"Me too," Angela said, butting in over the top of Steve. "I feel a lot better about myself and I feel more focused without being confused or frustrated, if that makes sense."

Simon, Jane and Steve all looked at Angela as they thought about their own situation.

"What about you, Simon?" Angela asked.

"I have to say that I agree," he responded. "I feel a lot more focused now too. But it has been a bit of a challenge for me as well, especially as those around me have noticed me changing."

"What do you mean?" Steve asked as he helped himself to another piece of garlic bread from the plate in the middle of the table.

"Well, my girlfriend has noticed quite a change in me. She said, similar to what Jane and I have just spoken about, that I seem more focused and energised. She said that I seemed to have more purpose now."

"That's great, isn't it?" Angela asked.

"Yes, but it has been a journey for her too, because she's had to get used to a new version of me and a version that seeks to spend more time with her, even for things like wedding planning."

They all looked at Simon with a look of astonishment that quickly turned to adulation.

"Yes, I know what you're thinking. Me…I'm enjoying wedding planning!"

They all laughed.

PRINCIPLES TO REMEMBER
Make It Stick...*Maintain Focus*

Maintaining Head Space

Head space is the time and space for you to consider why you're on this earth and what you're going to do with your time.

Maintaining head space requires making a conscious choice in the face of many distractions.

Sticky to Stuck

Developing the right habits allows you to go from sticky to stuck with your plans to fulfil your purpose.

TASKS FOR THE READER

Make It Stick...Maintain Focus

Making your plans to fulfil your purpose requires that you maintain head space to constantly consider why you're on this earth and what you're going to do with your time. It also requires you to develop the right habits to focus your day-to-day energy.

Task I: Maintaining Head Space

Maintaining head space ensures that you maintain time and space to consider who you are and what's important to you in terms of your purpose.

How will you seek to maintain your head space?

Action	By When

Task 2: Developing the Right Habits

Habits are what guide your day-to-day actions. By developing the right habits you can ensure that you unconsciously do things that will help you fulfil your purpose.

Use the table below to understand what habits you have and what habits you want to develop to support you in fulfilling your purpose.

What bad habits do I have that may prevent me from fulfilling my purpose?	What good habits do I have that support me in fulfilling my purpose?	What new habits can I develop to replace my bad habits with? What will I do each day to establish this habit?
		Habit 1: Habit 2: Habit 3:

CONCLUSION
The Secret Is Showing Leadership

The Day Arrives

"Listen Taylor, we're not going if you won't be there," Jane stated assertively as they all stood around Taylor's hospital bed.

It was two days before the ball to mark the end of their two-year development programme at World-Corp, and with only limited improvement in Taylor's condition they had all come to the same conclusion that it would be unfair if they went without him.

"Don't be so stupid," Taylor replied as he slowly but consciously moved his head to look at each of them in turn. "I won't hear of you not being there."

"But Taylor," Simon stated with a direct tone, "we don't want you to miss out."

"I'm not missing out," Taylor stated. "You guys have been great to me over the last eight months and I would see it as more of an insult if you didn't go."

Mark, who had continued visiting Taylor after their last session, suddenly entered the room.

"I agree with Taylor," Mark announced. "You guys deserve this celebration, after all look how far you've come."

They all looked at Mark and then back at Taylor, knowing that no matter how much they stood their ground they would not win.

"So the ball it is then," Taylor replied. "Just take lots of pictures and try to make sure that Steve behaves himself."

"Hey, who are you telling to behave himself?" Steve asked, knowing that Taylor was absolutely right.

The day of the ball arrived. Whilst they were excited to be celebrating the end of the programme, they all carried the same sense of guilt that their friend could not be with them. World-Corp had spared no expense for the occasion which was held in the main ballroom of one of London's most prestigious hotels. The hotel staff had set out what seemed like hundreds of large round tables, similar to the layout at their induction two years ago. On the centre of each of the tables was a beautiful bouquet of flowers which was surrounded by the settings of wine glasses and sparkling silver cutlery. Bottles of wine and water were also positioned strategically around the flowers.

At the front of the massive room was a wooden dance floor that was bounded on one edge by a stage. On one side of the stage was a speaker's lectern; on the other side was a DJ with his mass of equipment. The dimmed lights and soft music created a subtly stylish ambience that you would expect at any exclusive event.

On the table where the group would be sitting for their meal, they decided to leave a seat vacant as a mark of respect for their missing comrade. Liz, along with Simon's fiancée and Tod, were also invited to join them at their table to celebrate the completion of the first part of their professional journey.

"Did you tie that yourself?" Jane asked Simon who walked proudly towards their table with his fiancée on his arm.

"As a matter of fact I did," Simon stated, feeling quite proud that he'd taken the trouble to put on a black dinner suit and bow tie.

"Just call me Bond, James Bond," he then said, trying to seem debonair.

Simon's fiancée and Jane rolled their eyes and let out a short laugh at Simon's expense.

At the table, Steve was already sitting with Angela and Liz. Steve, true to form, had elected not to go for the standard black dinner suit option like the others, but instead chose to go for a pure white ensemble.

"Nice suit," Tod said with a smile as Steve stood up to greet them.

"Glad you like it," Steve replied with a smile as he stood up to shake Tod's and then Simon's hand.

Once everyone was seated, the proceedings commenced with a series of speeches from the Development Programme Manager and also from the CEO. At Jane's request, her uncle asked everyone to raise their glass to toast Taylor.

"Shall we dance?" Steve asked Angela once the plates for dinner had been removed and the music was about to start.

Before Angela could reply Steve was dragging her towards the dance floor not wanting to lose the opportunity to be first to cut his moves. Simon and his fiancée were quick to follow as other couples took Steve and Angela's lead.

"Don't worry about me," Liz said to Jane who obviously didn't want to leave Liz on her own. "I think I saw Mark earlier so I plan to grab him for a twirl."

Jane smiled and, without further ado, Tod put out his hand gesturing for a dance.

Liz wandered over to find Mark talking to Jane's uncle.

"A dance, Mr Pattern?" she asked with a smile.

"Sorry Tom," Mark said, redirecting his attention from Jane's uncle to Liz. "I've just had a better offer."

Tom smiled as he watched Liz lead Mark towards the dance floor.

After a few songs and many partner swaps, the entire group along with Liz and Mark formed a circle on the dance floor. Steve, not wanting to disappoint the crowd, chose to do his best Michael Jackson impersonation when the song *Thriller* came over the speakers. Just as Steve's performance ended, Mark pulled his mobile phone out of his suit pocket.

"Sorry guys, I'll be back in a moment," he said as he walked off towards the entrance to a small reception room that none of them had noticed before.

"That's me, too," Simon announced as he wiped the sweat from his brow.

Taking Simon's lead, they all followed him back to the table and sat down.

"What happened to Mark?" Jane asked Liz.

"I'm not sure, I think he had to take a call," Liz replied.

"I thought he just couldn't handle my moves," Steve added, sweeping back his hair with both hands.

As they each took a sip from their drinks, Mark reappeared at the entrance to the room into which he had disappeared.

"Liz, I think Mark wants you," Angela said, trying to decipher Mark's hand gestures.

"I'll be back in a minute," Liz said as she left the table to see what Mark wanted.

After a brief conversation with him, Liz returned to the others.

"Mark asked if you could all come over," she announced, standing in front of them.

One by one they stood up, looking at each other wondering what Mark wanted. Walking slowly into the room they found Mark standing next to a small round table that seemed to be positioned perfectly in the centre of the carpet. On the table sat a bottle of champagne in a frosted silver ice bucket that was surrounded by glasses. Liz, who was the last to enter the room, closed the doors behind them.

"I just wanted to congratulate you for everything you've achieved over the last two years," Mark started as they all stood astonished at the sentiment.

"Mark, you didn't have to do this," Jane said, feeling a little embarrassed by his words.

"It's important to celebrate, and I have to say that the journey you have travelled and how you've handled that journey has been nothing short of amazing. I personally have been incredibly proud to see how far of each of you has come. And I think that you should be proud of this too," Mark said as he moved his gaze slowly from Simon, to Jane, to Steve and then to Angela.

Mark then reached down and took the champagne from the bucket. He peeled back the foil and removed the wire cage. Finally, holding the cork between the fingers of his left hand, he twisted the bottle with his right hand resulting in an almighty pop as the cork flew across the room, hitting the door through which they'd entered.

After filling all of the glasses, Mark handed one to each of them. They then stood there in silence with a glass in their hand waiting for Mark to propose a toast. At that moment, time seemed to stop. Suddenly the noise from the party outside filled the air around them as the doors to the room were flung open.

"You're not going to toast without me, are you?" a familiar voice asked over the top of the music that flowed into the room.

Instantly they all spun round. It was Taylor, dressed immaculately in a black dinner suit sitting in a wheelchair with Alex standing behind him.

"Oh my God," Jane screamed as her glass slipped from her fingers and bounced on the carpet at her feet. "Taylor…is…is that you?"

"I found this guy hanging around outside so I thought I better bring him in," Alex announced with a smile.

Jane burst into tears she led the rush towards their friend.

"I…I can't believe it," Jane said, struggling to find the words.

As they reached him, Taylor raised his arms to receive the embrace that for a moment saw five individuals all connect to be one.

"But…but…you couldn't move," Simon exclaimed, not caring that he too was crying.

"Well…kind of," said Taylor, also with tears streaming down his face.

"I guess I just wanted to surprise you all," he continued, seeking to wipe his eyes.

"Champagne anyone?" Alex asked as he made his way over to the table where Mark and Liz were still standing.

"Absolutely," they all said as they rose from their crouching positions and watched Taylor wheel himself slowly towards the table.

"This is amazing," Angela said softly, seeing her friend move forwards with the power of his arms.

Showing Leadership – You and Beyond

"So, what shall we toast?" Jane asked excitedly once everyone had a glass in their hand.

"How about 'to friendship'?" Simon replied.

"Yes. To friendship," Mark said, "may it always be there to support you on your journeys."

"To friendship," they all said loudly as their glasses clinked.

As they sipped their champagne, Simon, Jane, Angela and Steve stood there still amazed to see Taylor in the flesh with them.

"So, Taylor…I mean…like…how…" Angela stammered. "We all thought you couldn't move."

"Well, let's just say that synchronicity happened," Taylor said as he smiled, looking towards Angela.

"See, as I lay in that hospital room each day unable to move I realised that I had a choice. I could be a victim, or I could take control over what I could influence and the one thing I definitely had influence over was my attitude."

Taylor paused as he shifted his gaze to Alex.

"And, you wouldn't believe it, on the very day I made the conscious decision to take control over my attitude, Alex showed up. We then spent a whole two hours talking solidly about Showing Leadership, which is exactly what I chose to do."

All their eyes were now fixed on Alex.

"Hey, I only dropped by to say hi," he said with a smile.

"So with the help of that man over there, and with the support of you guys each day when you turned up, that's exactly what I chose to do. I chose to define what success meant to me each day, and then I focused on what I could influence to achieve it and, day by day, things got better," Taylor continued.

"And you know what," he continued, softening his voice, "as I took control over my attitude and sought to Show Leadership, I realised that through doing this I could help others. I could go beyond me, much like what you guys have done. And I think that this was the most rewarding part of all; I could help those worse off than me. I could serve them is what I think Alex would say."

Again tears welled in their eyes as the intense feeling of pride for their friend overcame them. Even Mark and Alex struggled to hide their emotion.

"I can even wiggle my toes. The toes on my left foot are this week's challenge and then next week it is my right foot," Taylor announced with a smile, sensing the need to ease the mood.

Each of them let out a brief chuckle imagining what was happening within Taylor's shoes.

"To Taylor," Steve said loudly breaking the others' concentration. "May the wiggle in his toes turn into a wiggle in his hips."

There was an eruption of laughter as they raised their glasses again.

"To Taylor," they all shouted.

"And also to Mark, Alex and Liz," Steve continued.

"May we make even half the difference to others as each of you has made to each of us," Steve toasted.

"Hear hear," they all said in unison.

Without saying a word, Mark reached into his suit pocket and then handed Liz, Simon, Steve, Angela, Jane and Taylor a small laminated card each.

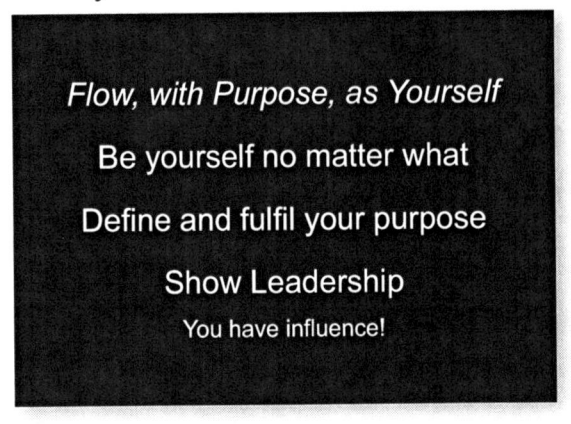

> *Flow, with Purpose, as Yourself*
>
> **Be yourself no matter what**
>
> **Define and fulfil your purpose**
>
> **Show Leadership**
> You have influence!

"We'll keep it with us always," Jane replied on behalf of the others as she looked at the card.

As they finished their champagne, they each stood there in silence savouring the moment.

"So Alex," Simon said, breaking the other's concentration, "when are you going to take us on the next stage of the journey?"

Alex looked towards Simon, who could see his eyes were starting to light up.

"Because I think I'd like to hear more about this serving others through Showing Leadership," Simon then stated.

"Me too," Steve added as they all looked towards Alex.

"All in good time," Alex replied softly, "all in good time…"

The End

Afterword
Beginning Your Journey

In following the journey of Simon, Angela, Steve, Jane and Taylor, it is easy to feel that you are starting behind the eight ball; *there is so much to do, and much time has passed.* However, as you've now read this book, can I encourage you to consider a few simple things:

- Your life is a journey, and on that journey the constant connection is you. This means that you always have a choice as to what you do in the present and what you plan to do with the future. Ultimately, you have a choice as to what you do on your journey!

- When you first arrive at work it is easy to become distracted. But if you take what you've learned about being a professional from this book and from those around you, and you put your lessons into practice, then you can regain the headspace you need to really make a difference. This will help you not only survive the onslaught of complexity and confusion that the professional world will throw at you, but you will also be able to get noticed by focusing your contribution.

- Once you regain some head space, it is also essential to use it proactively to define your purpose. Don't dwell on time past, or worry about the future. Instead, consider what your purpose is and then, as you begin to define it, make sure you take considered action to flow with purpose, as yourself, in the right stream throughout your life.

Through doing these things and by Showing Leadership, you will be able to focus your energy on gaining alignment and fulfilling your purpose. And as you do this, just remember that the journey you take is as important as the destination, so never forget to enjoy each and every day by remaining in the present.

So now you understand the journey, the next move is yours; *what are you going to do today?*

For further resources to help you on your journey, visit **www.grad-expectations.com**

Suggested Further Reading

Arden, P. (2003) *It's Not How Good You Are, It's How Good You Want to Be*, New York: Phaidon Press.

Johnson, S. (1998) *Who Moved My Cheese?*, London: Random House.

Johnson, S. (2003) *The Present: The Gift that Makes You Happy and Successful at Work and in Life*, Australia: Random House.

Lundin, S., Paul, H. and Christensen, J. (2000) *Fish: A Remarkable Way to Boost Morale and Improve Results*, London: Hodder and Stoughton.

Patterson, K., Grenny, J., McMillan, R. and Switzler, A. (2002) *Crucial Conversations: Tools for Talking when the Stakes are High*, London: McGraw-Hill.

Blanchard, K., Oncken, W. and Burrows, H. (1990) *The One Minute Manager Meets the Monkey*, London: HarperCollins.

Covey, S.R. (1989) *The 7 Habits of Highly Effective People*, Melbourne: The Business Library.

Vengel, A. (2000) *Influence Edge*, San Fransisco: Berrett Koehler Communications.

Goffee, R. and Jones, G. (2006) *'Why Should Anyone be Led by You?'* Massachusetts: Harvard Business School Press.

Kotter, J. and Cohen, D. (2002) *The Heart of Change: Real-life Stories of How People Change their Organisations*, Boston: Harvard Business School.

Agness, L. (2008) *Change Your Life with NLP*, Harlow: Prentice Hall.

Jaworski, J. (1996) *Synchronicity: The inner path of leadership*, San Francisco: Berrett-Koehler.

Robinson, D. and Aronica, L. (2009) *The Element*, London: Penguin Group.

Tolle, E. (1999) *The Power of Now*, London: Hodder and Stoughton.

About the Author

Rob Cross was born in Melton Mowbray but emigrated with his family to Melbourne, Australia as a toddler. He has degrees in both business and engineering. After an influential tenure with the Australian Air Force he returned to Britain in 2004, and was employed to deliver leadership courses to public, private and not-for-profit organisations. He currently works as a business and leadership development consultant focusing on developing tomorrow's leaders through providing specialist coaching and consultancy, as well as running training seminars and motivational speaking assignments. Rob Cross lives in London.

To find out more about Rob Cross go to www.rob-cross.com

Summary of Your Journey

Becoming a Professional

What are the 3 key things I will do from today to be more effective as a professional?

What will I do?	What outcome will I achieve by doing this?	How / When will I do this?

Who are you? Why are you here?

What is my Purpose?

My Purpose

What are my Values?

My Values

What are the key parts of my plan?

My Plan	
Who I Want To Be	Where I Want To Be
3 Years	3 Years
2 Years	2 Years
1 year	1 year
6 Months	6 Months
3 Months	3 Months
1 Month	1 Month

What are my 3 most powerful empowering beliefs?

My Empowering Beliefs		
Belief 1	Belief 2	Belief 3

Notes